GAINING GROUND
Intermediate Grammar

Cathleen Cake
Holly Deemer Rogerson
University of Pittsburgh

NEWBURY HOUSE PUBLISHERS, Cambridge
A division of Harper & Row, Publishers, Inc.
New York, Philadelphia, San Francisco, Washington
London, Mexico City, São Paulo, Singapore, Sydney

Library of Congress Cataloging-in-Publication Data

Cake, Cathleen.
    Gaining ground.

    1. English language--Text-books for foreign speakers.
2. English language--Grammar--1950-   I. Rogerson,
Holly Deemer. II. Title.
PE1128.C28   1986   428.2'4   85-21518
ISBN 0-88377-314-7

Cover photograph courtesy of Fay Foto Service
Cover by Carson Designs
Illustrations by Carol Ann Gaffney

NEWBURY HOUSE PUBLISHERS
A division of Harper & Row, Publishers, Inc.

Language Science
Language Teaching
Language Learning

CAMBRIDGE, MASSACHUSETTS

Copyright © 1986 by Newbury House Publishers, A division of Harper & Row, Publishers, Inc. All rights reserved. No part of this book may be reproduced or transmitted in any form or by any means, electronic or mechanical, including photocopying, recording, or by any information storage and retrieval system, without permission in writing from the Publisher.

Printed in the U.S.A.   First printing: February 1986
63-20766

Acknowledgments

We would like to offer our heartfelt thanks to a number of people at the English Language Institute at the University of Pittsburgh. Without their help this project would not have reached completion.

First of all, Karen Billingsley, who tirelessly typed both the original manuscript and repeated revisions.

The teachers at the ELI who used the prepublication manuscript for four terms in their grammar and writing classes: Cheri Micheau, Aleta Kerrick, Deborah Fink, Dorolyn Smith, Joe Sukenick, Joan Lucas, Tom Swinscoe, Susan Donio, Marie Eichler, Elizabeth Ashmore, and David Hunter. Many of their suggestions for revisions have been incorporated into the final manuscript, and they have helped us produce a far better text than we could have done on our own.

The students in the high-intermediate level who also made helpful suggestions which we used in our revisions.

And finally, Christina B. Paulston, Director of the English Language Institute, who gave us both permission to use the prepublication manuscript in the ELI classes and the secretarial help needed to complete the text.

Contents

To the Teacher   viii
The Situation   xii

1   *Tense Review*   1

Present Continuous vs. Present   1
Past Continuous vs. Past   6
Past Perfect vs. Past   10
Present Perfect vs. Past   13
Present Perfect Continuous vs. Present Perfect   17
Past Intention (*was/were going to* + VERB)   20
Future Time (*will vs. be going to*)   22
Future Time: Present and Present Continuous   24
Fine Points for Recognition   30
Summary   31

2   *Modals*   32

Part I   *Permission, Requests, Advice, Necessity*
Asking and Giving Permission (*can/could/may*)   32
Making and Answering Requests (*can/could/will/would*)   34
Giving Advice (*should, ought to*) and Stating Necessity
    (*must/have/has to*)   37
Expressing Prohibition (*must not*) and Lack of Necessity
    (*don't/doesn't have to*)   42
Giving Strong Advice (*had better*)   44

Part II   *Ability, Possibility, Expectation, Deduction*
Expressing Ability (*can/could*)   47
Expressing Possibility (*could/may/might*)   48
Expressing Expectation (*should/ought to*)   54
Expressing a Deduction (*must*)   58
Fine Points for Recognition   69
Summary   70

iv

3 Gerunds and Infinitives 72

Part I *Gerunds*
Gerunds as Subjects   72
Gerunds Following Prepositions   76
Gerunds as Direct Objects   78
Gerunds as Subject Complements   81

Part II *Infinitives*
Infinitive Phrases as Subject Complements   82
Infinitive Phrases as Direct Objects   84
Gerunds vs. Infinitives: Different Meanings   90
Verbs with Infinitives without *To*   93
Infinitive Phrases as Adjective Phrases   95
Infinitive Phrases as Adjective Complements   97
Infinitive Phrases as Subjects   99
Infinitive Phrases as Adverbials (*in order to*)   102
Fine Points for Recognition   106
Summary   108

4 Comparisons 110

Comparatives (*-er, more, less than*)   110
Equatives (*as . . . as, the same . . . as*)   114
Equatives (*like, as*)   115
Superlatives   118
Expressions of Degree (*so, such . . . that*)   119
Fine Points for Recognition   123
Summary   124

5 Relative Clauses 125

Subject Relative Pronouns   125
Restrictive vs. Nonrestrictive Relative Clauses   127
Object Relative Pronouns   130
Possessive Relative Pronouns   134
Relative Pronouns in Prepositional Phrases   136
Special Relative Pronouns (*when, where, why*)   140
Fine Points for Recognition   145
Summary   146

6 Conditionals 147

Type I: Present/Future Real (*if*)   147
Type I: Present/Future Real (*unless*)   151
Type II: Present Unreal   153
Type III: Past Unreal   157
Mixed Type: Types II and III   161
Fine Points for Recognition   164
Summary   166

7 *Passive* 167

Without a *By*-Phrase   167
With a *By*-Phrase   171
Indirect Object as the Passive Subject   174
Passive with Other Tenses   176
Passive Forms with Modals   178
Passive Causatives   180
Fine Points for Recognition   184
Summary   185

8 *Logical Connectors* 186

Part I *Coordination*
Coordinating Conjunctions to Connect Clauses   186
Positive Correlatives as Coordinating Conjunctions   188
Negative Correlatives as Coordinating Conjunctions   191
Coordinating Conjunctions: Subject-Verb Agreement   193

Part II *Subordination*
Subordinating Conjunctions Indicating Time Sequences (*after, before, until, by the time, when*)   195
Subordinating Conjunctions Indicating Cause (*because, since*) and Purpose (*so that*)   198
Preposition of Cause (*because of*)   201
Subordinating Conjunctions Indicating Contrast (*while, although, even though, though*)   202
Prepositions of Contrast (*despite, in spite of*)   205

Part III *Transition*
Transitions Indicating Sequence: Time Sequence or Logical Sequence   207
Transitions Indicating Cause/Effect (*consequently, therefore, thus*)   209
Transitions Indicating Contrast (*however, in contrast, on the other hand, nevertheless*)   211
Transitions Indicating Similarity (*similarly, likewise*)   213
Transitions Indicating Emphatic Restatement (*actually, indeed, in fact*)   215
Transitions Indicating Exemplification (*for example, for instance*)   216
Transitions: Adverbs of Exemplification   218
Transitions Indicating Addition (*moreover, in addition, furthermore, also, besides*)   219
Prepositions Indicating Addition (*besides, in addition to*)   221
Fine Points for Recognition   225
Summary   226

9 Noun Clauses 229

Part I *Statements*
Noun Clauses as Direct Objects (*that*) 229
Noun Clauses as Direct Objects (*if, wh-* words) 233
Noun Clauses as Subject Complements 236
Noun Clauses as Subjects 238
Noun Clauses as Adjective Complements 242
Noun Clauses as Objects of Prepositions 243
Noun Clauses with Uninflected Verbs 246

Part II *Indirect Speech*
Noun Clauses as Statements in Indirect Speech 249
Main Verbs in Indirect Speech 256
Yes/No Questions as Noun Clauses in Indirect Speech 259
Wh- Questions as Noun Clauses in Indirect Speech 261
Commands and Requests as Noun Clauses in Indirect Speech 264
Fine Points for Recognition 269
Summary 270

10 Participles 272

Participles as Adjectives 272
Participles as Adjective Phrases 277
Participles as Verbal Complements 280
Participles as Adverbial Phrases of Time, Reason, and Contrast 283
Participles as Adverbial Phrases of Manner 286
Fine Points for Recognition 289
Summary 291

Appendix I: Irregular Verbs 293

Appendix II: Adjectives, Nouns, and Verbs + Prepositions 295

Appendix III: Determiners, Articles (*a/an, the*), Demonstratives
(*this/these; that/those*), and Quantifiers 297

Answer Key for Recognition Exercises 303

Index 305

vii

To the Teacher

INTRODUCTION

This book is designed for use with intermediate and intermediate/advanced ESL/EFL students. Completion of the entire text takes from 75 to 100 classroom hours, depending on the initial proficiency level of the students. The range of TOEFL scores for students at the beginning of the course should fall on either side of 400. In English programs in which separate class hours are devoted to separate skill areas, Chapters 7, 8, and 9 can be covered during the writing class since the material in these chapters is most necessary for written English.

CHAPTER FORMAT

This book includes several features that make it easy to use. The first of these features is the Situation: a fictional university in the United States named Hoopersburg State University and a group of five students who are third-year students there. All the important features of the Situation are described, in paragraph form, on one page at the beginning of the book. Before beginning the first chapter of the book with your class, read over the Situation with your students and make sure that they understand who each character is, the relationships among the characters, and the setting of the Situation. A thorough understanding of the Situation will enable your students to understand more deeply the grammar points presented in the book.

The Examples at the beginning of each teaching point are based on the Situation. The meaning of the Example sentences should be clear to your students from their

viii

understanding of the Situation, permitting them to concentrate on how the new grammar communicates that meaning. The vocabulary used in these initial Examples is restricted to a core of words that recur throughout the book; your students need not struggle with the new vocabulary while they are dealing with the initial presentation of new grammatical patterns.

For each grammar point presented, following the Examples is an Explanation of both the Form and the Meaning of the new grammar pattern. The Form explanation is presented in chart format, with essential verb forms and punctuation clearly marked. At the bottom of each of these Form charts is a phrase or sentence that further exemplifies the pattern in question. In the Meaning section, the various functions of the pattern in focus are explained with additional example sentences to clarify each use of the pattern. These additional example sentences may or may not be based on the Hoopersburg situation. The new pattern is contrasted with similar patterns that have been presented previously in order to help the students understand the overall system of the language. Where appropriate, diagrams are used to show the relationship of similar patterns. Lists are included, where needed, to permit the student to apply the new pattern in a wider range of contexts. A variety of carefully sequenced Exercises follows the Explanation of each grammatical point.

In our experience, students have difficulty with some grammatical patterns primarily because of meaning rather than form, while with other patterns, the form is the primary stumbling block. For both patterns where we believe such difficulties may arise, we have begun the Exercise section with a Recognition Exercise, identified by the symbol of an open book in the margin. When the Recognition Exercise focuses on meaning, students are asked to make judgments about the meaning of the pattern; they should be permitted to refer back to the Explanation while doing the exercise. When the focus is on structure, the Recognition Exercise has students address the complex forms of grammatical patterns. We recommend that the Recognition Exercises be done in class so that the teacher can closely monitor the students' understanding of the pattern. The Recognition Exercises may be difficult for the students; however, we feel that it is not useful for students to practice language forms until they have a good understanding of both meaning and structure.

Following the Recognition Exercise there are Production Exercises, which are sequenced according to ease of student response. Of course, ease of response is determined by a variety of factors. We have found through classroom testing of this text that the two most important factors are the constraints on the student response and the degree to which the student response is revealed by the cue. For example, the answering of questions, which is usually thought to be a difficult task, was often found to be comparatively easy if the verb form in the response was revealed by the verb form in the question. A more difficult task than answering with a particular verb tense is filling in the appropriate verb tense in a given situation or paragraph. The Production Exercises have been divided into Oral Exercises, identified by the symbol of two people talking, and Written Exercises, identified by the symbol of a pencil. Typically the Oral Exercises precede the Written Exercises. Oral Exercises are intended to be done in class, and Written Exercises should be assigned for homework. Of course, any of the

Oral Exercises may be assigned as written homework even if they have been done in class since a variety of answers is usually possible.

Review Exercises appear at the end of each chapter and, in some chapters, at the end of the first part of the chapter. These exercises provide the students with extra practice on the points that were covered in the chapter. These Review Exercises force the students to review and integrate the pieces of knowledge that they have mastered in the chapter. These exercises may be Oral or Written.

At the end of each chapter are the Fine Points for Recognition for the chapter. This section presents related but more complex grammatical points for students capable of a more advanced level of work than the intermediate students for whom the book is primarily intended. The presentation includes Form and Meaning Explanations, as well as Examples. No Exercises are included with the Fine Points for Recognition because at this level the grammar points in these sections are more suitable for recognition than for production. Teachers with lower-level students can simply pass over this section.

At the close of each chapter is a Summary of the grammatical points covered in the chapter. The Summary includes the name of each pattern and one or more Example sentences taken from the chapter. This section was added to the book in response to student requests for an overview for each chapter.

APPENDICES

At the end of the book are three Appendices. Appendix I provides a list of the past tense and past participle of common irregular verbs. (It is assumed that students know most of these forms already.) Appendix II gives lists of Adjective + Preposition, Noun + Preposition, and Verb + Preposition combinations. These lists are particularly useful in conjunction with Chapter 3. Appendix III contains a summary of Determiner usage, most of which is assumed to be known by intermediate students.

ADAPTATION FOR LESS PROFICIENT STUDENTS

Teachers with weaker students can simplify this book in several ways. Where extended lists are presented (for example, in Chapter 3), the teacher can select a smaller number of items to be covered. In addition, Part 2 of Chapter 9 and all of Chapter 10 contain more difficult material and can be omitted. Of course, for such students, the Fine Points for Recognition should be omitted.

SEQUENCE OF CHAPTERS

The sequence of chapters in this book was determined primarily by two somewhat conflicting factors: usefulness and difficulty. In cases where these two criteria greatly conflicted, usefulness was given priority and the chapter was placed early in the book. Specific reasons for the placement of problematic chapters are the following:

While modals generally pose great difficulties for learners of ESL, they were placed in Chapter 2 because of their frequency and importance in delivering meaning in English. We felt that in this way the students could receive continued feedback on their use of modals throughout the term.

Gerunds are covered before infinitives in Chapter 3 because our observation of students' use of these two structures has been that they overuse the infinitive structure and avoid the gerund structure. We felt that learning the rules for gerund usage would more rapidly result in an improvement in their English. Also, as with the modals, doing this problematic but extremely useful area early permits much needed feedback over the remainder of the term.

Participles are placed in the final chapter for several reasons. First of all, we have observed that our students frequently have great difficulty with them. In addition, many instances of participial usage can be easily avoided, with no great loss of fluency.

FLEXIBILITY OF USE

Although the setting of the situation of this book is a university in the United States, care has been taken to ensure that the book is usable in a great variety of locales and situations. Culturally sensitive topics have been avoided. Question items typically relate to student life, goals, and daily life situations which can be answered by most ESL/EFL students. The large number of exercises in the text permits teachers to select those most appropriate for their classes.

The Situation

Many of the examples and exercises in this book center on university life at a fictional university called Hoopersburg State University. Read over the descriptions of the characters below and try to remember this information as you are studying the examples and exercises throughout the book. This situation gives a context for the grammar points introduced and should help you to understand the meaning of the grammar.

BILL

Bill is beginning his junior year. He is an engineering major and wants to enter a graduate program in engineering at a major U.S. university after graduating from Hoopersburg. His parents live near Hoopersburg, and they are paying his tuition for him.

JIM

Jim is a junior. He is a computer science major and plans to get a job after graduation. He has been engaged to Cindy for one year. Jim is paying for his schooling with a student loan. He's from New York City. Bill and Jim are roommates in the dorm.

CINDY

Cindy is a junior and her major is accounting. She is engaged to Jim, but she is not very eager to get married right away. She would like to establish a career after graduating. She and Jim were high school sweethearts. She is a very good student and has received a scholarship to pay for her college expenses.

WIZARD

Wizard is a junior at Hoopersburg, but he spent his freshman year at MIT. He wasn't a serious student at that time and, as a result, he failed several courses. Now that he has transferred to Hoopersburg, he has settled down and is getting good grades. Although he doesn't really need the money, he has a job at the computer center because he loves computers.

SID

Sid is a foreign student from India. He's a junior, majoring in math, and plans to continue his studies in math in graduate school. However, his family has financial problems, and he may have to return home.

GAINING GROUND

Tense Review 1

PRESENT CONTINUOUS vs. PRESENT

EXAMPLES
1. Most third-year engineering students take 16 credits at Hoopersburg State University, but Bill is taking 18 credits.
2. Cindy usually studies in her room. However, today she's working in the library.
3. Most engineering students feel that junior year is the hardest one.

EXPLANATION

Form

PRESENT CONTINUOUS			PRESENT	
am			VERB	-s
is	VERB	-ing	walks	
are				
is walking				

Meaning

Use the PRESENT CONTINUOUS for temporary or limited actions and habits. Such actions or habits occur at the time you are speaking or writing.

4. Sid isn't having any difficulty with his mathematics class this semester.
5. Are you attending any academic courses this term?

Use the PRESENT tense for

a. Factual material (natural law, definitions, explanations)

    6. Hot air rises.

b. States and conditions (see the list of verbs on pages 3-4).

    7. American food tastes very bland to most foreign visitors.

c. Habitual action without any time restriction

    8. I take my lunch to school.

EXERCISE 1-1 Present Continuous vs. Present

Directions
    Answer the questions.

1. What are other students at your school doing while you are having grammar class?
2. What is your roommate/friend doing right now?
3. What are the people in your family doing right now?
4. What part of town are you living in?
5. Are you taking other classes now?
6. Are your children attending a local school?
7. What is the weather like today? (Begin with "It...")
8. What do you tell your family about this city when you write/talk to them?

The following verbs are typically used in simple verb forms, not in continuous forms.

1. Verbs of sense perception:

   Examples: see, hear, feel, taste, smell

   Note: Watch, look at, listen to, can be used with CONTINUOUS. These verbs express intentional actions.

   (1) I see a red bird on top of the house (now).
   (2) He's watching TV (now).

   Also note: Use the CONTINUOUS form of verbs of sense perception only when the speaker is intentionally experiencing the action.

   (3) He's tasting the soup to see if it needs salt.
   (4) She's feeling the sandpaper, and it feels rough to her finger.

2. Verbs of opinion and some verbs of mental perception:
   Examples: know, believe, think, remember

   (1) She knows all those rules.
   (2) I believe that she will do well on the exam.

   Note: These verbs are often used with *that*.

   Note: Think can also be used in CONTINUOUS form for continuing mental activity.

   (3) He thinks that the rules are complicated.
   (4) He is thinking about these rules.

3. Verbs of emotion:

   Examples: hate, like, dislike, want, love

   (1) I love you.
   (2) He wants a different adviser.

4. Verbs of measurement:

   Examples: weigh, cost, equal, measure, fit

   (1) That package weighs 5 pounds.
   (2) That book costs $10.

   Note: Measurement can also be a temporary action that is performed by a person. The verb would then be used in the present continuous form.

   (1) The butcher is weighing the meat, and it weighs 3 pounds.
   (4) The salesperson is measuring the fabric. It measures 4½ yards.

5. Verbs of relationship:

   Examples: have, belong, own, contain, resemble, consist of, depend on, include, involve, lack, owe, need

   (1) He owns two homes.
   (2) That box contains 20 books.

   Note: Have can be used in CONTINUOUS form when it does not express possession.

   (3) He is having difficulty with his homework.
   (4) Are you having a good time?

6. Other stative verbs: appear, seem, be

   (1) Her children seem happy in their new school.
   (2) He appears healthy, but he is often sick.

EXERCISE 1-2   Present Continuous vs. Present

Directions
Some of the sentences below contain PRESENT CONTINUOUS where it is incorrect. Find these mistakes, underline them and then rewrite the sentences in the correct form.

Example
   I'm understanding tense much better now.
   → I understand tense much better now.

1. Sandpaper is feeling rough.
2. She's measuring her room for a new carpet.
3. We are knowing that we don't understand this lesson.
4. The students are needing more time for all the experiments in chemistry class.
5. We are having trouble with our landlord.
6. His special diet is consisting of fruits, vegetables, and dairy products.
7. My roommate is having a brand-new stereo.
8. I'm looking for a new apartment.
9. We are belonging to the photography club.
10. They are thinking about moving to a new city.

EXERCISE 1-3 Present Continuous vs. Present

Directions

With a partner use the words below to make two-line dialogues. Use the PRESENT CONTINUOUS or PRESENT in your questions. Answer with an appropriate verb form.

Example

fit — blue jacket
→ A: How does the blue jacket fit?
  B: It fits pretty well.
  watch — special TV series on the Vietnam War
→ A: Are you watching that special TV series on the Vietnam War?
  B: No, I missed the first program.
    Yes, I'm looking forward to the next program.

1. like — Mexican food
2. take — course in U.S. history
3. own — a tape recorder
4. sit — comfortable chair
5. write — in a diary
6. owe — $20
7. take — notes during class
8. remember — name of your writing teacher

EXERCISE 1-4 Present Continuous vs. Present

Directions

Write the present or present continuous form of the following verbs in the sentences below.

depend	live	possess	send	doubt
snow	worry	like	think	smell
feel	dislike	know	guess	

1. Bill and Jim _____ in the dormitory this term. Jim _____ a
                  a   b
   lot of sports equipment, so their room is full of stuff.

6 GAINING GROUND

2. I _____ my parents a picture of my classmates. When they receive
   a
   it, they will feel closer to me. They _____ a lot about me.
   b

3. Sid generally _____ American food, but of course, he _____
   a   b
   _____ that Indian food is much tastier.

4. Our plans for the weekend _____ on the weather. Since it
   a
   _____ right now, I _____ that we will go out very
   b   c
   much.

5. Everyone _____ good when the sun is shining.
   a

PAST CONTINUOUS vs. PAST

EXAMPLES
1. Wizard was working in the computer center last night from 7:00 to midnight.
2. Jim was talking on the phone with Cindy when Sid knocked on his door.
3. While Jim was talking on the phone to Cindy, Sid knocked on his door.
4. Bill was talking to his adviser at 3 p.m.
5. Bill was listening to records while Jim was studying.
6. Sid called his parents once a month last year.
7. Sid arrived in the United States 3 years ago.

EXPLANATION

Form

PAST CONTINOUS		
was	VERB	-ing
were		
was walking		

PAST	
VERB	-ed
walked	

Meaning

Use the PAST to express completed actions.

Use the PAST CONTINUOUS only in the following situations:

a. To emphasize the duration of a past action.

   8. I was sitting in the doctor's office all Monday afternoon.

b. To indicate a past action of duration that is interrupted by another action in simple past.

   9. Did he look around while he was backing up the car?
   10. I wasn't doing anything special when the electricity went off.

c. To indicate an action occurring at a specific time. This means that the action began sometime before the stated time and ended sometime after the stated time.

   11. We were having lunch at 12:30 yesterday.

d. To indicate two actions if both have duration and they occurred approximately simultaneously.

   12. While my roommate was making breakfast, I was taking a shower.

Use *while* with the continuous action (Examples 3, 5, 9, 12). Use *when* with the simple past (Examples 2, 10). Use *ago* with the simple past (Example 7).

SIMPLE PAST ACTION	CONTINUOUS PAST ACTION
Sid knocked on Jim's door	while Jim was talking on the phone

EXERCISE 1-5 Past Continuous vs. Past

Directions
Read the first sentence. Then judge the truth of the following sentences. Circle T if the sentence is true according to the first sentence. Circle F if it is false. Circle ? if the first sentence does not give enough information to judge the sentence true or false.

Example
1. We were watching TV at 8:15 last night.
   (T)/ F / ?   We were watching TV at 8:14.
   (T)/ F / ?   We were watching TV at 8:17.
   T / F /(?)   We were watching TV for a long time last night.

8   GAINING GROUND

2. While we were having breakfast, the phone rang.
   T / F / ?   The phone rang at the end of our breakfast.
   T / F / ?   The phone was ringing for a long time.
   T / F / ?   Eating breakfast took a long time.
   T / F / ?   The action of eating breakfast was longer than the action of the phone ringing.
3. I was listening to records while I was doing my homework.
   T / F / ?   I started to listen to records before I started to do my homework.
   T / F / ?   The action of doing my homework was shorter than the action of listening to music.

EXERCISE 1-6   Past Continuous vs. Past

Directions
   Answer the questions.

1. What happened while you were studying last night?
2. What was your roommate doing while you were studying on Sunday?
3. What were you doing when your roommate got home last night?
4. What were you doing while your friend was talking to his family on your phone?
5. What happened while you were driving to school this morning?
6. What were you thinking about while you were walking to school this morning?
7. What did you see while you were waiting for the bus this morning?
8. What were you doing at 9:00 last night?
9. What were you doing at 8:00 this morning?
10. What happened while you were eating breakfast this morning?

EXERCISE 1-7   Past Continuous vs. Past

Directions
   Give a logical sentence using the two verbs given to indicate one action interrupted by another action.

Example
   watch TV — ring
   → While I was watching TV, the phone rang.
   → I was watching TV when the phone rang.

1. take a shower — hear
2. cook — ring
3. do homework — begin
4. study — knock
5. cut onions — begin to cry
6. read — hear
7. drive — see
8. arrive — watch
9. listen — arrive
10. see — check homework

EXERCISE 1-8 Past Continuous vs. Past

Directions
Write the more appropriate verb form: past or past continuous. All the sentences are part of the same story.

1. Jim and Bill _____ a pizza when Wizard _____
                             a - (eat)   b - (return)
   from the computer center.

2. Wizard _____ very hungry and he _____ half the
                   a - (be)   b - (eat)
   pizza.

3. While they _____ , the boys _____ their plans for
                      a - (eat)   b - (discuss)
   the weekend.

4. While they _____ , Wizard _____ that a new
                     a - (talk)   b - (remember)
   comedy program _____ on TV.
                              c - (be)

5. He _____ on the TV and they _____ to watch.
          a - (turn)   b - (begin)

6. The program _____ funny.
                   a - (be)

7. When the program _____ , the boys _____ while
                         a - (end)   b - (laugh)
   they _____ back to their rooms.
          c - (walk)

PAST PERFECT vs. PAST

EXAMPLES
1. Bill had asked Dr. Hobson for advice before he registered.
2. Sid came to the United States after he had decided to major in math.
3. Until he began school at Hoopersburg, Jim had never lived away from home.

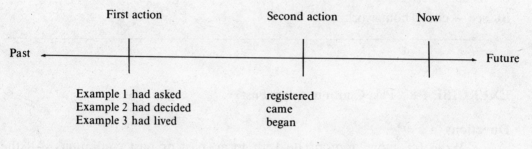

EXPLANATION

Form

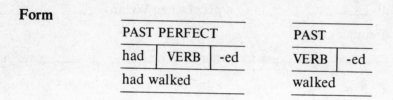

Meaning

Use the PAST PERFECT with the verb that describes the earlier of the two past actions. In other words, when you have a sequence of two past actions, use PAST PERFECT for the first action and the PAST TENSE for the second action.

4. The teacher had prepared the lesson carefully before he entered the classroom.
5. We had purchased tickets by phone before we arrived at the symphony.
6. Had he asked permission before he left the room?

Useful time expressions: before, after, until

First action	Second action
We had purchased tickets by phone	*before* we arrived at the symphony.
Had he asked permission	*before* he left the room?
After they had rented the apartment,	they noticed the heating problems.
After I had handed in the test,	I remembered the meaning of the word.
He had never lived alone	*until* he went to the university.
My watch had worked well	*until* I dropped it.

See Chapter 9 for the use of PAST PERFECT in indirect speech.
See Chapter 8 for the use of additional time expressions with the PAST PERFECT.

EXERCISE 1-9   Past Perfect

Directions
Read the first sentence. Then judge the truth of the following sentences. Circle T if the sentence is true according to the first sentence. Circle F if it is false. Circle ? if the first sentence does not give enough information to judge the sentence true or false.

1. He had studied English for 2 years before he came to the United States.
   T / F / ?   He studied English. Then he came to the United States.
   T / F / ?   He came to the United States recently.
   T / F / ?   His English study was just before he came to the United States.
2. After we had eaten dinner, he left.
   T / F / ?   He left during dinner.
   T / F / ?   We ate dinner. Next he left.
   T / F / ?   Dinner lasted a long time.
3. They ordered a pizza after they had drunk all the beer.
   T / F / ?   They ordered the pizza. Then they drank the beer.
   T / F / ?   They drank beer with their pizza.

EXERCISE 1-10   Past Perfect

Directions
Answer the questions.

1. What had you thought about doing before you decided to study here?
2. What advice had your parents given you before you began this course?
3. What had you read about this school before you arrived here?
4. What American movies had you seen before you began this course?

12 GAINING GROUND

5. Had you bought your books before your classes started?
6. Had you traveled to an English-speaking country before you began to study English?
7. Before you began to study here, who had you spoken English with?
8. How had you studied English before you began English classes here?

EXERCISE 1-11   Past Perfect vs. Past

Directions

Give a sentence using the two verbs and showing a time sequence in the past. Use *after* or *before* in each sentence. Be sure the sequence of actions is a logical one. Be creative!

Example

take a shower — eat
→ I ate breakfast after I had taken a hot shower.
→ Before I ate breakfast, I had taken a hot shower.

First action	Second action
1. eat	watch the news
2. go to the movies	study
3. finish my homework	go to bed
4. go to sleep	eat
5. turn off	end
6. study	come to the United States
7. travel	graduate from high school
8. try	live in the United States
9. have	go to school
10. drive	get a license

EXERCISE 1-12   Past Perfect vs. Past

Directions

Write the correct form: past or past perfect.

1. Bill and Jim _____ their freshman year at Hoopersburg 3 years
   a - (begin)
   ago. Before that, they _____ away from home. They also _____
   b - (never, live)   c - (never,

Tense Review **13**

_____ such a large school before. When they _____ at
attend)   d - (arrive)
Hoopersburg, they _____ many adjustments to make.
                        e - (have)

2. Wizard _____ to Hoopersburg 2 years ago. He _____
           a - (transfer)   b - (study)
for one year at MIT, but he had to leave because his grades were bad. Wizard

_____ very disappointed when he had to leave MIT; he
        c - (feel)
_____ to go there for a long time. Unfortunately, he _____
      d - (want)   e - (realize)
too late that he _____ too much time playing with the computer
                    f - (spend)
and not enough time studying.

PRESENT PERFECT vs. PAST

EXAMPLES
1. Bill and Jim have been roommates for 3 years.
   They moved into the dorm on the same day.
2. Jim has already applied for loans twice.
   He applied for the first time 2 years ago.
3. Sid has just gotten a letter from his family.
4. Bill has roomed with Jim since freshman year.

EXPLANATION

Form

PRESENT PERFECT		
have	VERB	-ed
has		
has walked		

PAST	
VERB	-ed
walked	

Meaning

a. Use **PRESENT PERFECT** for actions or states that began in the past
   and continue up to (and perhaps including) the present (Example 1).

                          have been roommates

←——→
      2 years ago   now

5. I haven't ever gone to San Francisco.
6. Has she ever lived in a dormitory?

Note: Such a time period is often indicated with *for* + time period or *since* + point of time. (Examples 1, 4)

b. Use PRESENT PERFECT for actions at indefinite past times.

7. We've already eaten at that restaurant three times.

c. Use PRESENT PERFECT to indicate a very recent action with *just*. You may hear people use *just* with the simple past tense, but in written style this is not correct.

8. Which topic have you just finished?

Useful time expressions: yet, already, just, still, never; for (+ period of time); since (+ point in time); ever (usually in questions and negatives) (Examples 5, 6)

9. She still hasn't found a job.
10. Have you bought the tickets for the game yet?

EXERCISE 1-13 Present Perfect

Directions

Read the first sentence. Then judge the truth of the following sentences. Circle T if the sentence is true according to the first sentence. Circle F if it is false. Circle ? if the first sentence does not give enough information to judge the sentence true or false.

1. He's eaten at that restaurant twice.
   - T / F / ?   He ate at that restaurant recently.
   - T / F / ?   He may eat at that restaurant again.
   - T / F / ?   He definitely will eat at that restaurant again.
2. They have studied Japanese.
   - T / F / ?   They are still studying Japanese.
   - T / F / ?   They may study Japanese in the future.
   - T / F / ?   They studied Japanese recently.
3. The class has just ended.
   - T / F / ?   The class lasted for a long time.
   - T / F / ?   The class ended very recently.

EXERCISE 1-14   Present Perfect

Directions
　　Choose *for* or *since* for each of the blanks.

1. He has lived in the dorm _____ 3 years.
2. That country has exported oil _____ 30 years.
3. She has been the prime minister _____ 1980.
4. That country has been independent _____ more than 100 years.
5. He has worked at that company _____ his whole life.
6. She has been an engineer _____ her graduation from college.
7. He hasn't been healthy _____ the war.
8. She hasn't come to class _____ a long time.

EXERCISE 1-15   Present Perfect vs. Present vs. Past

Directions
　　There are mistakes in some of the verbs below. Underline the mistakes and then give the sentences in their correct forms.

Example
　　　Sid <u>is</u> a student at Hoopersburg State University for 3 years.
　→ Sid <u>has been</u> a student at Hoopersburg State University for 3 years.

1. Jim has met Cindy 3 years ago.
2. Hoopersburg State University has a Computer Science Department since 1975.
3. Cindy received a scholarship after her freshman year of college.
4. Jim has decided to major in computer science during his sophomore year at Hoopersburg State.
5. From 1980 to 1982 Hoopersburg State University accepted 25 percent more international students than in the previous decade.
6. The university has opened a special International Student Advising Center in 1980.
7. Since the opening of the advising center, the university expands the services for its foreign students.
8. The center now provided a special host-family program so that foreign students can stay with American families.
9. It also offers free tickets for local sports and cultural events to all international students.
10. Sid takes advantage of all the special services of the center since the beginning of his sophomore year.

EXERCISE 1-16   Present Perfect vs. Past

Directions

Write a sentence in the present perfect or past about your country with the following time expressions.

Example

→ in 1976 — We had an election in 1976.
→ for 20 years — My country has been independent for 20 years.

1. last year
2. for 6 months
3. never
4. from 1970 to 1980
5. since 1980
6. in 1980
7. just
8. 5 years ago
9. ever
10. 100 years ago

Tense Review **17**

PRESENT PERFECT CONTINUOUS vs. PRESENT PERFECT

EXAMPLES
1. Cindy   has been studying / has studied   accounting for 3 years.
2. Bill's been doing his homework all afternoon. (He isn't finished yet.)
3. Jim has done his homework. (He is finished now.)

EXPLANATION

Form

PRESENT PERFECT CONTINUOUS			
have / has	been	VERB	-ing
has been walking			

PRESENT PERFECT		
have / has	VERB	-ed
has walked		

Meaning

PRESENT PERFECT CONTINUOUS can be used (but is not required) to emphasize the duration of the action in situations where the action began in the past and continues to the present.

4. We've been studying this chapter for 2 days.

When no specific time is mentioned, there is a difference in meaning between the continuous and noncontinuous sentences. Use of the continuous indicates the ongoing nature of the action or situation.

5. Carlos has been dating Rosa. They are going out tonight.
6. Carlos has dated Maria, but he isn't seeing her anymore.

Note: PRESENT PERFECT CONTINUOUS can only be used for continuous actions, not repeated actions.

7. I've already read the chapter three times, and I've been studying it all afternoon.

EXERCISE 1-17 Present Perfect Continuous

Directions

Read the first sentence. Then judge the truth of the following sentences. Circle the T if the sentence is true according to the first sentence. Circle F if it is false. Circle ? if the first sentence does not give enough information to judge the sentence true or false.

1. He's been living in the United States for 2 years.
   - T / F / ?   He began living in the United States 2 years ago.
   - T / F / ?   He has lived in the United States for 2 years.
   - T / F / ?   He doesn't live in the United States anymore.
2. I've been reading a good book.
   - T / F / ?   I have already finished the book.
   - T / F / ?   I began to read the book very recently.
   - T / F / ?   I am still reading the book.
3. He's been attending classes at night.
   - T / F / ?   He began attending classes at night a long time ago.
   - T / F / ?   He is still attending classes at night.
   - T / F / ?   He doesn't attend night classes anymore.

EXERCISE 1-18

Present Perfect vs. Present Perfect Continuous vs. Past

Directions

The following time line shows some events in Wizard's life. Assume that the point labeled *now* is today. Make as many statements as you can about Wizard.

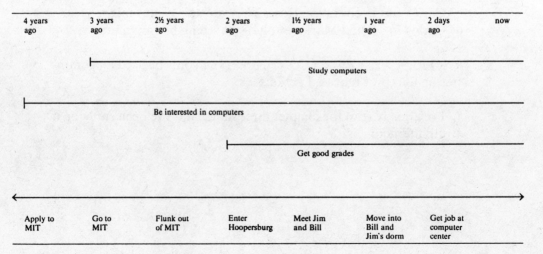

Examples

Wizard applied to MIT in 19____. (4 years ago)

He's been a student at Hoopersburg since 19____.

EXERCISE 1-19
Present Perfect vs. Present Perfect Continuous vs. Past

Directions

Answer the following questions truthfully. Remember to use the simple past tense if you mention specific events in the past and when they occurred.

1. How long have you been here?
2. How many good movies have you seen in the past 2 months?
3. Have you eaten Chinese food recently?
4. Have you met any new friends in the last 2 years?
5. Have you finished your assignments for tomorrow yet?
6. Who have you been writing letters to recently?
7. Which foreign cities have you visited?
8. Have you visited the museums here yet?
9. Have you learned how to spell the names of all your teachers yet?
10. What kinds of things have you been doing on the weekends here?

EXERCISE 1-20 Present Perfect vs. Past vs. Past Perfect

Directions

Write the correct verb forms. All the sentences refer to the same story.

1. My writing teacher last term ____*was*____ the best teacher I _____
                                               a - (be)   b - (ever,
   _____ in my life. I _____ more in her class than I _____
   have)   c - (learn)   d - (ever,
   _____ from any teacher before then. She _____ us a lot of
   learn)   e - (give)
   homework, but we _____ because we _____ more
                                   f - (NEGATIVE, care)   g - (make)
   progress than we _____ in any other class.
                               h - (ever, make)
2. Each week we _____ a composition. The teacher always
                        a - (write)
   _____ interesting topics. After she _____ our
      b - (choose)   c - (read)
   papers, we _____ another chance to improve them. It _____
                 d - (have)   e - (be)
   easier to find our mistakes after we _____ our papers for a while.
                                         f - (NEGATIVE, see)
   Of course, this system _____ that the teacher _____
                                g - (mean)   h - (correct)
   each paper two times. This _____ a lot of work for her, but it really
                                         i - (be)
   _____ us.
     j - (help)

20   GAINING GROUND

3. She _____ my teacher this term. I still see her, though, because we
         a - (NEGATIVE, be)
_____ friends since last term. In fact, she _____
       b - (be)   c - (just, call)
me up to invite me to a party at her house this weekend. I hope my old classmates

will be there. I _____ some of them for a long time.
                    d - (NEGATIVE, see)

PAST INTENTION (*was/were going to* + VERB)

EXAMPLES
1. Wizard was going to get a degree from MIT.
   (Unfortunately, he flunked out.)
2. Jim was going to marry Cindy last spring.
   (But she wanted to wait.)
3. Bill and Jim were going to move off campus.
   (But they didn't have the money.)

EXPLANATION

Form

PAST INTENTION		
was	going to	VERB
were		
was going to walk		

Meaning

This pattern is used to indicate a past intention which was not completed. Sometimes a second clause is added which explains why the intention was not fulfilled. However, this is not necessary.

4. Our class was going to have a picnic, but it rained.
5. Ahmed was going to study English for another term, but he decided to begin academic work instead.
6. Ahmed wasn't going to begin academic work so soon, but his father wanted him to begin.

EXERCISE 1-21 *was/were going to* + VERB

Directions
Read the first sentence. Then judge the truth of the following sentences. Circle T if the sentence is true according to the first sentence. Circle F if it is false. Circle ? if the first sentence does not give enough information to judge the sentence true or false.

1. She was going to hand in her paper on time last week.
    T / F / ?   She planned to hand it in on time.
    T / F / ?   She did not hand it in on time.
    T / F / ?   She took a long time to hand in her paper.
2. They were going to have a picnic tomorrow.
    T / F / ?   They are going to have a picnic tomorrow.
    T / F / ?   They had plans to have a picnic tomorrow.
    T / F / ?   Something changed their plans for a picnic.

EXERCISE 1-22 *was/were going to* + VERB

Directions
Give the reason why you did not do each of the following actions. Use the subject given.

Example
> my brother — study abroad
> → My brother was going to study abroad, but he got married.

1. I — learn Russian
2. my father — give me a car
3. the teacher — give an exam
4. the policeman — arrest me
5. my landlord — fix my refrigerator
6. I — go swimming on Saturday
7. the teacher — call on me
8. my friend — move
9. my mother — call me
10. my neighbor — lend me his car

EXERCISE 1-23 *was/were going to* + VERB

Directions

Tell something that you or someone else was planning to do. Use was/were going to + VERB. Then explain why you or the other person didn't do it.

Example

→ I was going to study at the National University at home, but I didn't pass the entrance exam.

FUTURE TIME (*will* vs. *be going to*)

EXAMPLES
1. Bill   will / is going to   apply for a summer job in his hometown.
2. Will Jim and Cindy / Are Jim and Cindy going to   get married after graduation?
3. Walt   will / is going to   spend the summer in Hawaii.

EXPLANATION

Form

GOING TO - FUTURE		
am		
is	going to	VERB
are		
is going to walk		

WILL - FUTURE	
will	VERB
will walk	

Meaning

Both forms indicate a future action. Often the two forms are interchangeable (see Examples 1, 2, 3).

Use *will* to signal a promise.

4. I'll help you find an apartment.
5. I won't bother you while you're studying.

Use *will* to volunteer spontaneously.

6. I'll answer it. (The phone is ringing.)

Use *be going to* to express a plan or an action which is planned.

7. I've been thinking about my birthday money. I'm going to put it in my savings account.
8. I have to go buy some ice cubes. I'm going to have a party tonight.

EXERCISE 1-24 Future: *will* vs. *be going to*

Directions
In the dialogue below *will* and *be going to* are sometimes interchangeable. The italicized words indicate a future promise, a voluntary action, or a plan. Write A for a promise; write B for a voluntary action; write C for a plan.

                Cindy: Look at those black clouds! It's going to rain this afternoon.
1. _____ Jim: And I didn't bring an umbrella. *I'm going to start* listening to the news so that this doesn't happen again.
                Cindy: Well, I'm going to leave now and get home before it starts to
2. _____   pour. *I'll see* you tomorrow.
3. _____ Jim: I don't think so. *I'm going to see* Dr. Hobson at 9:30, and I'll
4. _____   probably be busy all day. *I'll call* you sometime in the afternoon.
5. _____ Cindy: I don't know exactly when I'll be home. *I'm going to meet* some friends for lunch and then study in the library.
6. _____ Jim: Maybe I'll see you there. In any case we*'ll talk* sometime tomorrow.
                Cindy: OK. Don't get too wet!

EXERCISE 1-25 Future: *will* vs. *be going to*

Directions
Answer the following questions truthfully.

1. What are you going to do this weekend?
2. Where will you eat dinner tonight?
3. Who are you going to call this weekend?
4. How long are you going to stay here?
5. How will you spend your next vacation?
6. Will you see your family soon?

7. When are you going to have a party?
8. Which movie are you going to see this weekend?
9. Are you going to register for next semester?
10. How many people are you going to invite to dinner?
11. Who are you going to eat lunch/dinner with?
12. What will you do about making new friends here?

EXERCISE 1-26 Future: *will* vs. *be going to*

Directions
Complete the following sentences, using *will* or *be going to*, according to your own choice.

1. At the end of the term
2. After I finish my English courses,
3. In the year 2000
4. In one month
5. When my lease expires,
6. After my last final examination
7. The next time I see my parents
8. In a couple of days
9. Sometime in the future
10. Next year

FUTURE TIME: Present and Present Continuous

EXAMPLES
1. Walt is leaving for New York tonight at 9:30, and he'll be back Sunday evening.
2. The university isn't sponsoring any social activities over the weekend.
3. Sid is going home with Bill this weekend.
4. According to the brochure, flight 015 to New York arrives at 2:15 p.m. Sunday afternoon.

EXPLANATION

Form

PRESENT	
VERB	-s
walks	

PRESENT CONTINUOUS		
am		
is	VERB	-ing
are		
is walking		

Meaning

Both PRESENT and PRESENT CONTINUOUS can signal a future action which is planned or scheduled. In contrast to *will/be going to*, these forms express great certainty about an action in the immediate future. Use a time expression with both forms.

Note: Verbs of leaving and arriving, beginning and ending are frequently used in these forms.

5. Are you taking the next TOEFL?
6. Intramural tennis tournaments don't take place until later in the term.

EXERCISE 1-27 Future: Present and Present Continuous

Directions

The itinerary below gives information about the President's trip to New York next week. Comment on his schedule.

	Time	Activity	Place
MONDAY	10 a.m.	arrival	J. F. Kennedy Airport
	12 p.m.	lunch	Plaza Hotel, NYC
	2 p.m.	speech on foreign policy	UN General Assembly
	5 p.m.	meeting with NATO allies	UN Building
	7 p.m.	dinner and speech	Labor Union Convention
TUESDAY	8 a.m.	breakfast and meeting with advisers	Plaza Hotel
	10 a.m.	meeting with NY governor	Federal Building
	12 p.m.	departure	J. F. Kennedy Airport

Example

→ The President gives / is giving a speech at 2:00 on Monday. The UN General Assembly meets / is meeting at 2:00 Monday.

EXERCISE 1-28   Future: Present and Present Continuous

Directions

Discuss activities, performances, and events which are scheduled for this week/weekend/month. (Refer to a local or school newspaper for exact times and locations.)

Example

→ The Pittsburgh Steelers   are playing / play   the Miami Dolphins on Sunday at 2:00.

→ A new art show   opens / is opening   at the Museum Tuesday.

EXERCISE 1-29   Future: Review

Directions

Write the future form of the verb. For some sentences more than one form of the future is appropriate.

1. Starting next week I _____ a class in self-defense on Saturday
                          a - (take)
mornings. The self-defense class _____ at 10:00 a.m., so I
                                       b - (meet)
_____ plenty of time to do other things in the afternoon.
     c - (have)
2. This summer the annual arts festival _____ the second week of
                                           a - (take place)
July. A friend of mine _____ in the festival. Last year he sold all his
                         b - (participate)
paintings, so he _____ more of his work this year.
                     c - (bring)
3. Jim and Cindy _____ married the summer after graduation. They
                      a - (get)
_____ all of their college friends in addition to their families. The
    b - (invite)
wedding ceremony _____ at the Baptist Church, and they
                          c - (be)
_____ a reception at Cindy's parents' home afterward.
    d - (have)
4. There _____ a meeting of everyone in our neighborhood this
             a - (be)
Thursday evening. We _____ about the recent robberies on the
                             b - (talk)
block. A policeman _____ and _____ us advice
                         c - (come)   d - (give)
about stopping crime.

Tense Review

EXERCISE 1-30 Future — Review

Directions
More than one form of the future is possible in many of the blanks. Write the letter(s) of all the possible future forms in each of the blanks.

    a. will + VERB   c. PRESENT TENSE
    b. be going to + VERB   d. PRESENT CONTINUOUS

Example

Wiz ____a, b, d____ to Hawaii for his summer vacation. His father
            1 - (go)
_____ him some extra money and _____ for the
  2 - (send)   3 - (pay)
airfare. While he is there, Wiz _____ with his cousins, who have
                                   4 - (stay)
already rented a condominium near the beach.

    He has already decided that he _____ every morning at the beach.
                                      5 - (spend)
Wiz learned how to surf 2 years ago. This summer he _____ his style
                                                    6 - (perfect)
and _____ a competition in August. He probably _____
    7 - (enter)   8 - (be able to meet)
a lot of girls on the beach, too.

    As everything stands now, he _____ Los Angeles on May 15. His
                                         9 - (leave)
flight _____ in Honolulu at 12 noon, so he _____
    10 - (arrive)   11 - (have)
some time to look around Honolulu before he drives to his cousins' place.

EXERCISE 1-31 Review

Directions
Look at the following time line. Describe the events and periods in Jim and Cindy's lives, using the verb tenses you have just been studying.

Example
→ Jim and Cindy got engaged 1 year ago.

	4 years ago	3 years ago	2 years ago	1 year ago	now
CINDY	Applies to Hoopersburg State U.	Enters Hoopersburg State U.	Gets a scholarship	Gets engaged	
JIM	Applies to Hoopersburg State U.	Enters Hoopersburg State U. Begins computer science Gets student loan	Decides to major in computer science	Gets engaged	Decides to get a job after graduation

Additional periods:
- Jim and Cindy meet for the first time (3 years ago)
- Jim begins rooming with Bill (2 years ago)
- Cindy decides to major in accounting (1 year ago)
- Cindy has a scholarship (from 2 years ago onward)
- Jim has a student loan (from 3 years ago onward)

EXERCISE 1-32 Review

Directions
Ask your classmates questions about Jim and Cindy using the time line.

Example
→ How long had they known each other before they got engaged?
   Two and a half years.

Tense Review   29

EXERCISE 1-33   Review

Directions
Tell the class about a famous person in the history of your country.

Example
→ Abraham Lincoln was President of the United States during the American Civil War.

EXERCISE 1-34   Review

Directions
Make questions based on the time line of Sid's life. Ask your classmates to answer.

Example
→ How long has Sid had financial troubles?
→ For about 1½ years.

Time line: Sid's Life

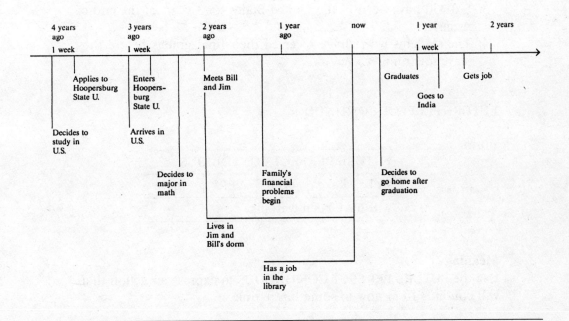

30 GAINING GROUND

FINE POINTS FOR RECOGNITION

FUTURE PERFECT

Form

FUTURE PERFECT			
will	have	VERB	-ed
will have walked			

Meaning

Use the FUTURE PERFECT to express an action that will occur or be completed by a specified future time.

Useful time expressions: by. before. on. in

EXAMPLES
1. By next summer Jim and Bob will have graduated.
2. In February Jim and Cindy will have known each other for 3½ years.
3. Sid will have been in the United States for 3 years at the end of August.
4. The students won't have received their final grades before they leave for summer vacation.

FUTURE PERFECT CONTINUOUS

Form

FUTURE PERFECT CONTINUOUS				
will	have	been	VERB	-ing
will have been walking				

Meaning

Use the FUTURE PERFECT CONTINUOUS to express an action that will continue from now to some future time.

Useful time expressions: by. before. on. in

EXAMPLES

1. Sid will have been living in the dorm for 2 years in June.
2. Wiz will have been working with computers for 4 years when he graduates.
3. In September Bill, Sid, and Jim will have been attending Hoopersburg State University for 3 years.

SUMMARY

1. PRESENT
   Bill *has* class at 9:00 every day.
2. PRESENT CONTINUOUS
   This term Bill *is taking* 18 credits.
3. PAST
   Jim *came* to Hoopersburg 3 years ago.
4. PAST CONTINUOUS
   While Jim *was talking* on the phone, Sid knocked on the door.
5. PAST PERFECT
   Sid came to the United States after he *had decided* to major in math.
6. PRESENT PERFECT
   Bill and Jim *have been* roommates for 3 years.
7. PRESENT PERFECT CONTINUOUS
   Cindy *has been studying* accounting since her freshman year.
8. WAS/WERE GOING TO + VERB
   Jim *was going to marry* Cindy last spring.
9. WILL/GOING TO + VERB
   Wiz *is going to/will spend* the summer in Hawaii.
10. PRESENT and PRESENT CONTINUOUS as FUTURE
    Sid *is going* home with Bill this weekend.

Modals   2

Part I   Permission, Requests, Advice, Necessity

ASKING AND GIVING PERMISSION (*can/could/may*)

EXAMPLES

1. (Informal)   Can I use your eraser?   Sure.
2. (Formal)   Could I look at your map, please?   Yes.
3. (Formal)   May we leave now, please?   Yes.

EXPLANATION

Form

ASKING PERMISSION				
Can				
May	I	VERB	please	?
Could	We			
Could I open the window please?				

GIVING PERMISSION
Yes.
Sure.
OK.

REFUSING PERMISSION		
Sorry	,	REASON
No		

32

Meaning
For asking permission *can* is used in informal situations.

4. Can I borrow your calculator?
   Sorry, I'm using it right now.

Could or *may* is used in formal situations.

5. Could I have another form, please?
   Yes.
6. May I put my books here, please?
   Yes.

For refusing permission *no* is usually limited to formal situations. *Sorry* is used in both formal and informal situations. It is polite to give an explanation or reason for your refusal.

Note: To be polite you should use *please* when asking permission.

EXERCISE 2-1 Asking and Giving Permission

Directions
Ask the person indicated for permission. A second person should respond to the question.

Example
      teacher — leave/room
→ A: May I please leave the room?
   B: Yes, you may. / Certainly.

1. friend — use/calculator
2. teacher — use/pencil

3. classmate — see/schedule of courses
4. teacher — call/at home
5. teacher — borrow/book
6. friend — borrow/pencil
7. stranger — sit/here
8. stranger — open/window
9. professor — return/this (tomorrow)
10. friend — use/pencil sharpener

EXERCISE 2-2 Asking and Giving Permission

Directions

Ask permission to do something in each of the following situations. Before you begin, tell whom you are addressing.

1. You broke your glasses. Your assigned seat is in the back of the writing class.
2. You forgot your grammar book and the teacher is beginning an exercise in it.
3. You're having dinner at your teacher's house, and you would like more bread.
4. Your headphones aren't working in your language laboratory class. The seat next to yours is empty.
5. You are filling out a form in the registrar's office, and you must use a pencil. You have only a pen.
6. You want to get a cat. You're sharing an apartment with friends.
7. In class, the window next to you is open and you are cold.
8. Your research paper is due on Wednesday, but you know that you can't finish typing it until Friday.
9. A friend is arriving at the airport this evening, and you want to use your roommate's car to pick him up.

MAKING AND ANSWERING REQUESTS (*can/could/will/would*)

EXAMPLES
1. (Informal)   Can you shut the window?   OK.
2. (Formal)   Could you explain that again, please?   Yes.
3. (Informal)   Will you shut the door, please?   Sure.

Modals   **35**

EXPLANATION

Form

MAKING A REQUEST

Will				
Can	you	VERB	please	?
Would				
Could				

Could you open the window please?

AGREEING TO A REQUEST

Yes.
Sure.
OK.

REFUSING A REQUEST

Sorry		REASON
No	,	

Sorry, I have a cold.

Meaning

A REQUEST means asking another person to do something for you. (Permission concerns your own actions.)

For making a request *will, can,* or *would* is used in informal situations.

4. Can you pick me up in front of the library? Sure.
5. Will you turn that down while I'm on the phone, please? OK.

Could is used in formal situations.

6. Could you show me how you did that, please?
   No, I can show you after class.

Note: The answers to requests are the same as the answers for giving permission (see page 32).

EXERCISE 2-3 Making Requests

Directions

Read the first sentence. Then judge the truth of the following sentences. Circle T if the sentence is true according to the first sentence. Circle F if it is false. Circle ? if the first sentence does not give enough information to judge the sentence true or false.

1. Could you show me where the men's shirts are, please?
   T / F / ?   This request is in the past.
   T / F / ?   This request is at a suitable level of politeness for addressing a stranger.
2. Will you shut the window?
   T / F / ?   The speaker wants the window shut now.
   T / F / ?   The speaker is speaking politely to a stranger.
3. Would you turn off the lights before you leave, please?
   T / F / ?   The situation is very informal.
   T / F / ?   The speaker is addressing a friend.
4. Can you lend me your dictionary for a minute?
   T / F / ?   The speaker is addressing a friend.
   T / F / ?   The situation is very formal.

EXERCISE 2-4 Making Requests

Directions

Make the following requests to the people indicated. A second person should answer the requests.

1. friend — lend a dime
2. teacher — spell that word
3. stranger — open the door
4. classmate — move chair
5. classmate — shut the window
6. teacher — explain that answer
7. policeman — give directions
8. store clerk — help find a gift
9. friend — pass the salt
10. coworker — turn out the lights

EXERCISE 2-5 Making Requests

Directions

Make a request for each of the following situations. Before you begin, tell whom you are talking to.

1. You are ready to start a test, but you don't have a pencil.
2. Your professor invites you to her home for dinner and you don't know where she lives.
3. You are waiting for a bus with some strangers and don't have your watch on.
4. The person behind the counter at the doughnut shop gives you a cup of coffee but no sugar.
5. You are hot in class, and another student is sitting closer to the window.
6. You get on an elevator, and a stranger is standing in front of the panel of buttons.
7. You are at the window in the cashier's office of the university, and you don't understand your bill.
8. You are getting on a city bus, and you are not sure where your stop is.
9. Your reading teacher uses a word that you want to look up in your dictionary, but you don't know how to spell it.
10. Your friend understands the homework exercise and you don't.

EXERCISE 2-6 Making Requests

Directions

For each of the situations given, indicate the possible request form(s) that is/are most appropriate. Explain your choice briefly.

        a. Will   b. Can   c. Would   d. Could

1. You are on a bus and you want the person who is standing in front of the rack of schedules to hand you one of them.
2. You can't get the lid off a jar of mustard, and you want your roommate to help.
3. You didn't quite catch the example your grammar teacher just gave.
4. You didn't understand your doctor when she was explaining how often you should take your medicine.
5. You want your former landlord to mail your security deposit to your new address.
6. You want your roommate's little brother to tell her that you called.
7. You want to move the desk in your room. You ask your roommate to help you.
8. Your friend is going grocery shopping. You ask her to buy a newspaper for you.

38   GAINING GROUND

GIVING ADVICE (*should, ought to*) and STATING NECESSITY (*must, have/has to*)

EXAMPLES
1. You   must / have to   sign your passport to make it valid.
2. You   should / ought to   wear clean clothes to school.
3. You   must / have to   wear shoes to school.

EXPLANATION

Form

GIVING ADVICE – PRESENT

should	VERB
ought to	

should write
ought to write

GIVING ADVICE – PAST

should	have	VERB	-ed
ought to			

should have written
ought to have written

STATING NECESSITY – PRESENT

must	
has to	VERB
have to	

must sign
has to sign

STATING NECESSITY – PAST

had to	VERB

had to sign

Note: Must have cannot be used to indicate past necessity.

See page 58 for the meaning of *must have*.

Meaning
These are the MODAL VERBS most commonly used to give advice or to discuss whether an action is advisable or necessary.

Giving advice

Should and *ought to* are synonyms. Use *should* or *ought to* when the action is advisable, but not absolutely necessary.

4. You   should / ought to   do your homework. (or the teacher will be angry)

Note: Ought to is rarely used in questions and negatives, so avoid using it in those situations. Use *should* for questions and negatives.

5. You shouldn't interrupt the teacher.
6. Should he tell the professor that his report will be late?

Use *should have* and *ought to have* for past situations when the action was advisable but did not happen.

7. You should have stayed home last night and rested. (You didn't stay home last night.)
8. It's raining now. I should have brought an umbrella. (I didn't bring one.)

Stating necessity

Use *must* or *have to* when the action is absolutely necessary:

See Example 1:   A passport is not valid without a signature.
See Example 3:   You are not permitted in school without shoes.

Use *had to* to express a past necessity.

9. In elementary school I had to wear a uniform.

EXERCISE 2-7   Giving Advice and Stating Necessity

Directions

Read the first sentence. Then judge the truth of the following sentences. Circle T if the sentence is true according to the first sentence. Circle F if it is false. Circle ? if the first sentence does not give enough information to judge the sentence true or false.

1. I ought to finish this paper by tomorrow. I have other homework due on Friday.
   T / F / ?   Something horrible will happen if I don't finish it.
   T / F / ?   I have to finish it by tomorrow.
   T / F / ?   It is a good idea to finish it by tomorrow.
2. She has to maintain a C average.
   T / F / ?   She must maintain a C average.
   T / F / ?   A C average is necessary for her.
3. They should have bought their tickets earlier.
   T / F / ?   They bought their tickets earlier.
   T / F / ?   They should buy their tickets soon.

40 GAINING GROUND

EXERCISE 2-8 Giving Advice

Directions
Give advice for the situation, using *should* or *ought to*.

Example
My teacher's wife had a baby.
→ I should congratulate him.
→ Our class ought to buy the baby a present.

1. The picture on my TV isn't very clear.
2. I need to get some exercise.
3. The weather forecast predicts cold weather for today.
4. The paint in my bedroom is in bad condition.
5. My brother is planning to visit London this summer.
6. I can see a strange man outside my neighbor's house.
7. My sister doesn't know what to study at the university.
8. I need a costume for a party this weekend.

EXERCISE 2-9 Giving Advice

Directions
Comment on the following situations, using *should(n't) have*.

Example
He failed the test.
→ He should have studied more.

1. I was late for class this morning.
2. She's all wet from the rain.
3. It's 10:00 a.m. and I'm really hungry.
4. He got a parking ticket today.
5. I overslept this morning.
6. I got a headache from watching TV last night.
7. They wanted to go to Hong Kong, but there were no more seats on the plane.
8. We got lost when we were driving through the city.

Modals 41

EXERCISE 2-10   Stating Necessity

Directions
Write the correct tense of *have to* in the blanks below.

Example
Jim ___*had to*___ apply for a student loan so he could afford to go to college.

1. Before Jim received the student loan, he _____ submit his father's financial statement.
2. He _____ reapply for the loan every year since then.
3. Jim _____ repay the loan after he graduates.
4. At the beginning of his junior year Bill _____ request a bigger loan to cover the increase in tuition.
5. Since he began studying, Jim _____ follow a very strict budget.
6. Jim _____ be careful about every dollar he spends.

EXERCISE 2-11   Stating Necessity

Directions
State what is necessary for the situation, using *have/has to* or *must*.

Example
I'm going to the United States to study.
→ I must apply for a visa.
→ I have to get a passport.

1. Steve doesn't have any food in his refrigerator.
2. My telephone bill is due the day after tomorrow.
3. I received my new driver's license, but I haven't signed it yet.
4. Susan is very sick. The doctor gave her some medicine.
5. The teacher asked me to come to his office after class.
6. Tuition for this term is due by the end of the week.
7. I want to drive to the beach tomorrow. My car needs gas.
8. I want to place a call to London. The operator doesn't speak my language.

EXERCISE 2-12 Giving Advice and Stating Necessity

Directions

Give advice or state what is necessary for the situation, using *should, ought to, must,* or *have/has to*.

Example

Mary wants to eat some Chinese food.
→ She should try the Ming Garden Restaurant on First Street.
→ She should have gone with us to Chang's last week.

1. John's rent is due tomorrow. The landlord will throw him out if he doesn't pay on time.
2. Now that Mary is living at college, her parents really miss her.
3. Registration ends tomorrow. Bill hasn't registered yet, and he doesn't have the money to pay a late fee.
4. It's May and I need some summer clothes.
5. Jim is working on his U.S. income tax form. The tax form is due on April 15.
6. I haven't talked to my friend Sally in 2 weeks.
7. My TV isn't working very well.
8. The teacher won't accept handwritten papers.
9. I'm gaining weight.

EXPRESSING PROHIBITION (*must not*) and LACK OF NECESSITY (*don't/doesn't have to*)

EXAMPLES
1. You must not drive without a license.
2. Americans don't have to carry ID cards.

EXPLANATION

Form

PROHIBITION - PRESENT		
must	not	VERB
must not drink		

LACK OF NECESSITY – PRESENT
do / does	not	have to	VERB

doesn't have to sign

LACK OF NECESSITY – PAST
did	not	have to	VERB

didn't have to sign

Meaning

In affirmative sentences, *must* and *have to* have the same meaning. In negative sentences, however, their meanings are different.

Use *must not* to express something that is not permitted (i.e., something that is prohibited). There is no past form for this meaning of *must not*.

3. You must not write your research paper in pencil. (Pencil is not permitted.)

Use *don't/doesn't have to* to express something that is permitted, but is not necessary. Use *didn't have to* to express something that was not necessary.

4. You don't have to type your research paper. (Typed papers are permitted, but not necessary.)
5. We didn't have to do any homework last night. (Our teacher was sick yesterday.)

EXERCISE 2-13 Expressing Prohibition and Lack of Necessity

Directions

Read the first sentence. Then judge the truth of the following sentences. Circle T if the sentence is true according to the first sentence. Circle F if it is false. Circle ? if the first sentence does not give enough information to judge the sentence true or false.

1. You must not pick the flowers in the park.
   T / F / ? There is a punishment for picking them if you are caught.
   T / F / ? Picking them is forbidden.
2. He doesn't have to take the entrance exam.
   T / F / ? He isn't permitted to take it.
   T / F / ? He should take it.
   T / F / ? The exam isn't necessary.
3. She didn't have to sign the contract.
   T / F / ? Her signature was not required.
   T / F / ? She was not permitted to sign the contract.

EXERCISE 2-14   Expressing Prohibition and Lack of Necessity

Directions

Paraphrase the following situations using *must not* or *don't/doesn't have to*.

Example

Health insurance is optional for students.
→ Students don't have to get health insurance.

1. The air pollution device on Wizard's car is broken. The law requires all cars to have a functioning air pollution device.
2. We can choose whether or not to attend the final class; it's optional.
3. A special permit is required to park in the lot. I don't have such a permit.
4. American citizens are not required to have a visa to visit Canada.
5. You are not permitted to leave until I collect the test booklets.
6. The final exam in my history class is a closed book exam.
7. Voting is not obligatory in U.S. elections; it's optional.
8. Utilities are included in the monthly rent of my apartment.

GIVING STRONG ADVICE (*had better*)

EXAMPLES
1. You'd better do your homework (or the teacher will give you a zero).
2. He'd better do well on the final exam (or he won't pass the course).
3. You'd better not be late (or you'll miss the plane).

EXPLANATION

Form

GIVING STRONG ADVICE		
had better	(not)	VERB
had better go		

Meaning

The meaning of *had better* is very similar to that of *should* and *ought to*. However, *had better* is slightly stronger because it always includes some implied or stated bad consequence of not following the advice.

Use *had better* only when giving advice to an equal or a subordinate, never to a superior.

Often *should*, *ought to*, and *had better* are interchangeable but not always. In the examples below, *should* and *ought to* are appropriate but not *had better*:

4. If you go to Hawaii, you should stay at Waikiki.
5. You should get a cat to keep you company.
6. You should try this new herbal tea. It's great.

EXERCISE 2-15 Giving Strong Advice

Directions
Give a comment of strong advice for the situations using *had better*.

Example
Pete is failing his math course.
→ He'd better do well on the final exam.

1. You know you're going to be absent tomorrow.
2. The doctor told you to take the medicine for 5 days.
3. This street is a no-parking zone.
4. The swimming pool is very deep, and there is no life guard on duty.
5. The brakes on my car are making a strange noise.
6. I think there is something wrong with my tooth.
7. Smoke is coming out of the TV.
8. They predict that the river will flood this week.

EXERCISE 2-16 Advisability and Necessity — Review

Directions
Answer the questions, using the modal verbs of advisability and necessity.

1. Name some things that you ought to do, but that are not absolutely necessary.
2. Name some things that are not permitted in some countries, but are permitted in your country.
3. Name some things that you have to do every week.
4. Name some things that you have to do in some countries, which you don't have to do in your country.

EXERCISE 2-17 Giving Advice — Review

Directions

For each situation tell your friend how he or she should have avoided the problem. Then, give him or her some advice to use now.

1. Your friend had a terrible accident with her car. She had no insurance and she wasn't wearing a seat belt. The police say she was speeding.
2. Your friend is unhappy with his new apartment. It has roaches, the heat doesn't work, and someone stole his TV last week.
3. Your friend's girlfriend is angry with him. He forgot her birthday. Her parents didn't like his behavior.

EXERCISE 2-18 Permission and Requests — Review

Directions

For each of the following situations, (1) make a request and (2) ask permission. Tell whom you are talking to.

1. post office
2. library
3. friend's house
4. football game
5. grocery store
6. bus
7. airport
8. department store
9. movie theater
10. pharmacy

Modals   **47**

Part II   Ability, Possibility, Expectation, Deduction

EXPRESSING ABILITY (*can/could*)

EXAMPLES
1. Sid can speak English well.
2. When he was a child, Sid could speak only Hindi.
3. When Wiz was in high school, he could already use a home computer.
4. Sid could have gone to a university in India.

EXPLANATION

Form

ABILITY – PRESENT		ABILITY – PAST		ABILITY – PAST			
can	VERB	could	VERB	could	have	VERB	-ed
can speak		could speak		could have studied			

Meaning
Use *can* to express a present skill or ability.

5. I can't play the guitar, but I'd like to learn.
6. Can you ride a bicycle?

Use *could* to express a past personal skill or ability. The skill or ability is usually a result of practice or training.

7. When could you first understand TV in English?

Use *could have* to express a past opportunity.

8. The pilot could have refused to take the hijackers to Cuba. (He was able to refuse, but he didn't refuse.)

Note: Could have expresses the idea that an action was possible, but it did not happen.

48 GAINING GROUND

EXERCISE 2-19   Expressing Ability

Directions
Answer the questions.

1. What can you do better than most people?
2. What can a two-year-old child do?
3. What can very strong men do?
4. What can't very old people do?
5. According to the Bible and the Koran, what could Moses do?
6. What can't animals do?
7. What could you do as a child that you can't do now?
8. What could you do better than your brothers or sisters when you were a child?

EXERCISE 2-20   Expressing Past Opportunity

Directions
Name five things that you could have done in your life which you didn't do. Explain why you didn't do each thing.

Example
→ I could have visited London last year, but my father wanted me to help at his shop.
→ I could have taken calculus last term, but I decided to wait until next year.

EXPRESSING POSSIBILITY (*could/may/might*)

EXAMPLES
1. It might rain later on. (I can see dark clouds on the horizon.)
2. Sid may get a special scholarship next year. (Sometimes foreign students receive the award.)
3. Bill could get B's in all his courses this term. (So far he has C's, but the final exams count for 50 percent of the grade.)
4. Sid's father might have lost his job.
5. Don't call her now, she may be sleeping.

EXPLANATION

Form

POSSIBILITY - PRESENT			
could	VERB		
might			
may	be	VERB	-ing

could be waiting
might wait

POSSIBILITY - PAST			
might	have	VERB	-ed
may			

might have waited

Meaning

All three MODALS express a weak possibility. *May* indicates a greater degree of certainty than *could* and *might*. These MODALS express a possibility, but not a probability.

NEGATIVES: When *not* appears in the sentences with these MODALS, *might* and *may* keep the same meanings.

6. You might not like the taste of root beer.

Although affirmative *can* is not used to show possibility, negative *can't* is used and has the same meaning as *couldn't*. Both *can't* and *couldn't* indicate great certainty.

7. This bill   can't / couldn't   be correct. I've never called Paris in my life!

Scale of certainty:

EXERCISE 2-21 Expressing Possibility

Directions

Read the sentence carefully. Circle the letter of the sentence below with the same meaning.

Example

You might not like the taste of root beer.
a. You probably did not like root beer.
b. It is very probable that you will not like root beer.
ⓒ It is possible that you will not like root beer.

1. I may have change for a dollar. Let me check.
    a. I have change for a dollar.
    b. I'm sure that I have change for a dollar.
    c. It seems possible that I have change.
2. The mail could be here already.
    a. The mailman delivered the mail earlier.
    b. There's a possibility that the mail is already here.
    c. I'm sure the mail is already here.
3. This can't be my bag of groceries.
    a. It is not possible that this bag is mine.
    b. This is my bag of groceries.
    c. It is not certain that this bag is mine.
4. The flight from Toronto might arrive late.
    a. It was possible that the flight was late.
    b. It is possible that the flight will be late.
    c. It is probable that the flight will be late.

Modals   51

Past time:
All three MODALS may refer to the present or a future time. *May have*
and *might have* express past possibility; remember *could have* usually
expresses past ability not past possibility (see page 47).

8. The professor may have finished correcting our exams already.

Note: Use the CONTINUOUS form of the verb to express a continuing
action. There is no change in meaning of the MODAL.

9. John's line is busy. He could be talking to his parents.

EXERCISE 2-22   Expressing Past Possibility

Directions
Write the appropriate form of the verb.

Example

The street looks wet.

→ They may ___*have cleaned*___ it a few minutes ago.
                (clean)

1. Ali arrived late at Chen's party last night.

   a. He may _____ the bus.
                    (miss)
   b. He might _____ a flat tire.
                    (have)
   c. He might _____ to buy some soda on his way to the party.
                    (go)
   d. He may not _____ the way to Chen's house.
                    (know)

2. The tunnel under the river was closed this morning.

   a. There may _____ an accident in the tunnel.
                    (be)
   b. They may _____ it in order to work on it.
                    (close)
   c. There might _____ too much carbon dioxide in it.
                    (be)

3. Class was canceled yesterday.

   a. The professor may _____ sick.
                    (be)
   b. They might _____ the class for a different time.
                    (schedule)
   c. The professor may _____ out of town.
                    (go)

EXERCISE 2-23 Expressing Possibility

Directions
Choose the correct verb form. CONTINUOUS verb forms may be appropriate in some sentences.

Example
It might __b__ later on.
a. rained   c. raining
b. rain   d. to rain

1. My car may _____ new brakes.
   a. needs   c. to need
   b. be needing d. need
2. Your check could _____ today. It'll be here by tomorrow for sure.
   a. to arrive   c. arrive
   b. be arriving d. arrived
3. The man can't _____ of natural causes. He was hit on the head.
   a. dying   c. has died
   b. died   d. have died
4. The plane from London is late. There may _____ bad weather there.
   a. being   c. have
   b. been   d. have been
5. Be quiet! The baby may _____ .
   a. sleep   c. be sleeping
   b. slept   d. have slept
6. I know my friend is home, but she doesn't answer the phone. She might _____ a shower.
   a. be taking   c. took
   b. takes   d. take
7. There could _____ some more juice in the refrigerator.
   a. be   c. is
   b. being d. been
8. The university might _____ the tuition next year.
   a. have raised   c. raise
   b. raising   d. raised
9. I didn't go to see my parents in August. I could _____ them during the next vacation.
   a. have visited c. have visit
   b. visit   d. be visiting

Modals 53

EXERCISE 2-24 Expressing Possibility

Directions

Give the appropriate form of the verb.

Examples

Don't call her now. She may ____*be sleeping*____.
                                          a - (sleep)
Steve looked upset this morning. He might _*have received*_ some bad
                                                    a - (receive)
news from home.

1. John and Bill are still in the classroom with the professor. She may
   _____ the homework.
         a - (explain)
2. I called my family last week, but no one answered. They might_____
                                                                              a - (be)
   out of town that day.
3. The children usually play out in the garden, but I don't see them. They could
   _____ in the park.
         a - (play)
4. When I got to the party, no one was there. They may _____ to a
                                                                    a - (go)
   bigger apartment.
5. I went to see my friend last night, but she wasn't there. She may_____
                                                                                   a - (be)
   at the library.
6. I can't find my wallet. I may _____ it on the bus.
                                          a - (lose)
7. Ted and I agreed to meet at the library, but he isn't here yet. He might
   _____ at the other door.
         a - (wait)
8. One of the tires on my car is flat. I may _____ some glass.
                                                        a - (run over)
9. My husband isn't home yet. He may _____ late.
                                                a - (work)
10. I've just found an ashtray on the floor. The baby might_____ it off
                                                                        a - (knock)
    the table.

EXERCISE 2-25 Expressing Possibility

Directions
Comment on the following situations using *could*, *may*, or *might*.

Example
> I have an appointment with Dr. Bowman at 10:00, but she's not here.
> → She could be in the main office. Try room 320.
> → She might have had class until 10:00, so maybe she's coming.

1. It's June, and you see some big clouds on the horizon.
2. There's a new student in your class. His name is Abdullah, but you don't know where he is from.
3. Your friend is absent today. Yesterday he or she felt fine, so you are surprised at his or her absence.
4. You are waiting for the bus. One usually comes every 10 minutes, but there haven't been any buses for 25 minutes.
5. You and your friends agreed to meet at 10:30. It's now 10:50 and one of your friends still hasn't arrived.
6. In 2 weeks you have a 3-day weekend, but you haven't made definite plans yet.
7. Your roommate has lost his or her umbrella. Think of some possible places for the umbrella.
8. You have been calling your family for 3 days, but no one answers the phone.

EXPRESSING EXPECTATION (*should/ought to*)

EXAMPLES
1. According to the schedule, flight 33 should / ought to be here in 20 minutes.
2. With all the rain so far this year we shouldn't have any water shortages this summer.
3. Sid, Bill, and Jim should / ought to graduate in spring next year.

EXPLANATION

Form

EXPECTATION	
should	VERB
ought to	
should arrive	
ought to arrive	

Meaning

Should indicates more certainty than *may, might*, or *could*. The speaker expresses a feeling that an action or condition is probable or expected.

4. We should be in Florida at this time next week. Spring vacation starts this weekend.
5. Hoopersburg State University should win the football championship this season. The team hasn't lost a game yet.

Note: Should + not indicates the same degree of certainty as *should*.

Note: Should usually refers to the future, but it may refer to the present.

6. There should be a lot of information about jazz in the university library since the Music Department here is excellent.

Note: Should have / Ought to have rarely has the meaning of past expectation. See Fine Points for Recognition at end of chapter.

Scale of certainty:

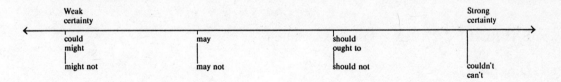

EXERCISE 2-26 Expressing Expectation

Directions
Read the sentence carefully. Circle the letter of the sentence below with the same meaning.

Example
Flight 33 should be here in 20 minutes.
   a. The plane will definitely be here in 20 minutes.
   (b.) The plane is expected to arrive in 20 minutes.
   c. It's possible that the plane will arrive in 20 minutes.

1. The car keys should be in my coat pocket.
   a. I'm positive that the keys are in the pocket.
   b. I'm not very sure that the keys are in the pocket.
   c. I'm fairly sure that the keys are in the pocket.
2. There shouldn't be much traffic today.
   a. The driver knows that there won't be any traffic.
   b. The driver doesn't expect much traffic.
   c. The driver isn't very sure about the traffic.
3. The police should catch the robber easily.
   a. It's necessary that the police will catch the robber.
   b. It's possible that the police will catch the robber.
   c. It's very probable that the police will catch the robber.
4. Your plants should grow quickly by the kitchen window.
   a. The plants will very probably grow quickly.
   b. The plants will definitely grow quickly.
   c. The plants will possibly grow quickly.

EXERCISE 2-27 Expressing Expectation

Directions
Answer the following questions, using *should* or *ought to*.

1. When do you expect to receive a letter from your family?
2. When do you expect to finish your English studies?
3. When do you expect to get home today?
4. What grade do you expect on the next test?

5. Where do you expect to meet your friends for lunch?
6. When do you expect to begin your academic studies?
7. How often do you expect to receive a bank statement?
8. How much do you expect your tuition to be next term?
9. How do you expect the weather to be next month?
10. How much do you expect your telephone bill to be this month?

EXERCISE 2-28 (*could/may/might* vs. *should*)

Directions

Make two comments on the following situations. Use different modals for different degrees of certainty.

Example

A man robbed a local bank. Many bank customers and employees saw the man's face very clearly.
→ The robber may have already left the city.
→ The police should find the man easily.
→ The witnesses may disagree about the man's description.
→ The witnesses shouldn't have any difficulty identifying him.

1. Tuesday is a national holiday.
2. I'm not sure how much it costs to go to the dentist.
3. It's spring, but the weather is rainy and cold.
4. I ordered some books from a catalog, and I have been waiting for them for 3 weeks.
5. A friend of mine moved 3 weeks ago, but he hasn't received his security deposit from his former landlord yet.
6. Registration for next term begins soon, but I haven't received any information from the university or my adviser.
7. We haven't had a test in this class in a while, and we have almost finished the chapter.
8. I have an A average in my homework and a B average in my tests and quizzes.

58   GAINING GROUND

EXPRESSING A DEDUCTION (*must*)

EXAMPLES
1. Bill and Jim must be about 20 if they are college juniors. (Most students begin college at 18.)
2. That old man must not hear very well. (He's wearing a hearing aid.)
3. It must be raining outside. (I can hear the raindrops on the roof.)
4. Cindy must have worked hard during her freshman year. (She received a scholarship her sophomore year.)

EXPLANATION

Form

		VERB		
must	(not)	be	VERB	-ing

DEDUCTION – PRESENT

must be waiting

DEDUCTION – PAST				
must	(not)	have	VERB	-ed

must have waited

Meaning

Must indicates that the speaker is very certain. The speaker has made an inference or deduction based on experience or on visible evidence.

5. Wizard must be very intelligent. He gets good grades, but he doesn't study very hard.
6. Cindy must feel proud of her good grades.

Note: In contrast to *should, must* is generally used for the present time, not the future.

Note: When *not* is added, there is no change in the speaker's degree of certainty. Do not use a contraction for this meaning of *must not*.

7. Jim's father must not earn a lot of money. (Jim has to get a loan for his tuition.)
8. You must not have shut the car window last night. The seats are wet.

Note: Have/had to is never used to express a deduction.

9. Barbara must be taking a lot of difficult courses. She is spending all her time in the library.
10. She must have taken easier courses last semester. She didn't study very much.

Scale of certainty:

```
Weak                                                                    Strong
certainty                                                               certainty
◄───────┬──────────────┬──────────────┬──────────────┬──────────────►
        could          may            should         must
        might                         ought to
        
        might not      may not        should not     must not         couldn't
                                                                      can't
```

EXERCISE 2-29   Expressing a Deduction

Directions
Write C below if the sentence expresses a strong certainty or deduction. Write N if the sentence expresses a necessity. Some sentences have more than one interpretation.

Example

    __C__   Bill and Jim must be around 20 years old.

    __N__   Sid must get a job on campus soon. His father isn't sending him money anymore.

1. _____ Bill and Jim must enjoy being roommates.
2. _____ Sid must worry about his family.
3. _____ Sid must renew his passport before the end of summer.
4. _____ Cindy must maintain a B average to keep her scholarship.
5. _____ Sid must miss his family sometimes.
6. _____ Hoopersburg State University must be a good place to study.
7. _____ Hoopersburg State University must permit qualified students of all races and religions to enroll.
8. _____ Wiz must regret not studying harder at MIT.

EXERCISE 2-30 Expressing a Deduction

Directions
   Give the appropriate form of the verb.

Examples

   They were angry at the waiter. They must _have waited_ a long time for their food.
   a - (wait)

   There are a lot of people sitting at gate 11. They must _be waiting_ for the plane from Athens.
   a - (wait)

1. The Prime Minister and his advisers are meeting. They must _____ the war.
   a - (discuss)
2. The earthquake yesterday was a bad one. It must _____ some buildings.
   a - (destroy)
3. The game is over and everyone is clapping. Our team must _____ .
   a - (win)
4. People are using umbrellas. It must _____ .
   a - (rain)
5. My neighbor is going to move tomorrow. She must _____ a nicer apartment.
   a - (find)
6. Mr. Gibson isn't here yet. He must _____ the bus.
   a - (miss)
7. The Parker family is taking their vacation in Texas again this year. They must _____ it there last year.
   a - (like)
8. I can't find my roommates anywhere in the dormitory. They must _____ in the library.
   a - (study)
9. The children's bicycles are not in the garage. They must _____ them to the park.
   a - (ride)
10. The department store is very crowded today. They must _____ some special sales.
    a - (have)

EXERCISE 2-31 *had to* VERB vs. *must have* VERB-ed

Directions
   Write the correct past modal. Remember *had to* VERB expresses past necessity and *must have* PAST PARTICIPLE expresses a past deduction.

Example

You see a policeman writing a ticket for a parked car. The money in the meter _must have run out_.
a - (run out)

There was a fire alarm at 5:30 a.m., and the firefighters _had to drive_
a - (drive)
to the other side of town.

1. Police cars and ambulances with their sirens and lights are going toward the north side of town. There _____ an accident.
a - (be)
2. The streets and sidewalks are wet this morning. It _____ last night.
a - (rain)
3. One of our classmates was absent from class because he _____ his
a - (take)
wife to the doctor.
4. Your friend's car has a big dent in the door on the driver's side. Someone _____ him. After the accident he _____ the police
a - (hit)   a - (notify)
and his insurance company.
5. Your roommate had a reservation on flight 93 from Houston but she wasn't on the plane. She _____ the plane. Maybe she had trouble with connec-
a - (miss)
tions because she _____ to Houston from Dallas earlier that day.
a - (fly)
6. The students who arrived late missed registration so they _____ a
a - (pay)
fee of $25.
7. My friends didn't pass the examination and _____ a retest.
a - (take)

EXERCISE 2-32 Expressing a Deduction

Directions
Comment on the following situations, using *must* to express a deduction.

Example
    Jim needs a loan to pay his tuition.
    → Jim's father must not earn a lot of money.
    → Jim must think that education is important.

1. You see a fire truck with flashing red lights stop at a nearby building.
2. You notice that there are a lot of advertisements and TV commercials in the United States for dog and cat food.

3. Yesterday your classmate had a headache and felt tired. Today he is not in class.
4. You receive your telephone bill and it lists two calls to Chicago. You don't know anyone in Chicago.
5. A famous university requires a TOEFL score of 600 for all graduate students.
6. A coffee shop near campus is always crowded—day and night.
7. Most graduates of the Computer Science Department at Hoopersburg State University get good jobs after graduation.
8. As you drive by the baseball stadium one afternoon you notice a lot of traffic and parked cars.
9. An apartment house in your neighborhood has a private swimming pool and tennis courts.
10. One of your classmates jogs 7 miles every day.

EXERCISE 2-33 *must* vs. *should*

Directions

Make as many comments on the following situation as you can. Use both *must* and *should*. (Remember, *should* usually refers to the future and *must* to the present.)

Example

The train usually stops at your station around 7:35. It is already 7:40, but the train hasn't arrived yet.
→ It should be here any minute.
→ There must have been some problem at the last station.

1. A good friend of yours is getting married soon, but you haven't received an invitation yet.
2. The national elections are scheduled for next month, and the three major candidates are still campaigning actively.
3. The World Cup soccer matches begin soon.
4. The City Council approved the plan to extend the city subway system.
5. The federal and state governments plan to build a dam in our region for electric power and irrigation.
6. The nurses went on strike last night at Mercy Hospital.
7. Your friend complains that he has terrible headaches, and he has made an appointment to see a specialist.
8. The highway between downtown and the airport will be under construction for the next 3 months.

Modals   **63**

EXERCISE 2-34   *could/may/might/should/must*

Directions

Write the correct form of the verb.

Example

Wiz may not __*have liked*__ the atmosphere at MIT.
a - (like)

It may _____ this afternoon.
a - (rain)

1. Cindy may _____ for 16 credits next semester.
a - (register)

2. Wiz's grades at MIT must _____ his parents.
a - (disappoint)

3. During the second term of their junior year, Bill, Jim, and Sid should

_____ most of their required courses.
a - (complete)

4. Jim and Cindy could _____ in a university closer to home, but
a - (enroll)

they wanted to leave the big city.

5. They might not _____ at home in Hoopersburg when they first
a - (feel)

arrived.

6. Jim and Cindy must _____ living in a small town now, since they
a - (enjoy)

plan to live somewhere similar to Hoopersburg.

7. Tuition fees at Hoopersburg State University may _____ next year
a - (rise)

or the year after.

8. An increase in tuition should _____ some complaints from many
a - (cause)

students' parents.

9. Sid can't _____ about his father's business problems when he first
a - (know)

came to the United States.

10. During his first term at Hoopersburg State University, Sid might _____
a - (be)

lonely and homesick.

EXERCISE 2-35 could/may/might/must

Directions
Answer the questions, using the past forms of the modals. If you use *must have*, give supporting reasons for your deduction.

Example
Why did your teacher come late to class yesterday?
→ She might have overslept.
→ She must have had trouble with her car. She told me last week that it often won't start in the morning.

1. How did Neil Armstrong feel when he walked on the moon?
2. Why was the airport closed yesterday morning?
3. Why was the woman released from jail?
4. Why did your neighbors install an alarm system in their house?
5. How did the wild animals on Hawaii get there? (Hawaii is a volcanic island in the Pacific.)
6. Why did the police close some streets downtown last night?
7. How did the fire on the plane start?
8. How did he break his legs?

EXERCISE 2-36 have to/could — Review

Directions
Answer the questions.

1. What could you do as a child that you can't do now?
2. When you applied to this program, what did you have to do?
3. What science courses could you take in your high school?
4. What did you have to do when you first moved into your room or apartment?
5. What languages could students learn in your high school?
6. What did you have to do to get a scholarship?
7. What could you do better than your brothers or sisters when you were a child?
8. How much did you have to pay for your plane ticket to _____ ?

EXERCISE 2-37 *could/should, ought to/might* — Review

Directions

Give advice to the person indicated about the situations below. Use the past forms of the modals.

Example

A friend missed his or her flight to San Francisco because he or she arrived late at the airport.
→ You should have taken the earlier limousine.
→ You could have driven and left your car at the airport.

1. Your classmate is upset because the teacher didn't accept his or her late composition.
2. Your brother or sister studied literature at the university, and now he or she can't find a job.
3. Your roommate is very tired because he or she couldn't fall asleep last night.
4. Your classmate is very unhappy because he or she has discovered that his or her new apartment has a broken heater.
5. Your high school friend is dissatisfied at his or her U.S. university because it doesn't offer all the courses he or she wants.
6. Your friend is very annoyed because his or her neighbors played their stereo loudly till 2 a.m. last night.
7. Your friends are very upset because someone stole their new TV from their apartment.
8. Your friends are upset because the river flooded their new house and ruined most of the furniture.

66 GAINING GROUND

EXERCISE 2-38 Review

Directions

The choice of modal in each sentence below is appropriate, but there is a mistake in the tense or form of the verb. Find the mistake, underline it, and write the correct verb phrase.

Example

It must be raining last night. *have rained*

You might have gave me the wrong number. *given*

1. _____ Our neighbor must has bought a new car.
2. _____ I hadn't to pay the late fee.
3. _____ My parents could have call while I was taking a shower.
4. _____ Please be quiet! The patient may be sleep!
5. _____ The driver who caused the accident might be drunk at the time.
6. _____ A round trip ticket to Hawaii must to cost at least $800.
7. _____ My old roommate might not living in Atlanta anymore.
8. _____ The library ought have a lot of information about solar energy.
9. _____ Another student in the class might borrowed the books you wanted.
10. _____ I could have run fast as a child, but now I'm out of shape.

EXERCISE 2-39 Review

Directions

Circle the correct modal.

Example

Flight 79 (should)/ must arrive tonight around 8:30.

1. Sid   could / can   have studied in his country.
2. Bill and Jim   might / must   get along well since they've been roommates for more than 2 years.
3. Sid   may / has to   receive a special scholarship for his tuition next term.
4. Wiz   should / must   get all As this term since he's the best student in all his classes.

5. Cindy and Jim   may / should   not have discussed their career goals in detail when they got engaged.
6. With her scholarship Cindy   doesn't have to / must not   worry about any school expenses for the rest of her college days.
7. Dr. Parker   should / must   have scheduled a meeting with all of his advisees, but he was too busy last week.
8. Dr. Parker   might / must   talk to all of them before registration because he   has to / can   sign their registration papers.
9. Sid   could speak / could have spoken   English as a child, but he- had to / should   learn American pronunciation when he came to Hoopersburg.
10. Wiz   must / should   have studied harder as a freshman.

EXERCISE 2-40   Review

Directions

Make three comments on each situation below. Use a variety of modals. Try to make present and past sentences.

Example

People are walking out of a movie theater and they are laughing and smiling.
→ They must have enjoyed the movie.
→ It could be a drama with a funny ending.
→ We should see that movie.

1. Flight 715 to Madrid didn't leave on time because someone called the airport and reported a bomb on the plane.
2. There was a big traffic jam this morning. A tall truck tried to go through the tunnel, but it got stuck.
3. The garbage collectors decided to go on strike starting tomorrow.
4. There will be a series of free concerts in the park during the summer.
5. Last night the electricity was out on the north side of town for 3 hours.
6. A graduate of this program died and left the school $750,000 in his will.
7. I read in the newspaper that two U.S. diplomats were asked to leave the U.S. Embassy in Moscow and return to Washington.
8. More than 50,000 people attended the fireworks last night.

EXERCISE 2-41 All Modals — Review

Directions

Fill in the chart with the correct forms of the present and past MODALS. The MODALS have different past forms for different meanings. Use the verb *write*.

Meanings	PRESENT	CONTINUOUS	PAST
Asking permission	_____ _____		
Making requests	_____ _____ _____ _____		
Advisability	_____ _____		_____ _____
Necessity	_____ _____		_____
Ability	_____		_____
Possibility	_____ _____	_____ _____	_____ _____
Expectation	_____ _____	_____ _____	_____ *
Deduction	_____ _____	_____ _____	_____ _____

* See Fine Points for Recognition.

Modals   **69**

FINE POINTS FOR RECOGNITION

A. MODALS + PERFECT CONTINUOUS

Form

MODAL	PERFECT CONTINUOUS			
should				
could				
may	have	been	VERB	-ing
might				
must				

Meaning

The action of the verb occurred in the past, and the action was a continuous one. See the previous lessons for the meanings of the MODALS.

EXAMPLES

1. The injured pedestrian should have been paying closer attention to the traffic.
2. Most of the people believed the witness, but he could have been lying about his involvement in the crime.
3. During the 1950s the spy might have been working for two different governments at the same time.
4. According to the evidence the pilot must have been changing altitude at the time of the explosion.

B. PAST EXPECTATION

Form

PAST EXPECTATION			
should			
ought to	have	VERB	-ed

Meaning

This form usually expresses past advice (see page 38). In some cases it can also express past expectation. The context will determine the intended meaning.

70 GAINING GROUND

Note: Often the action expressed did not actually happen (see Examples 2, 3).

EXAMPLES
1. Flight 55 should have arrived 20 minutes ago according to the schedule. (We don't know if the plane arrived or not.)
2. The African runner should have won the marathon since he holds the world record. (He didn't win the marathon.)
3. The bank should have sent your statement at the end of the month. (They didn't send it as expected.)

SUMMARY

1. PERMISSION
   Can I *use* your eraser?
   Could I *have* another form, please?
   May I *leave* now?

2. REQUESTS
   Can you *shut* the window?
   Would/Could you *explain* that again, please?
   Will you *shut* the door, please?

3. ADVISABILITY and NECESSITY
   You *should/ought to do* your homework.
   I *should have brought* an umbrella.
   You *have to/must wear* shoes to school.
   Wiz *had to transfer* to a less competitive school.
   He *had better do* well on the final examination.

4. PROHIBITION and LACK OF NECESSITY
   You *must not drive* without a license.
   Americans *don't have to carry* ID cards in the United States.
   We *didn't have to do* any homework last night.

5. ABILITY
   Can you *ride* a bicycle?
   When *could* you first *understand* TV programs in English?
   The pilot *could have refused* to take the hijackers to Cuba.

6. POSSIBILITY
   It *might rain* later on.
   Sid *may get* a special scholarship.
   This bill *can't/couldn't be* correct!
   Don't call her now. She *may be sleeping.*
   Sid's father *might have lost* his job.
   Wizard *may not have liked* the atmosphere at MIT.

Modals **71**

7. EXPECTATION
   Flight 33 *should/ought to be* here in 20 minutes.
   With all the rain this year, we *shouldn't have* a water shortage this summer.

8. DEDUCTION
   Bill and Jim *must be* about 20 years old.
   That old man *must not hear* very well.
   It *must be raining* outside.
   Cindy *must have worked* hard during her freshman year.

Gerunds and Infinitives   3

Part I   Gerunds

GERUNDS AS SUBJECTS

EXAMPLES
1. Looking for a job is difficult.
2. Living in the dorm costs a lot.
3. Jim's asking Cindy to marry him surprised Bill.

EXPLANATION

Form
The term GERUND refers to the -ing form of a verb used as a noun.
The GERUND is the form of the verb most commonly used as a noun.

GERUNDS may be simple (i.e., one word):

Traveling is educational.
Swimming is fun.

Or the GERUND may be in a GERUND PHRASE:

Traveling by plane is expensive.
Finding an apartment takes a lot of time.

72

Note: The form of the verb used with a GERUND as its subject is always third person singular.

If the GERUND PHRASE has a subject, the subject should be in the possessive form:

His arriving late annoys me.
Mary's getting that job was a surprise.

Do not use a subject for the GERUND if the statement is general *or* if the subject of the gerund is obvious from the sentence or context.

4. Writing in pencil is not permitted on that exam.
5. Taking the medicine made him sleepy.

You will hear nonpossessive forms used in speech, but practice using the possessive form which is correct in speech and writing. All of the sentences here show GERUNDS or GERUND PHRASES as subjects.

Meaning
Most nouns refer to people, objects or ideas; however, a GERUND refers to an action.

NEGATIVE GERUNDS:
Put *not* before the GERUND to make the GERUND negative.

6. Not sleeping enough is bad for your health.
7. Not paying your phone bill will result in termination of your service.

EXERCISE 3-1 Gerunds as Subjects

Directions
Read the following sentences. After each sentence is a statement that is either true or false. Circle the T if the statement is true; circle the F if the statement is false.

1. Making friends in a new country takes time.
   T / F   People don't usually find new friends quickly in a new country.
2. Bill's talking in his sleep woke up Jim last night.
   T / F   Jim talked in his sleep and woke Bill up last night.
3. Not responding to a written invitation is impolite in the United States.
   T / F   A polite person in the United States answers a written invitation.
4. His winning the lottery was a big surprise to us.
   T / F   We were surprised because we won the lottery.
5. Transferring to a new school takes a lot of planning.
   T / F   Wiz made a lot of plans before he transferred to a new school.
6. A driver's not stopping at a red light is against the law.
   T / F   All drivers must stop at a red traffic light.

EXERCISE 3-2 Gerunds as Subjects

Directions
Complete the following sentences.

Example
→ Looking for a job is *difficult*_____.
→   *frustrating*_____.

1. Smoking cigarettes can be _____.
2. Driving fast is _____.
3. Not drinking enough water is _____.
4. His forgetting his homework was _____.
5. Helen Keller's graduating from college _____.
6. Not learning to swim is _____.
7. Speaking English is _____.
8. Going camping is _____.

Gerunds and infinitives 75

EXERCISE 3-3 Gerunds as Subjects

Directions
Complete the following sentences with a gerund or gerund phrase.

1. _____ is against the law.
2. _____ takes a lot of time.
3. _____ takes a lot of money.
4. _____ takes a lot of patience.
5. _____ is embarrassing.
6. _____ upsets me.
7. _____ is frightening.
8. _____ takes a lot of planning.
9. _____ annoys me.
10. _____ costs a lot.

EXERCISE 3-4 Gerunds as Subjects

Directions
Your friend or classmate makes suggestions for a weekend or vacation activity. You don't like the suggestions and point out the problems.

Example
S1: Let's go to the movies.
S2: Going to the movies costs too much on the weekend.
S1: Let's stay home and read.
S2: Staying home is boring on the weekend.

EXERCISE 3-5 Gerunds as Subjects

Directions
Using gerund phrases, complete the following sentences with your impressions and observations about a new city.

1. _____ surprised me at first.
2. _____ shocked me.
3. _____ impressed me.
4. _____ disappointed me.

76   GAINING GROUND

5. _____ frightens me.
6. _____ disgusts me.
7. _____ makes me laugh.
8. _____ bores me.

GERUNDS FOLLOWING PREPOSITIONS

EXAMPLES
1. Bill is satisfied with living in the dorm.
2. Sid is interested in going to graduate school.
3. Wizard is embarrassed about flunking out of MIT.

EXPLANATION

Form
Use a GERUND or GERUND PHRASE after a preposition. The GERUND is the *only* form of the verb that may follow a preposition.

4. I respect him for doing his job well.
5. Don't leave without turning off the lights.

Use the possessive form to show the subject of the action of the GERUND PHRASE.

6. Can I depend on your not telling anyone?

Note: Some verbs, adjectives, and nouns are used with specific prepositions. See Appendix II. Remember that *to* is often a preposition.

7. I'm not used to speaking English yet.

Meaning
The GERUND refers to an action instead of a person, object, or idea.

EXERCISE 3-6 Gerunds following Prepositions

Directions
Answer the following questions with a gerund (phrase).

1. What are you thinking about doing this weekend?
2. What do you look forward to doing during your next vacation?
3. What have you recently apologized for?
4. What has your roommate complained about lately?
5. What have you become accustomed to doing in the United States?
6. In your country what were you responsible for in your job?
7. What do you plan on doing after this term?
8. What were you afraid of doing as a child?
9. What are you proud of?
10. What have you thanked your roommate for lately?

EXERCISE 3-7 Gerunds following Prepositions

Directions
Make suggestions to classmates for the situations given below. Use the expression "How about," which is a common suggestion form in English.

Example
    activities for the weekend
    → How about going to a concert? How about taking a bike trip?

1. activity for the whole class this weekend
2. activity for the next vacation
3. plans for a picnic
4. ways to improve listening and speaking skills
5. ways to find a new apartment
6. ways to find information in the library
7. ways to meet Americans
8. plans for a class party

EXERCISE 3-8 Gerunds following Prepositions

Directions
Use gerunds to write sentences with the following phrases.

Example
> approve of
> → The police didn't approve of my driving over the speed limit.

1. object to
2. think about
3. incapable of
4. insist on
5. grateful for
6. care about
7. adjust to
8. be used to
9. instead of
10. prevent someone from
11. reason for
12. in danger of
13. succeed in
14. angry about
15. thank someone for

GERUNDS AS DIRECT OBJECTS

EXAMPLES
1. Did Jim finish correcting his computer program?
2. Wizard enjoys working in the computer center.
3. Cindy resisted getting engaged to Jim.

EXPLANATION

Form

Subject	VERB	(POSSESSIVE)	(not)	GERUND
He suggested their not going by car.				

Meaning
When the meaning of your sentence requires that another verb follow the particular verbs listed below, use a GERUND or GERUND PHRASE, not an INFINITIVE.

4. He excused their being rude.
5. I can't help making mistakes when I type.

Verbs grouped according to meaning:

			Unrelated verbs:
dislike	keep	admit	can't help
mind	resume	deny	endure
resist	appreciate	excuse	fear
avoid	enjoy	complete	imagine
defer	favor	finish	recall
delay	suggest	quit	risk
miss		stop	
postpone			

Note: There are some other verbs that can be followed by either a GERUND PHRASE or an INFINITIVE PHRASE. You will learn these verbs in Part II of this chapter.

EXERCISE 3-9   Gerunds as Direct Objects

Directions

Read the first sentence. Then judge the truth of the following sentences. Circle T if the sentence is true according to the first sentence. Circle F if it is false. Circle ? if the first sentence does not give enough information to judge the sentence true or false.

1. John's arrival delayed my parents' leaving.
    T / F / ?   John was leaving.
    T / F / ?   John was delayed.
    T / F / ?   My parents were delayed.
2. She feared taking the test.
    T / F / ?   She was going to take the test.
    T / F / ?   A lot of people were taking the test.
3. She appreciated my bringing a gift.
    T / F / ?   She brought a gift.
    T / F / ?   I brought a gift.
    T / F / ?   I appreciated the gift.

EXERCISE 3-10   Gerunds as Direct Objects

Directions
Answer the following questions using a gerund or gerund phrase.

1. What do you enjoy on weekends?
2. What did you finish yesterday?
3. What do you avoid?
4. What do you suggest doing on a nice day?
5. What do you recall doing a year ago?
6. What do you fear?
7. What do you appreciate about your parents?
8. What do you dislike most about school?
9. What can't you help doing when you are studying?
10. What did the government delay?

EXERCISE 3-11   Gerunds as Direct Objects

Directions
Complete each sentence with a gerund or gerund phrase.

1. The trip up the mountain was dangerous. He risked _____.
2. I don't like apartments. I favor _____.
3. In some countries, you can finish college before you go into the military. In other words, you can't defer _____.
4. After the Surgeon General had announced that smoking led to cancer, many Americans quit _____.
5. When I was at home, I used to enjoy _____.
   Now that I'm here, I really miss _____.
6. The heating system in their house was bad, so they had to endure _____ _____ all winter.
7. His parents are very strict. They dislike _____.
8. When I return home, I plan to resume _____.
9. I hate to wash dishes, but I don't mind _____.

EXERCISE 3-12 Gerunds as Direct Objects

1. Tell (in a few sentences) about something you like doing. Include some of the following verbs plus gerund phrases:
   appreciate   enjoy   favor
2. Tell (in a few sentences) about something you don't like doing. Include some of the following verbs plus gerund phrases:
   dislike   endure   mind   resist
3. Tell (in a few sentences) about some past and possible future events in your life. Include some of the following verbs plus gerund phrases:
   complete   finish   keep   quit   resume
4. Tell (in a few sentences) about a person accused of some crime. Include some of the following verbs plus gerund phrases:
   admit   deny   excuse   suggest
5. Tell (in a few sentences) about something which you don't like to do and try to avoid. Include some of the following verbs plus gerund phrases:
   avoid   defer   delay   miss   postpone

GERUNDS AS SUBJECT COMPLEMENTS

EXAMPLES
1. Wizard's problem is not studying enough.
2. Bill's hobby is collecting rocks.
3. His favorite activity on Sunday is watching TV.

EXPLANATION

Form

Subject	BE	(not)	GERUND
Her job is managing the office.			

The GERUND is the form of the verb most commonly used as a subject complement.

4. A lie is not telling the truth.
5. Happiness is eating an ice cream cone on a hot day.
6. Was his mistake taking too many courses in one term?

Meaning
The GERUND refers to an action instead of a person, object, or idea.

EXERCISE 3-13   Gerunds as Subject Complements

Directions

Answer the following questions using gerunds or gerund phrases as subject complements.

1. What is your hobby?
2. What is your worst problem in school?
3. What is your favorite weekend activity?
4. What is your favorite rainy day activity?
5. What is your favorite outdoor activity?
6. What is your favorite winter pastime?
7. What is your favorite summer pastime?
8. What is the most difficult part of learning English?
9. What is your purpose for studying English?
10. What is your greatest accomplishment to date?

Part II   Infinitives

INFINITIVE PHRASES AS SUBJECT COMPLEMENTS

EXAMPLES
1. Jim's goal is to get a good job before he marries Cindy.
2. Wizard's dream is to own his own computer company.
3. Cindy's intention is to finish her paper before the vacation.

EXPLANATION

Form

Subject	BE	to	VERB	(...)

His goal is to win the game.

An INFINITIVE PHRASE may consist of

a. only an infinitive: to win
b. an infinitive plus an object: to win the prize
c. an infinitive with a subject (and object): for him to win (the prize) (see p. 95)

Meaning
Usually, GERUND PHRASES are used as subject complements. However, with such subjects as *goal, dream, objective,* and *intention,* INFINITIVE PHRASES usually serve as subject complements.

Note that these subjects (dream, intention, etc.) concern the future and are not current realities.

4. The army's objective was to capture the town.
5. His aim is to be president.
6. The committee's proposal is to cut the funding of the program.

NEGATIVE INFINITIVE PHRASES
Put *not* before the to + VERB to make the INFINITIVE PHRASE negative.

7. Sid's intention is not to stay in the United States after graduation.
8. The pilot's plan is not to fly through the storm.

EXERCISE 3-14 Infinitive Phrases as Subject Complements

Directions
Answer the questions, using an infinitive phrase as the subject complement.

Example
What is your goal after graduation?
→ My goal is to get a good job.

1. What is your goal in life?
2. What is your dream in life?
3. What is your homework for tomorrow in your writing class?
4. What is your duty to your family?
5. What is your intention in the United States?
6. What is the objective of most international students in the United States?
7. What is your goal in this course?
8. What is your weekly assignment in your reading class?

84   GAINING GROUND

INFINITIVE PHRASES AS DIRECT OBJECTS: Type 1

EXAMPLES
1. Bill hesitated to ask Jim for a loan.
2. Jim learned to write computer programs 3 years ago.
3. Wizard had to promise not to spend all his time with the computers.

EXPLANATION

Form

Subject	VERB 1	to	VERB 2	(. . .)
He hoped to win the game.				

Meaning

Note that the subject of the INFINITIVE is the same as the subject of the main verb.

Example: John agreed to leave. (John agreed. John left.)

Verbs grouped according to meaning:

agree	attempt	appear
consent	endeavor	seem
promise	seek	
		begin*
offer	arrange	cease*
volunteer	plan	continue*
	prepare	proceed

Unrelated verbs:

bother	hate*
can afford	hesitate
can't bear	hope
claim	learn (how)
decide	neglect*
demand	pretend
deserve	refuse
fail	tend
happen	threaten

*These verbs can also be used with a GERUND as their direct object with no difference in meaning.

Example: He hates   to get up early. / getting up early.

4. He never bothers to check his paper.
5. She planned to finish the job by Friday.
6. He claims to be a doctor, but he refuses to show his credentials.
7. Did you happen to read the newspaper last night?
8. While they were playing, the children pretended to be cowboys and Indians.
9. He failed to arrive on time and could not take the test.

Gerunds and infinitives   85

EXERCISE 3-15   Infinitive Phrases as Direct Objects: Type I

Directions
   Answer the questions, using an infinitive phrase as the direct object.

Example
   What did he claim to be?
   → He claimed to be a doctor.

1. What do many children refuse to do?
2. What do you sometimes neglect to do?
3. What did you offer to do last week?
4. What do you hope to do next year?
5. What do you seek to do here?
6. What do some students pretend to do in class?
7. What will you endeavor to do when you finish studying English?
8. What did you promise your parents before you left home?
9. What don't you bother to do on weekends?
10. What do you hesitate to do here?
11. What can an average person afford in your country?
12. What did you happen to do last week?
13. What do people tend to do when the weather is nice?
14. What did you attempt to do when you first came here?
15. What are you preparing to do by studying English?

EXERCISE 3-16   Infinitive Phrases as Direct Objects: Type I

1. Using some of the following verbs, tell what your future plans are.
   seek   attempt   endeavor   plan
2. Using some of the following verbs, tell what agreement you made with your family before you left home.
   agree   consent   offer   promise
3. Using some of the following verbs, tell about something that you don't like.
   hate   hesitate   demand   refuse

86   GAINING GROUND

INFINITIVE PHRASES AS DIRECT OBJECTS: Type II

EXAMPLES
1. Bill's adviser will probably instruct him to take that course.
2. They hired Wizard to help at the computer center.
3. Jim persuaded Cindy to get engaged.

EXPLANATION

Form

Subject	VERB 1	Object	to	VERB 2	(. . .)

The coach told us to win the game.

This pattern must be used when the verbs below are in the VERB 1 position.

Meaning

Notice that the *object* here is functioning as the *subject* of the INFINITIVE.

Example: I asked *him* to leave. (*He* will leave.)
We expect *the train* to be on time. (The train will be on time.)

Verbs grouped according to meaning:			*Unrelated verbs:*	
appoint	force	order	*advise	hire
select	compel	command	believe	invite
		require	cause	tempt
teach	encourage		challenge	trust
train	persuade	tell	enable	warn
	urge	instruct	*forbid	
notify				
remind	*allow			
	*permit			

Verbs used with an object and the INFINITIVE "to be":
consider   guess   judge   know   report

*Note: These verbs can also be used with a GERUND as their direct object with no difference in meaning. The INFINITIVE pattern is usually preferred.

Example: They permitted   him to leave. / his leaving.

EXERCISE 3-17 Infinitive Phrases as Direct Objects: Type II

Directions
Answer the questions, using the VERB + object + to + VERB pattern.

Example
Who ordered the people to stay indooors?
→ The police ordered them to stay indoors.

1. Who encouraged you to study English?
2. Who reminds you to do your work?
3. Whom do you judge to be the most famous person in your country?
4. What do your parents warn you not to do?
5. What did your parents compel you to do when you were a child?
6. What did your friends tempt you to do when you were a child?
7. What do your parents trust you to do while you're in the United States?
8. What does the U.S. Immigration Service require foreigners to do to enter the country?
9. What do your teachers urge you to do?
10. What does this class challenge you to do?
11. What have your friends persuaded you to do?
12. What did your boss hire you to do?

EXERCISE 3-18 Infinitive Phrases as Direct Objects: Type II

Directions
Write a sentence with each of the verbs below. Use an infinitive phrase as a direct object.

1. appoint
2. notify
3. urge
4. require
5. hire
6. warn
7. report
8. consider
9. allow
10. advise

88   GAINING GROUND

INFINITIVE PHRASES AS DIRECT OBJECT: Type III: VERBS WITH BOTH PATTERNS

EXAMPLES
1. Bill wanted Jim to clean the room, but Jim didn't want to do it.
2. Wizard helped Bill to write his program.
3. Didn't the professor expect Bill to write it by himself?
4. Bill had intended to do it by himself, but he had a lot of problems with it.

EXPLANATION

Form

Subject	VERB 1	Object	to	VERB 2	(. . .)

They expected (him) to win the game.

Use the verbs below in either of these two INFINITIVE patterns, depending on your meaning.

Meaning
When the object appears in the sentence, it functions as the subject of the INFINITIVE.

5. He begged her not to go.

Verbs grouped according to meaning:			*Unrelated verbs:*
ask	desire	like*	choose
beg	expect	love*	help†
request	intend	prefer*	need
	want		

*These verbs can also be used with a GERUND as their direct object with no difference in meaning.
†*Help* can also be used with a "bare infinitive." See page 95.

6. She asked to leave.
7. We should choose John to do the job.
8. I expected the plane to arrive by 10:00.

EXERCISE 3-19 Infinitive Phrases as Direct Objects:
Type III: Verbs with Both Patterns

Directions
Answer the questions, using one of the two patterns.

1. What do your parents want you to do in the future?
2. What do you prefer to do?
3. What does the teacher ask you to do in class?
4. What does the teacher expect the students to do at home?
5. When you have a problem, what do you want your friends to do?
6. What do you intend to do after your English class?
7. What did you help your friend to do last week?
8. What do you want your government to do?
9. What do you expect your government to do concerning education in the future?
10. What did the teacher choose you to do?

EXERCISE 3-20 Infinitive Phrases as Direct Objects: All Types — Review

Directions
There is a mistake in some of the sentences. Underline the mistakes and then rewrite the sentences in their correct forms.

Example
He is determined go home.
→ He is determined to go home.

1. I know to be a thief.
2. My mother urged to stay home.
3. She managed to complete the test.
4. I threatened him to shoot.
5. I agreed her to stay.
6. The machines ceased to work after the fire.
7. I refused them to return the money.
8. He persuaded me to come to the party.
9. He preferred come early.
10. They notified to leave next week.

EXERCISE 3-21 Infinitive Phrases as Direct Objects:
All Types — Review

Directions
Complete the sentences in each situation, using infinitive phrases.

1. Last night a bank was robbed.
   The police expected _____.
   The police notified _____.
   During the trial the court decided _____
   and required _____.
2. I wanted to move into a new apartment.
   By looking in the newspaper, I attempted _____.
   Unfortunately, I can't afford _____.
3. Our class is planning a picnic for next weekend.
   I volunteered _____.
   The teacher reminded _____.
   Some of the other students prefer _____.
4. My phone was almost disconnected.
   I failed _____.
   The telephone company refused _____,
   but I persuaded _____.

GERUNDS vs. INFINITIVES: Different Meanings

EXAMPLES
1. Bill remembered to set his alarm on the night before the GRE's.
2. Bill remembers visiting his great-grandfather many years ago.
3. Cindy means to become an accountant.
4. Becoming an accountant means taking a lot of business courses.

EXPLANATION

Form
The verbs below can be used with either a GERUND PHRASE or an INFINITIVE PHRASE as their direct objects.

Meaning

VERB	+ to + VERB	+ VERB -ing
mean	= intend I didn't mean to hurt your feelings.	= signify Learning a foreign language means memorizing a lot.
try	= attempt He tried to finish the test on time.	= experiment You should try adding sugar to that bitter coffee.
remember	Did you remember to lock the door?	= recall I can't remember locking the door; let's go check.
forget	He forgot to sign his application.	= not recall I won't forget spending this time with you.

Note the sequence of actions:

5. Did you remember to lock the door?
   First, you remember. Then, you lock the door.
6. I can't remember locking the door; let's go check.
   First, you lock the door. Then, you can't remember.

EXERCISE 3-22 Gerunds vs. Infinitives — Different Meanings

Directions
Answer the following questions using the appropriate pattern.

1. What did you remember to do before you left home today?
2. What did you mean to do when you started this program?
3. What do you remember doing when you were a child?
4. What did you forget to do before you left your country?
5. What do you try to do when you are studying?
6. What does studying hard mean to you?
7. What do you try to do on weekends?
8. What did you remember to do last night?
9. What did you try to do when you first came here?
10. What did you forget to do last week?

EXERCISE 3-23 Gerunds vs. Infinitives — Different Meanings

Directions
Fill in the blanks with the GERUND or the INFINITIVE of the verb given.

Example

Bill remembers ___*visiting*___ his great-grandfather many years ago.
   a - (visit)

1. I sometimes forget _____ the door, but my roommate always remembers.
   a - (lock)
2. Moving to a new town means _____ my friends.
   a - (leave)
3. She tried _____ the plant more, but it died anyway.
   a - (water)
4. Catching the 8:00 bus means _____ at 6:30.
   a - (get up)
5. Although they left when they were children, my parents remember _____ in a small town.
   a - (live)
6. He tried _____ his homework before class.
   a - (finish)
7. If you don't know a word, try _____ your dictionary.
   a - (use)
8. They meant _____ late Sunday night.
   a - (return)
9. Do you remember _____ to school for the first time?
   a - (go)
10. I will never forget _____ the capital.
    a - (visit)

Gerunds and infinitives   **93**

VERBS WITH INFINITIVES WITHOUT *TO*

EXAMPLES
1. Bill's adviser   made / had   him take five courses this term.
2. Wizard let Bill look at his program.
3. Then he helped him write his own program.

EXPLANATION

Form

Subject	CAUSATIVE VERB	Object	VERB	(. . .)
	VERB OF SENSE PERCEPTION			

The coach made him leave the game.
The coach saw him leave the game.

Use the verbs below with a "bare" INFINITIVE (without *to*) as their direct object.

Note: Help is also used with *to* and is used in both patterns:
    help + (to) + VERB
    help + object + (to) + VERB

Note: Do not confuse the PRESENT PERFECT with this use of *have*.
Compare:

   a. The policeman *has shown* drivers his badge and ID. (PRESENT PERFECT)
   b. The policeman *has* drivers *show* their licenses.

Meaning

Group 1: Causatives	Group 2: Verbs of Sense Perception	
have	feel	notice
help	hear	see
let	observe	smell
make	overhear	watch

4. The teacher saw the students cheat on the test.
5. I didn't hear you come in.
6. Can you smell the gas come on?

This special *have*-structure has a causative meaning. The two sentences below are similar in meaning:

    c. The policeman usually has drivers show their licenses.
    d. The policeman usually causes drivers to show their licenses.

The verbs of sense perception are used in this pattern only with verbs that express single actions, not continuous actions.

  7. The woman saw the child cross the street.

Note: In Example 7 you cannot use the verb *play* because it expresses a continuous action.

EXERCISE 3-24 Causatives

Directions
Answer the questions, using *let, make, have.*

1. What did your parents make you do when you were in elementary school?
   Example: They made me go to church every week.
2. What did your father have you do for him when you were a teenager?
   Example: He had me wash the car every two weeks.
3. What did your parents let you do when you became 16 years old?
   Example: They let me carry a key to the house.

EXERCISE 3-25 Verbs with Infinitives without *to*

Directions
Complete each sentence, using a bare infinitive.

Example
    Bill's adviser made him *take an extra course*   .

1. I let my brother _____.
2. My mother made me _____.
3. When I was coming to school, I saw _____.
4. During the explosion, I felt _____.
5. My friend helped me _____.
6. In the library, I overheard a classmate _____.

7. After the accident the policeman made the witnesses _____.
8. The coach had the team members _____.
9. While she was looking out of her window, the old lady noticed the children _____
_____.
10. Every 6 months I have the mechanic at the garage _____.

EXERCISE 3-26   Infinitive Phrases as Direct Objects

Directions
Answer the questions below.

1. What had your father made you do before you left home?
2. What does your family expect you to do in the future?
3. What did you see a man do on the bus this morning?
4. What did you remind your friend to do yesterday?
5. When you were 10 years old, what didn't your parents let you do?
6. What did your younger brother or sister ask you to do?
7. What did you notice your neighbor do last week?
8. What did your teacher forget to do last week?
9. What did your teacher have you do yesterday?
10. What did you make your child do yesterday?

INFINITIVE PHRASES AS ADJECTIVE PHRASES

EXAMPLES
1. Cindy didn't have time to help Jim with his homework.
2. Wizard wanted some coffee to drink.
3. Bill didn't have money to give Jim for the pizza.

EXPLANATION

Form

(...)	NOUN	to	VERB	(...)

There are many books to read for that course.

Meaning
Use INFINITIVE PHRASES to complete the meaning of nouns.

Look at the examples above. The INFINITIVE PHRASES explain the meaning of the nouns they follow. The INFINITIVE PHRASES answer the question *what*?

    What time?
    What coffee?
    What money?

4. There is a variety of things to buy in a department store.
5. The way to go downtown is by bus.
6. Who's the best person to do that job?

EXERCISE 3-27 Infinitive Phrases as Adjective Phrases

Directions
Complete the sentences with an infinitive adjective phrase.

Example
    I don't have time...
    → I don't have time to watch TV tonight.

1. The U.S. government doesn't have enough money...
2. She bought some pretzels...
3. It's time...
4. There are a lot of courses...
5. I don't know the way...
6. The library has lots of books...
7. Do you have some changes...?
8. I have some questions...?
9. The professor... is Dr. Johnson.
10. The place... is Napoli's Pizzeria.

Gerunds and infinitives **97**

INFINITIVE PHRASES AS ADJECTIVE COMPLEMENTS

EXAMPLES
1. Wizard's handwriting is hard to read.
2. Computer programs are interesting to work on.
3. Bill's not tall enough to be on the basketball team.

EXPLANATION

Form

(. . .)	ADJECTIVE	(for + Object)	to	VERB

This is easy for me to understand.

If a subject is necessary for the INFINITIVE, use *for + Object*.

4. That homework will be difficult for Bill to finish.

Meaning
Use INFINITIVE PHRASES after adjectives to complete the meaning of the adjectives.

To indicate *excess* use *too* before the adjective.

(. . .)	too	ADJECTIVE	(for + Object)	to	VERB

This is too difficult for him to understand.

5. This coffee is too hot to drink.
6. That homework will be too difficult for Bill to finish.
7. Is he too busy to go to the movies with us?

To indicate *sufficiency*, use *enough* after the adjective.

(. . .)	ADJECTIVE	enough	(for + Object)	to	VERB

Her pronunciation is clear enough for me to understand.

8. His score is high enough for him to pass the course.
9. The weather is warm enough for us to swim.
10. That jacket is heavy enough to wear in the winter.

EXERCISE 3-28 Infinitive Phrases as Adjective Complements

Directions
Complete the sentences with an infinitive as an adjective complement.

Example
> Eggs are good ...
> → Eggs are good to eat for breakfast.

1. That article is difficult ...
2. It's too hot ...
3. That jacket is too light ...
4. I'm too busy ...
5. His English is good enough ...
6. It's too windy ...
7. Professor Johnson is easy ...
8. His lectures are too fast ...
9. That movie is scary enough ...
10. Soccer is exciting ...

EXERCISE 3-29 Infinitives as Adjective Complements

Directions
Comment on the situation using *too* or *enough*.

Example
> Jose couldn't do his reading homework.
> → It was too difficult to read.

1. Setsuko works for an American company as a translator.
2. Mike doesn't wear his glasses to drive.
3. Pam turned on the light before she began to do her homework.
4. Sally has a lot of parties at her apartment.
5. Anita borrowed a computer to do her math problems.
6. When the phone rang, Bob turned down the stereo.
7. Steve added some sugar to his coffee.
8. The coach wouldn't let Doug play on the basketball team.

Gerunds and infinitives **99**

INFINITIVE PHRASES AS SUBJECTS: 1. *IT* AS SUBSTITUTE SUBJECT

EXAMPLES
1. It's easy for Wizard to write computer programs.
2. It takes a lot of time for Cindy to do her homework.
3. How much does it cost to go to college in the United States?

EXPLANATION

Form

It	be + ADJECTIVE	(for + Object)	to	VERB	(...)
	cost ...				
	take ...				

It is expensive for a student to have a car.
It costs a lot for a student to have a car.
It takes a lot of money for a student to have a car.

It is unusual in English to use an INFINITIVE PHRASE as the subject in the subject position of a sentence. To avoid infinitives in subject position, use *it* as a substitute subject (or use a gerund phrase). *It* occurs most commonly with the verbs *cost* and *take*, and with adjectives.

    a. *To learn English* is difficult.
       It's difficult *to learn English*.
    b. *To drive a small car* is economical.
       It's economical *to drive a small car*.

4. Is it costly to eat meals out?
5. It takes patience to work with children.
6. It was difficult not to get impatient at all the delays.

Use *for + Object* to indicate the subject of the INFINITIVE (Examples 1, 2).

7. It's common *for him to miss class*.
8. It's possible *for us to go there by plane*.
9. It has been exciting *for us to travel around the country*.

When the subject of the INFINITIVE is stated with *for*, the INFINITIVE PHRASE may appear in subject position:

    c. *For him to miss class* is common.
    d. *For an athlete to qualify for the Olympics* takes a great deal of effort.

Meaning
There is no change in meaning when *it* replaces an INFINITIVE PHRASE in subject position.

EXERCISE 3-30 Infinitive Phrases as Subjects: *It* as Substitute Subject

Directions
Make sentences with the phrases below, using the *it* pattern with an infinitive.

Example
>   frightening for children ... in the dark
> → It's frightening for children to be alone in the dark.

1. easy for me ... in this class
2. difficult for students in a foreign country
3. economical for students
4. typical for university students
5. takes me a great deal of effort
6. costs a lot in my country
7. takes a lot of time ... when you are learning a foreign language
8. dangerous ... in the city
9. takes a lot of time here
10. difficult ... when you talk to foreigners

INFINITIVE PHRASES AS SUBJECTS: 2. *IT* AS SUBSTITUTE SUBJECT

EXAMPLES
1. It's nice of Wizard to help Bill with his program.
2. It was generous of Bill to lend Sid that money.
3. It was rude of Cindy to hang up on Jim.

EXPLANATION

Form

It	Be	ADJECTIVE	Of + Object)	to	VERB	(...)
It was careless of me to lose my umbrella.							

Meaning
Note the difference in the relationship between the adjective and the following object in these two sentences:

a. It was good for him to take that vacation. (i.e., The vacation was good for him.)
b. It was good of him to send us a postcard. (He was good to send us a postcard.)

Use *adjective + of + Object* when the adjective describes the subject of the INFINITIVE PHRASE.

4. It was obnoxious of you to make noise during class. (You were obnoxious.)
5. It's wise of tourists to carry traveler's checks. (Tourists are wise.)
6. It was stupid of us not to bring the camera. (We were stupid.)

EXERCISE 3-31 *It* as Substitute Subject with Infinitives

Directions
Make sentences with the words below, using the Adjective + *of* pattern.

Example
    nice — Wiz
    → It was nice of Wizard to help Bill with his homework.

1. generous — my friend
2. nice — our teacher
3. clever — my classmate
4. wise — my father
5. foolish — I
6. careless — the driver
7. foolhardy — my friend
8. brave — my father
9. perceptive — my mother
10. ridiculous — my neighbor

INFINITIVE PHRASES AS ADVERBIALS (*in order to*)

EXAMPLES
1. Bill left to go to the library.
2. Cindy stayed home to study.
3. Wizard went to the computer center to finish his program.

EXPLANATION

Form
The INFINITIVE PHRASE usually appears at the end of the sentence without a comma. It is sometimes possible for the phrase to appear at the beginning with a comma separating it from the subject.

To finish his degree, Wiz transferred to Hoopersburg State University.

Meaning
Use INFINITIVE PHRASES to mean *in order to*. These INFINITIVE PHRASES show the reason for the action.

4. He came to the United States to study English.
5. Where did she go shopping to buy spring clothes?
6. He stopped working to have a snack.

EXERCISE 3-32   Infinitive Phrases as Adverbials

Directions
Answer the questions, using an infinitive phrase as an adverbial. You may give a long or short answer.

Example
      Why did you go downtown?
→ I went to buy a pair of shoes.
→ To buy a pair of shoes.

1. Why do you want to learn English?
2. Why do people drink diet sodas?
3. Why is he going to the library?
4. Why are you calling your friend?
5. Why do banks lend people money?

6. Why did you watch the news last night?
7. Why did you call your family last week?
8. Why do you want to borrow $1,000?
9. Why are you filling out that form?
10. Why are you taking aspirin?

EXERCISE 3-33 *too* and *enough* — Review

Directions

Add either *too* or *enough* to the sentences below. Use the correct word order.

Example

He's not *tall enough* to be on the basketball team.
　　　　　a - (tall)

1. Today it's _____ to fry an egg on the sidewalk.
　　　　　　　a - (hot)
2. The rent for the two-bedroom apartment is _____ for me to pay.
　　　　　　　　　　　　　　　　　　　　　　a - (expensive)
3. Some plants are _____ to grow in our climate.
　　　　　　　　　a - (delicate)
4. Peggy's car isn't _____ for everyone to fit into.
　　　　　　　　　a - (big)
5. The food in that restaurant is _____ to eat.
　　　　　　　　　　　　　　　a - (salty)
6. His voice is _____ to hear across the room.
　　　　　　　a - (loud)
7. Our swimming team wasn't _____ to win the championship.
　　　　　　　　　　　　　　a - (good)
8. The grass in the park is probably _____ for us to sit on right now.
　　　　　　　　　　　　　　　　　　a - (wet)

EXERCISE 3-34 Gerund vs. Infinitive — Review

Directions

Paraphrase the sentences below using a gerund phrase. In some sentences you may need to change the word order.

Example

　　Some of my friends like to spend their money on movies.
　→ Some of my friends like spending their money on movies.

1. As we entered the door, the telephone started to ring.
2. The teacher forbids us to look in our books during tests.
3. Our teacher also prefers us to speak English during class.

104 GAINING GROUND

4. It takes a lot of time to make a stamp collection.

5. For us to speak English all day is very tiring.

6. After the firemen had put out the fire, the wood continued to smoke.

7. It may take hours of work for you to solve these problems.

8. It was dangerous for the tourist to photograph the airport.

EXERCISE 3-35   Gerund vs. Infinitive — Review

Directions

Circle the correct phrase to complete the sentence.

Example

We appreciate _____ to the party.

(a.) your inviting us   b. you to invite us   c. to invite us

1. The bank robbers threatened _____ the customers.
   a. hurting   b. to hurt   c. the guard to hurt

2. The doctor has warned _____ more frequently.
   a. Mr. Brown's exercising   b. to exercise   c. Mr. Brown to exercise

3. The pilot delayed _____ until he had spoken with the airport officials.
   a. landing   b. to land   c. the plane to land

4. When I hear certain kinds of music, I can't help _____ my foot.
   a. tapping   b. to tap   c. myself to tap

5. The students in his classes consider _____ an excellent teacher.
   a. Dr. Ketchum's being   b. to be   c. Dr. Ketchum to be

6. The Caplans wouldn't let _____ outside after 7:00.
   a. their children's playing   b. their children to play   c. their children play

7. Our teacher may refuse _____ the test.
   a. postponing   b. to postpone   c. us to postpone

8. The driver didn't deny _____ the speed limit.
   a. going over   b. to go over   c. the policeman to go over

9. The stewardess reminded _____ their seatbelts on during the takeoff.
   a. the passengers' keeping   b. to keep   c. the passengers to keep

10. While we were at the post office, we happened _____ Pam and Judy.
    a. seeing   b. to see   c. see

EXERCISE 3-36 Gerund vs. Infinitive — Review

Directions
Underline the mistake in every sentence below. Write the correction above the sentence.

Example
It was careless *of* ~~for~~ me to lose my umbrella.

1. I'm used to get up at 7:00 every morning.
2. Will you let me to borrow your notes until tomorrow?
3. It's dangerous for they to play with matches.
4. We failed finishing the exam before the time was up.
5. My parents trusted us telling the truth.
6. Some people object to live in a big city.
7. Our teacher requires to sit in the same chair every day.
8. The reporter agreed don't print the story until the following day.
9. A friend of mine suggested us taking a picnic lunch to the mountains.
10. I like no getting up early on the weekends.
11. The teacher demanded me to read the note.
12. Gina singing is very enjoyable.

EXERCISE 3-37 Gerund vs. Infinitive — Review

Directions
Fill in the blank with the correct form of the verb.

Example

Bill hesitated ____*to ask*____ Bill for a loan.
　　　　　　　　　a - (ask)
He excused their ____*being*____ rude.
　　　　　　　　　　a - (be)

1. The politician promised _____ crime in the cities.
　　　　　　　　　　　　　　　　a - (reduce)
2. The passengers had already prepared _____ the plane, when the
　　　　　　　　　　　　　　　　　　　　　　　a - (leave)
stewardess announced a delay.
3. The coach suggested _____ a healthier diet.
　　　　　　　　　　　　　　a - (eat)
4. The children pretended not _____ their mother when she called
　　　　　　　　　　　　　　　　　　　a - (hear)
them.

106 GAINING GROUND

5. He admitted not _____ his homework very carefully.
   a - (do)
6. Would you mind _____ these books for me?
   a - (carry)
7. The policeman demanded _____ my driver's license.
   a - (see)
8. I can't afford _____ a vacation this year.
   a - (take)
9. After lunch the workers will resume _____ the street.
   a - (repair)
10. The speeding driver failed _____ the stop sign, and the police-
    a - (notice)
    woman gave him a ticket.

FINE POINTS FOR RECOGNITION

A. GERUND PHRASES AS APPOSITIVES
   GERUNDS or GERUND PHRASES can serve as appositives.
   Remember that an appositive is a noun or noun phrase which
   describes or explains the noun it follows.

Examples
1. My hobby, skiing, is expensive.
2. The topic of this debate, reducing inflation, interests many people.
3. They quickly reached their goal, mastering English.

B. PERFECT GERUND
   A few verbs which require GERUND direct objects may have
   PERFECT GERUND objects. This form of the GERUND (*having* +
   PAST PARTICIPLE) emphasizes a time contrast between the action
   of the main verb and the action of the GERUND verb.

Examples
1. She denied having robbed the jewelry store.
2. I remember having met you before.
3. He admitted having cheated on the exam.
4. He appreciated having received her help.

C. PERFECT INFINITIVE
   A few verbs which require INFINITIVE direct objects with the
   pattern VERB + *to* + VERB may have PERFECT INFINITIVE
   objects. This form of the INFINITIVE (*to* + *have* + PAST
   PARTICIPLE) emphasizes a time contrast between the action of the
   main verb and the action of the INFINITIVE verb.

Gerunds and infinitives **107**

Examples
1. The students seem to have misunderstood the directions on the quiz.
2. He pretended not to have been frightened during the earthquake.
3. The driver appears to have lost control of the car on the ice.
4. He claims to have seen men from another planet.

GERUND Verbs		GERUND or INFINITIVE	
admit	fear	attempt	like
appreciate	finish	begin	love
avoid	imagine	can't bear	neglect
can't help	keep	cease	prefer
complete	mind	continue	propose
consider*	miss	hate	start
defend	postpone		
defer	quit	**GERUND or INFINITIVE**	
delay	recall	**(different meanings)**	
deny	recommend	forget	remember
despise	resent	mean	try
detest	resist		
dislike	resume	**GERUND or INFINITIVE†**	
endure	risk	**(Group II)**	
enjoy	stop	advise	forbid
excuse	suggest	allow	permit
favor			

*Also Group II INFINITIVE   †Use with INFINITIVE is
 + to be   preferred.

INFINITIVE Verbs (Group I)		INFINITIVE Verbs (Groups I and II)	
agree	manage	ask	help
aim	need	beg	intend
appear	offer	choose	request
arrange	plan	desire	want
bother	pledge	expect	wish
can afford	prepare		

INFINITIVE Verbs (Group II)

appoint	know‡
believe	notify
cause	oblige
challenge	order
command	persuade
compel	remind
dare	require
drive	select
enable	teach
encourage	tell
find	tempt
force	train
guess‡	trouble
hire	trust
instruct	urge
invite	warn
judge‡	

INFINITIVE Verbs (Group I), continued:

care	pretend
claim	proceed
consent	promise
decide	refuse
demand	resolve
deserve	seek
endeavor	seem
fail	tend
happen	threaten
hesitate	undertake
hope	venture
learn (how)	volunteer

INFINITIVE Verbs without *to*

feel	make
have	notice
hear	overhear
help	see
let	smell

‡Use with "to be."

SUMMARY

1. GERUND — SUBJECT
   Looking for a job is difficult.
   Not sleeping enough is bad for your health.

2. GERUND — FOLLOWING A PREPOSITION
   Sid is interested in *going to graduate school*.
   Can I depend on *her not telling anyone*?

3. GERUND — DIRECT OBJECT
   Did Jim finish *correcting his computer program*?
   She suggested *their not going by car*.

Gerunds and infinitives **109**

4. GERUND — SUBJECT COMPLEMENT
   Bill's hobby is *collecting rocks*.
   A lie is *not telling the truth*.

5. INFINITIVE — SUBJECT COMPLEMENT
   Jim's goal is *to get a good job after graduation*.
   The pilot's plan was *not to fly through the storm*.

6. INFINITIVE — 1. DIRECT OBJECT
   Bill hesitated *to ask Jim for a loan*.
   He has to promise *not to come home too late*.

7. INFINITIVE — 2. DIRECT OBJECT
   They hired *Wiz to help at the Computer Center*.
   They persuaded *the professor not to give an exam that week*.

8. INFINITIVE — "Bare"
   Wizard *let* Bill *look* at his program.
   I *heard* you *come* in.

9. INFINITIVE — ADJECTIVE PHRASES
   Cindy didn't have time *to help Jim with his homework*.
   Who's the best person *to do that job*?

10. INFINITIVE — ADJECTIVE COMPLEMENT
    Wizard's handwriting is hard *to read*.
    She's *too* busy *to go to the movies*.
    He's not tall *enough to be on the basketball team*.

11. INFINITIVE — 1. SUBJECT
    It's easy *for* Wizard *to write computer programs*.
    It takes a lot of time *for* Cindy *to do her homework*.

12. INFINITIVE — 2. SUBJECT
    It's nice *of* Wizard *to help Bill with his program*.
    It was stupid *of* me *not to bring my camera*.

13. INFINITIVE — ADVERBIAL
    Bill left *to go to the library*.
    She stopped working *to have a snack*.

Comparisons 4

COMPARATIVES (-*er, more, less than*)

EXAMPLES
1. Wizard is richer than Bill and Jim.
2. Jim is taller than Bill (is), but Bill is more athletic.
3. Wizard is happier at Hoopersburg than he was at MIT.

EXPLANATION

Form

ADJECTIVES

-er than	more than	IRREGULAR	less than
One syllable tall – taller short – shorter hot – hotter	*All others* foolish – more foolish flowery – more flowery intelligent – more intelligent	good – better bad – worse far – farther	*All adjectives* less tall less simple less foolish less intelligent
Two syllables (-ow, -le, -y) yellow – yellower simple – simpler lazy – lazier			

Note: The addition of -er may involve spelling changes.

a. For two-syllable words which end in -y, change the -y to -i, and add -er.
b. For one-syllable words which end in a single vowel followed by a single consonant, double the consonant and add -er.

4. Courses for seniors are more difficult than freshman courses.
5. Hoopersburg is less famous than MIT.

Meaning
Use these forms to compare two elements (for example, people, objects).

Form

ADVERBS

-er than	more than	IRREGULAR	less than
One syllable fast – faster hard – harder	*All others* quickly – more quickly carefully – more carefully	well – better bad – worse	*All adverbs* less quickly than less carefully than

6. Bill has to study harder than Wizard.
7. You should drive more slowly (than you usually do).
8. Wiz studied less diligently at MIT.

Meaning
Use these forms to compare two actions.

Form

NOUNS

	more than	less than	fewer than
count nouns noncount nouns	more books more sugar	less sugar	fewer books

9. Wizard has fewer problems now than he used to.
10. Grammar class has less homework than writing class.
11. There are more men than women in the computer science department.

Meaning
Use these forms to compare two elements.

In order to emphasize the degree of comparison:

    a. Add *much* to all comparative forms except count nouns:
        much happier
        much faster
        much more intelligent
        much more quickly
        much more sugar
        much less sugar

    b. Add *many* to comparative forms of count nouns:
        many more books
        many fewer books

Note the use of *compared to/with*:

12. Compared to Bill, Jim is *tall*.
13. Compared with Jim and Bill, Wiz has *a lot of* money.
14. Bill studies *a lot*, compared to Wizard.

Notice that it is not necessary to use the comparative forms with *compared to/with*.

EXERCISE 4-1 Comparatives

Directions

There are mistakes in some of the comparatives. Underline the mistakes and rewrite the sentence in its correct form.

Example

He is intelligen<u>ter</u> than I am.
→ more intelligent

1. She works harder as most students.
2. That house was more expensive than the others in this neighborhood.
3. He spends the more time in the library than his roommate.
4. That bike is gooder than mine because it is heavyer.
5. John speaks faster than the other students.
6. My sister eats more slowlier than I do.

EXERCISE 4-2 Comparatives

Directions

Describe the students in your class, using comparatives.

Example

Maria has longer hair than Gloria.

EXERCISE 4-3 Comparatives

Directions

Describe your hometown by comparing it to the place where you are living now. (Possible topics: population, cost of living, amount of pollution, traffic, number of skyscrapers, friendliness of the people.)

Example

Tokyo is much bigger than _____ .

EQUATIVES (*as . . . as, the same . . . as*)

EXAMPLES
1. Bill is the same age as Jim.
2. Cindy isn't as tall as Jim.
3. Wizard doesn't do as much studying as Bill.

EXPLANATION

Form

as	ADJECTIVE	as
	ADVERB	
	much NOUN (noncount)	
	many NOUN + s (count)	

the same	(NOUN)	as
the same price as		

as tall as
as carefully as
as much money as
as many books as

Meaning
Use these forms to indicate equal characteristics of two elements (e.g., people, objects).

4. Sid's grades are as good as Cindy's.
5. The other students don't take as many vacations as Wiz does.
6. Are the terms at MIT the same length as they are at Hoopersburg?
7. He studies as diligently as the other students do.

EXERCISE 4-4 Equatives

Directions
There are mistakes in some of the equatives. Underline the mistakes and write the correct form of the equative.

Example
He is as tall<u>er</u> as I am.
    as tall as

1. That book is the same expensive as this one.
2. He isn't as handsome that his brother.
3. Her lecture was the same long as his lectures always are.

4. That cat can run as fast as that dog.
5. She scored as better as I did on the exam.
6. He received the same score than he received last time.

EXERCISE 4-5 Equatives

Directions

Using *as . . . as* and *the same . . . as*, compare the educational system in your country with a similar system in another country. (Possible topics: difficulty, size of schools, class size, lengths of elementary school, high school, etc.)

Example
The school year in _____ is as long as it is in the United States.

EXERCISE 4-6 Equatives

Directions

Using *as . . . as* and *the same . . . as*, compare clothing in your country with clothing in another country. Remember that you can use negatives with these patterns if necessary.

Example
Women's skirts in my country are not as short as they are in the United States.

EQUATIVES (*like, as*)

EXAMPLES
1. Wiz drives like a maniac.
2. Cindy studies every day as a good student should.
3. Bill is like a brother to Sid.

EXPLANATION

Form

(a lot)	like	NOUN
(a little bit)		

a lot like her father
a little bit like her mother

as	CLAUSE
as her mother always did.	

Note: Like is a preposition; *as* is a subordinating conjunction.

Meaning

Use these forms to bring together two similar elements. The second element explains or describes the subject or verb of the sentence.

4. The Hoopersburg campus is a lot like a small city.
5. Wiz works long hours in the computer center, as only someone who loves his work can.
6. Reading a good adventure book is like being* there yourself.

*Note the use of gerunds with *like*.

Note: Questions of the form: "What is _____ like?" are not asking for an answer using *like* or *as*. Rather, these questions ask for a simple description.

Example: a. What is your hometown like?
It has a population of 100,000 and has many beautiful trees.
b. What is John like?
He's tall, has light hair, and laughs a lot.

Note: Use *as* + NOUN to mean in the role of NOUN.

Example: c. He worked as a truck driver over the summer.
d. She appeared as a writer in the play.

EXERCISE 4-7 Equatives

Directions

Use *like* or *as*.

Example

He eats __*like*__ a horse.

1. Do _____ I say, not _____ I do.
2. She swims _____ a fish.
3. She makes pumpkin pie _____ my grandmother did.
4. He typed his paper, _____ he had been instructed to do.
5. This melon tastes _____ a cantaloupe.
6. He runs _____ a bird flies.
7. This perfume smells _____ wild flowers.
8. She completed the form _____ the law requires.

EXERCISE 4-8 Equatives

Directions
    Comment on the topics, using *like*.

Example
    George Washington
    → George Washington was like a father to the United States.

1. your dorm room
2. your mother's cooking
3. your hometown
4. learning a foreign language
5. your best friend
6. your little brother or sister
7. your classroom
8. relaxing at home
9. living away from your family
10. having a pet

118   GAINING GROUND

SUPERLATIVES

EXAMPLES
1. The computer science department has the most students.
2. Jim is the most diligent of the boys.
3. Cindy is the fastest runner on the team.
4. The engineering department is one of the largest departments at Hoopersburg.

EXPLANATION

Form

ADJECTIVES

the -est	the most _____	IRREGULAR	the least
One syllable tall – tallest hot – hottest	*All others* foolish – most foolish intelligent – most intelligent	good – the best bad – the worst far – the farthest	*All adjectives* the least tall the least simple the least foolish
Two syllables (-ow, -le, -y) yellow – yellowest simple – simplest lazy – laziest			

ADVERBS

One syllable fast – fastest hard – hardest	*All others* quickly – most quickly carefully – most careful	well – the best badly – the worst less – the least	*All adverbs* the least hard the least quickly

NOUNS

	the most books (count) the most sugar (noncount)		the fewest books the least sugar

Note: The addition of -est may involve spelling changes (see page 111).

Note: The may be replaced by any of the possessive adjectives (my, his, our, etc.).

Meaning

Use these forms to express the maximum or minimum degree of the adjective or adverb. The use of the superlative always implies the comparison of three or more elements (e.g., people, things).

5. In golf the person with the fewest hits wins.
6. His worst mistake was buying the car without driving it.
7. What is the least difficult part of learning English?
8. He studies the hardest just before exams.
9. Of all the women in the race, she ran the most quickly.

EXERCISE 4-9 Superlatives

Directions

Give a true sentence about people and things you know with the superlative forms.

Example

   most diligent
   → Maria is the most diligent student I know.

1. most helpful
2. greatest
3. most beautiful
4. laziest
5. most interesting
6. most delicious
7. most pleasant
8. funniest
9. saddest
10. most spectacular

EXPRESSIONS OF DEGREE (*so, such . . . that*)

EXAMPLES

1. Sid was so worried about his family that he had trouble sleeping.
2. Computer science is such a popular department that admission is very competitive.
3. Cindy is so independent that Jim has to learn to do some things alone.

EXPLANATION

Form

such	a	ADJECTIVE	NOUN (count)	that	DEPENDENT CLAUSE (result)
			NOUN (noncount)		

It was such a simple course that many students got As.
They were making such loud noise that we couldn't talk.

so	ADJECTIVE	that	DEPENDENT CLAUSE (result)
	ADVERB		

The course was so simple that many students got As.
They were shouting so loudly that we couldn't talk.

Meaning

Use these forms to show that an extreme degree of the adjective (adverb, noun) has led to some result (expressed in the final dependent clause).

4. He was so tired that he fell asleep on the bus.
5. She was such a good violinist that she received a scholarship to study in Europe.
6. It rained so hard that the streets flooded.
7. That bakery makes such good bread that I never buy it anywhere else.

EXERCISE 4-10 *so, such . . . that*

Directions

Complete the sentences.

1. The bus was so crowded that
2. The curry was so spicy that
3. He has such a bad cold that
4. She was so angry at her roommate that
5. They had such a good time at the amusement park that
6. The rain lasted so long that

7. My plane arrived so late that
8. The boys were so hungry that
9. The teacher gave such a hard test that
10. It was such a good movie that

EXERCISE 4-11 *so, such . . . that*

Directions
    Make sentences with the following words, using *so* or *such . . . that*.

Example
    friendly → My neighbors are so friendly that they are like my family.

1. dirty
2. delicious ice cream
3. dangerous
4. popular restaurant
5. difficult job
6. famous
7. clever
8. high prices
9. messy handwriting
10. noisy

EXERCISE 4-12 Review

Directions
    Give at least five sentences, comparing the food in your country with the food in another country.

Example
    The food in the United States is not as spicy as the food in _____.

EXERCISE 4-13 Review

Directions

Give at least five sentences, comparing television in your country with television in another country.

Example

→ Japanese television has more game shows than American television.

EXERCISE 4-14 Review

Directions

Answer the questions.

Example

Are you older than your brothers?
→ No, one brother is older than I am. The other one is younger.

1. Is your English class this term as difficult as it was last term?
2. What is your family like?
3. What was the most tragic moment in your country's history?
4. What did your brother work as during summer vacation?
5. What was the happiest moment of your life?
6. Who served as your adviser when you first started this program?
7. What is your favorite place like in your country?
8. What did you wear the last time you went to a costume party?
9. Are you the same as you were five years ago?
10. Is this city at the same altitude as your hometown?

EXERCISE 4-15 Review

Directions

There are mistakes in some of the comparatives/equatives/superlatives below. Underline the mistake and write the correct form.

Example

She swims <u>as</u> a fish. *like*

1. I am not as tall than my brother.
2. The seashore is most beautiful part of my country.

Comparisons **123**

3. A Mercedes isn't as expensive as a Rolls Royce.
4. I've read less books this term than I read last term.
5. She does math like a computer.
6. He'll have much more questions next week.
7. The patient is more sicker than the doctors thought.
8. I did my most careful work in that course.
9. I study more efficiently in the morning than at other times of the day.
10. This factory causes more pollution than any other in the city.

FINE POINTS FOR RECOGNITION

A.
Examples
1. The longer I study, the more frustrated I get.
2. Bring your friends along to the party: the more, the merrier.

Form

the COMPARATIVE	(...)	,	the COMPARATIVE	(...)

Meaning
Use this form to indicate that two actions are parallel (i.e., an increase in one action means an increase in the other action).

Note that the action may be only implied (Example 2).

The more (people at the party), the merrier (the party will be).

B.
Examples
1. That child grows taller and taller every year.
2. As it got dark outside, the house became colder and colder.
3. He grew more and more tired as the evening progressed.

Form

VERB	ADJECTIVE -er	and	ADJECTIVE -er
	more		more ADJECTIVE

Meaning
Use these forms to emphasize an increase in the degree of the adjective during a period of time.

124 GAINING GROUND

C. EXPRESSIONS OF DEGREE

Examples

1. He is such an expert that he never needs advice.
2. He is such a liar that no one wants to talk to him.

Form

such	a	NOUN (count)	that	DEPENDENT CLAUSE (result)

Meaning

Use this form with nouns that are inherently very negative or positive. (Compare with pages 119–120.)

SUMMARY

1. COMPARATIVES
   Jim is *taller than* Bill.
   Wiz has *more money than* Bill and Jim.
   The tickets were *more expensive than* she had expected.

2. EQUATIVES (*as . . . as, the same . . . as*)
   Bill is *the same* age *as* Jim.
   Bill isn't *as* tall *as* Jim.

3. EQUATIVES (*like, as*)
   Wiz drives *like* a maniac.
   Cindy studies every day *as* a good student should.

4. SUPERLATIVES
   Jim is *the most diligent* of the boys.
   The computer science department has *the most* students.
   The engineering department is one of *the largest* departments at HSU.

5. EXPRESSIONS OF DEGREE
   Sid was *so* worried about his family *that* he had trouble sleeping.
   Computer science is *such* a popular department *that* admission is very competitive.

Relative Clauses   5

SUBJECT RELATIVE PRONOUNS

EXAMPLES
1. The department which has the most students is computer science.
2. Sid lives in the room which is next to Jim and Bill's.
3. Who is the student who lives next to Jim and Bill?

EXPLANATION

Form

(...)	NOUN	who / which	VERB	(...)

I like the professor who teaches my calculus class.
I like the book which has an answer key.

Clauses beginning with *which* or *who* are called RELATIVE CLAUSES. The clauses in these examples are called *subject* RELATIVE CLAUSES because the relative pronoun (*which* or *who*) is the subject of its clause.

Using RELATIVE CLAUSES is a way to combine two sentences concerning the same noun:

a. *The department* is computer science.
b. *The department* has the most students.
   The department *which has the most students* is computer science.

125

c. Sid lives in *the room*.
d. *The room* is next to Jim and Bill's.
   Sid lives in the room *which is next to Jim and Bill's*.

Meaning
Use a RELATIVE CLAUSE following a noun in order to give more information about the noun.

In subject RELATIVE CLAUSES, use *who* to refer to people and use *which* to refer to everything else.

EXERCISE 5-1   Subject Relative Pronouns

Directions
Circle the correct relative pronoun. Put brackets around the entire relative clause.

Example
   The department   [who / (which)   has the most students] is computer science.

1. The student   who / which   lives next to Sid plays his stereo too loudly.
2. Jim sold his books to a freshman   who / which   lives down the hall.
3. Cindy is thinking about moving to a dorm   who / which   is more centrally located.
4. Who is the math major   who / which   is helping Jim with his homework?
5. Writing computer programs is the thing   who / which   gives Bill the most problems in his engineering courses.
6. The animal   who / which   is the symbol for Hoopersburg State University is the lion.

Relative clauses **127**

RESTRICTIVE vs. NONRESTRICTIVE RELATIVE CLAUSES

The examples on page 125 are *restrictive* RELATIVE CLAUSES because the information in the RELATIVE CLAUSE is necessary in order to "restrict" (uniquely explain) the noun it follows.

1. The department which has the most students is computer science.

The following examples are *nonrestrictive* RELATIVE CLAUSES. The noun described by the nonrestrictive RELATIVE CLAUSE is uniquely identified even without the RELATIVE CLAUSE; the RELATIVE CLAUSE provides additional information only.

Separate nonrestrictive RELATIVE CLAUSES from the main clause with commas (or with one comma if the RELATIVE CLAUSE ends the sentence). Remember, in general, commas separate nonessential information from the rest of the sentence. In speech, there are pauses before and after nonrestrictive RELATIVE CLAUSES.

2. The computer science department, which has many students, is located in Crawford Hall.
   (There is only one computer science department. The information about the number of students is extra information.)
3. Sid, who is from India, lives next to Jim and Bill.
   (Sid's name uniquely identifies him. We don't need the information about India in order to know who Sid is.)

THE RELATIVE PRONOUN *that*
You can replace *who* and *which* with *that* in restrictive relative clauses in speech and in informal writing. *That* is the relative pronoun most commonly used in the speech of Americans.

Note: Never use *that* as the relative pronoun in a nonrestrictive RELATIVE CLAUSE.

4. The department that has the most students is computer science.
5. Sid lives in the room that is next to Jim and Bill's.
6. Who is the student that lives next to Jim and Bill?

Note: In the following examples, notice the use of commas and relative pronouns.

7. Hoopersburg State University, which is located in the western part of the state, has a total enrollment of 12,000.
8. Jim and Bill live in the dormitory   which / that   is located one block from the Student Union.

EXERCISE 5-2 Restrictive vs. Nonrestrictive Relative Clauses

Directions
Circle the letter of the correct explanation of the sentence.

Example
The local university, which has both day and night classes, is only 20 minutes from here.
a. There's one university in the area.
b. There's more than one university in the area.

(a is circled)

1. I received a bill today from the doctor who performed my operation.
   a. I go to one doctor.
   b. I go to more than one doctor.
2. The convertible that is parked in front of our house belongs to my uncle.
   a. There's only one convertible on the street.
   b. There's more than one convertible on the street.
3. We usually catch the early morning bus, which leaves about 6:45 a.m.
   a. There's only one early morning bus.
   b. There's more than one early morning bus.
4. My roommate who owns the stereo lets all of us use it.
   a. I only have one roommate.
   b. I have more than one roommate.
5. Leave your name and address with the secretary, who will send you an application as soon as possible.
   a. There's only one secretary.
   b. There's more than one secretary.
6. The revolution, which occurred in 1796, resulted in the independence of the country.
   a. The country had only one revolution.
   b. The country had more than one revolution.

EXERCISE 5-3 Subject Relative Pronouns

Directions
Complete the sentences with a subject relative clause beginning with *who* or *which*.

Example
> Sid is the student...
> → Sid is the student who is from India.

1. Bill is the junior...
2. Wizard is the student...
3. Cindy is the girl...
4. Computer science is the department...
5. Sid is the student...
6. Dr. Hobson is the adviser...
7. Thompson Hall is the dormitory...
8. Hoopersburg State is the university...

EXERCISE 5-4 Subject Relative Pronouns

Directions
Use sentences with subject relative clauses to describe some of the people in your school.

Example
> → Mohammed is the student who wears glasses.

EXERCISE 5-5 Subject Relative Pronouns

Directions
Answer the questions, using subject relative clauses.

Example
> What is an oil tanker?
> → It's a large ship which carries oil.

1. Who was Abraham Lincoln?
2. What is Washington, D.C.?
3. What is a hitchhiker?
4. What is a hardware store?
5. What is a vending machine?
6. What is a dentist?

130 GAINING GROUND

 7. Who was Gandhi?
 8. What is a tutor?
 9. What is a convertible (car)?
10. What is an adviser?
11. What is a bilingual dictionary?
12. Who was George Washington?
13. Who was Madame Curie?
14. What is an escalator?
15. Who was Albert Einstein?

OBJECT RELATIVE PRONOUNS

EXAMPLES
1. The hardest course which Jim is taking is math.
2. The university which Wizard attended before Hoopersburg was MIT.
3. The girl whom Wizard had helped at the computer center last week called him yesterday.

EXPLANATION

Form

(...)	NOUN	which / whom / that*	SUBJECT	VERB	(...)

The professor whom they like is teaching the course.
The course that they enjoy meets at 2:00.

*Use *that* only in restrictive clauses.

In these examples, the relative pronoun (*which* or *whom*) is the object in the RELATIVE CLAUSE.

    a. The hardest *course* is math.
    b. Jim is taking the *course*.
       The hardest course *which Jim is taking* is math.

c. The *girl* called him yesterday.
d. Wizard had helped the *girl* at the computer center last week.
The girl *whom Wizard had helped at the computer center last week* called him yesterday.

Meaning

In object RELATIVE CLAUSES use *whom* to refer to people and *which* to refer to anything else. Many Americans use *who* in place of *whom* in speech and informal writing. However, you should use *whom* in academic writing.

4. The student whom I had met during the summer became my roommate.

Optionally, use *that* or ϕ (no relative pronoun) as the restrictive object relative pronoun for people or things in speech and informal writing.

e. The hardest course that Jim is taking is math.
f. The hardest course Jim is taking is math.
g. The girl that Wizard had helped called him.
h. The girl Wizard had helped called him.

NONRESTRICTIVE

Object RELATIVE CLAUSES can also be nonrestrictive. Never use *that* as the relative pronoun in a nonrestrictive relative clause.

5. Cindy, whom Jim met in high school, is majoring in accounting.
6. Calculus II, which Bill took freshman year, is a required course for some majors.

In the following examples, note the use of commas and relative pronouns.

7. The university   which / that   they attend is a state school.
8. Jim is thinking about buying a calculator   that / which   he saw on sale yesterday.
9. Dr. Hobson, whom all the computer science students respect, always makes time to talk with his advisees.
10. Sid wants to move into a room   which / that   he can share.
11. Is the university   which / that   they attend a state school?
12. Jim and Bill's dorm, which they really like, is the most popular dorm on campus.

EXERCISE 5-6 Object Relative Pronouns

Directions
Combine the sentences using an object relative clause. Make verb tense changes where necessary.

Example
> The university is a state school. They attend the university.
> → The university which / that they attend is a state school.

1. The bus broke down. We took the bus.
2. The boys ordered Cokes. They quickly drank the Cokes.
3. They hate the professor. The professor is teaching the course.
4. The bus came early. Cindy missed the bus.
5. Sid needs the book. It's missing from the library.
6. Jim found a kitten in the parking lot. It was lost.
7. Wizard found a job. The job is at the computer center.
8. They had some Indian food. Sid prepared it.
9. Bill talked to a girl at the party. A friend of his brought her to the party.
10. Wizard called the man. The man had offered him a job.

EXERCISE 5-7 Object Relative Pronouns

Directions
Answer the questions, using object relative clauses.

Example
> What are sneakers? → They are shoes which you wear for sports.

1. What is a take-home exam?
2. What is a bus pass?
3. What is an open-book exam?
4. What is a slide rule?
5. What is a backpack?
6. What is a savings account?
7. What is chess?
8. What is a required course?
9. What is an air conditioner?
10. What is a registered letter?

Relative clauses

EXERCISE 5-8 Object Relative Pronouns

Directions
Write the letter of the correct relative pronoun in the blank.
a. only *which*   c. *which* or *that*
b. only *whom*   d. *whom* or *that*

Example
____c____ The hardest course _____ Jim is taking is math.

1. _____ The car _____ Wiz drives is a two-door red Mustang convertible.
2. _____ The convertible _____ Wiz's father bought for him is the only one of its kind on campus.
3. _____ Wiz often gives rides to students _____ he sees waiting for the campus bus late at night.
4. _____ He parks the car at a parking lot _____ the university provides for the students.
5. _____ The fee for parking, _____ is by permit only, is $50 per term.
6. _____ The man _____ the university pays to watch the parking lot knows all the students who park on campus.
7. _____ This guard, _____ all the students call "Jonesy," has worked for Hoopersburg State University for years.
8. _____ The parking space _____ Wiz usually takes is right next to Jonesy's little office.
9. _____ Jonesy usually goes home as soon as Wiz returns from the computer center, _____ he generally leaves around midnight.
10. _____ Wiz goes into the dorm and Jonesy goes to a little apartment _____ he rents near campus.

EXERCISE 5-9 Object Relative Pronouns

Directions
Can you omit the relative pronouns from any sentences in the previous exercise? If so, which sentences?

134   GAINING GROUND

POSSESSIVE RELATIVE PRONOUNS

EXAMPLES
1. Sid, whose family lives in India, is having financial problems.
2. The friend whose notes Bill borrowed called; he needs them to study tomorrow.
3. Hoopersburg State awarded a scholarship to Cindy, whose grades were the best of all the applicants.

EXPLANATION

Form

(. . .)	NOUN	whose	NOUN	SUBJECT VERB	(. . .)
				VERB	

The professor whose class they are taking is interesting.
The professor whose class meets at 2:00 is interesting.

In these examples, the relative pronoun (*whose*) is possessive and must be followed by a noun.

    a. *Sid* is having financial problems.
    b. *Sid's* family lives in India.
       Sid, *whose family lives in India*, is having financial problems.

    c. *The friend* called.
    d. Bill borrowed *the friend's* notes.
       The friend *whose notes Bill borrowed* called; he needs them to study tomorrow.

Note: The relative pronoun *whose* + NOUN may function as a SUBJECT or OBJECT in the RELATIVE CLAUSE.

4. I've never heard of the movie director whose films they are showing on campus this week.
5. Do you happen to remember the name of the singer whose record was number one in 1980?

Meaning
Whose usually refers to an animate antecedent. It is possible, however, to find examples of *whose* which refer to a nonpersonal antecedent.

    e. The cities *whose* populations have decreased in the last decade need to attract new businesses to their areas.

Note: Possessive RELATIVE CLAUSES can also be nonrestrictive.

6. Albert Schweitzer, whose interests included classical music and theology, is best known for his medical work in Africa.

EXERCISE 5-10 Possessive Relative Pronouns

Directions
Combine the sentences, using a possessive relative clause.

Example
I've never heard of the movie director.
They are showing the director's films on campus this week.
→ I've never heard of the movie director whose films they're showing on campus this week.

1. They spoke to the neighbor.
   The neighbor's dog was barking all night.
2. The teacher reprimanded the student.
   The student's paper was late.
3. The police contacted the woman.
   I hit the woman's car.
4. The chemistry department invited the man to give a lecture.
   The man's paper had won an award.
5. The college received $10,000.
   The college's basketball team had won the championship.
6. The car went off the road.
   The car's tire was flat.
7. The police found the man's wallet.
   He'd been mugged.
8. The student went to the police.
   The student's car had been stolen.
9. The cat's tail is white.
   The cat belongs to me.
10. The artist is giving a lecture.
    We are studying his work in our class this week.

EXERCISE 5-11 Possessive Relative Pronouns

Directions
Use sentences with possessive relative clauses to describe some of the people in your school.

Example
Maria is the student whose cousin is in the basic level class.
Ms. Walker is the one whose car someone stole.

EXERCISE 5-12 Possessive Relative Pronouns

Directions
Write six sentences about famous people in your country—either historical or contemporary. Use possessive relative clauses in your sentences.

Example
John F. Kennedy, whose presidency lasted not quite 3 years, had to respond to many crises during his term of office.

RELATIVE PRONOUNS IN PREPOSITIONAL PHRASES

EXAMPLES
1. Sid, about whom everyone is worried, still hasn't heard anything from his family.
2. Computer science is the department for which Hoopersburg State is best known.
3. The dean is the person to whom students must apply for permission to work on campus.

EXPLANATION

Form

FORMAL

(...)	NOUN	PREPOSITION	whom / which	SUBJECT	VERB	(...)

The professor to whom we spoke explained the schedule.
The class about which I asked him meets in the afternoon.

(...)	NOUN	whom / which	SUBJECT	VERB	PREPOSITION	(...)

INFORMAL

The professor whom we spoke to explained the schedule.
The class which I asked him about meets in the afternoon.

In these examples, the relative pronouns (*whom, which*) are the objects of prepositions in the RELATIVE CLAUSE.

    a. *Sid* still hasn't heard anything from home.
    b. Everyone is worried about *Sid*.
       Sid, *about whom everyone is worried*, still hasn't heard anything from home.

    c. Computer science is *the department*.
    d. Hoopersburg State is best known for *the department*.
       Computer science is the department *for which Hoopersburg State is best known*.

The following are examples of informal English:

4. Sid, whom everyone is worried about, hasn't heard anything from home.
5. Computer science is the department which Hoopersburg State is best known for.
6. The dean is the person whom students must apply to for permission to work on campus.

Note: Many Americans use *who* in place of *whom* in speech and informal writing.

7. Sid, who everyone is worried about, still hasn't heard anything from home.

RESTRICTIVE VS. NONRESTRICTIVE
Clauses with relative pronouns in prepositional phrases can be restrictive or nonrestrictive.

8. I have already forgotten the name of the man that I was introduced to.
9. Albert Einstein, to whom the professor referred in his lecture, worked at Princeton University after he came to the United States.

That may be used in restrictive RELATIVE CLAUSES *but* only in a limited way.

e. The plane for which we have been waiting had engine trouble.
f. The plane which we have been waiting for had engine trouble.
g. The plane that we have been waiting for had engine trouble.

Note: You may not use *that* in a sentence like "e" when the preposition is at the beginning of the RELATIVE CLAUSE.

Note: You may omit *that* in these clauses (just as in object RELATIVE CLAUSES).

h. The plane we have been waiting for had engine trouble.

In the following examples, note the range of possible relative pronouns.

10. The oral exam   which / that / ϕ   we were so nervous about took only 10 minutes per person.
11. How long did the written exam   which / that / ϕ   you weren't nervous about take?

EXERCISE 5-13   Relative Pronouns in Prepositional Phrases

Directions

The sentences below are either formal or informal. Change each one to the other form of the relative clause.

Example

I have already forgotten the name of the man to whom I was introduced.
→ I have already forgotten the name of the man who / that I was introduced to.

1. The record album to which we were listening last night belongs to my roommate.
2. The charity organization which he sent money to helps orphans go to college.
3. The stranger to whom I lent $5 disappeared.
4. The old friend I ran into last night used to live in my dorm.
5. The problem about which he had consulted a lawyer has been solved.
6. The bus for which we are waiting must be late.
7. The decision about which we've been thinking for the past week is a difficult one.
8. The person you are thinking of moved away last year.
9. The disease which he is suffering from is incurable.
10. The occasion which these clothes are suitable for is an elegant party.

EXERCISE 5-14   Relative Pronoun in Prepositional Phrases

Directions
    Answer the questions, using relative clauses.

Example
    What radio station do you usually listen to?
    → The radio station that I usually listen to is WPIZ.

1. What subjects do you like to talk about with your friends?
2. What kind of pictures do you like to look at in a museum?
3. What problems in your country are you most concerned about?
4. What club or organization do you belong to?
5. What aspect of American life are you impressed with?
6. What sports are you interested in?
7. What accomplishment are you proud of?
8. Which decision of the government are you happy about?
9. Which of your classes are you tired of?
10. Which part of the United States are you familiar with?

EXERCISE 5-15 Relative Pronoun in a Prepositional Phrase

Directions
Write sentences, using a relative pronoun in a prepositional phrase.

Example
wait for → The person that I was waiting for never showed up.

1. agree with
2. apologize to (+ person) for (+ thing)
3. listen to
4. complain about
5. interested in
6. object to
7. approve of
8. search for
9. suffer from

SPECIAL RELATIVE PRONOUNS (*when, where, why*)

EXAMPLES
1. Bad grades were the reason why Wizard left MIT.
2. Midnight is the time when Wizard usually returns to the dorm.
3. The library is the place where Bill studies.
4. There are a number of reasons why the city has decided to expand the subway system.
5. At a time when they should have been in bed, the children were up watching TV.

EXPLANATION

Form

(…)	NOUN	why / when / where	SUBJECT	VERB	(…)

Room 225 is the place where they have class.
Ten o'clock is the time when they have class.
The equipment is the reason why they meet in that room.

Meaning
When, *where*, and *why* are used in place of the following prepositional phrases:

    a. Bad grades were the reason *for which* Wizard left MIT.
    b. Midnight is the time *at which* Wizard usually returns to the dorm.
    c. The library is the place *in which* Bill studies.

When, *where*, and *why* are especially common in spoken English.

Note: These clauses can be restrictive or nonrestrictive.

  6. I'll meet you in the park at the place where we had our picnic last year.
  7. We don't want to meet in our classroom, where we can't have food.

EXERCISE 5-16   Special Relative Pronouns: *when, where, why*

Directions
    Complete the relative clauses.

Example
        Bad grades were the reason why ...
    → Bad grades were the reason why Wizard left MIT.

1. That dorm is the place where ...
2. During the war was the time when ...
3. The high price was the reason why ...
4. The park is the place where ...
5. The excellent location of the house was the reason why ...
6. The end of the term is the time when ...
7. Hollywood is the place where ...
8. Winter is the time when ...

EXERCISE 5-17 Special Relative Pronouns: *when, where*

Directions
Answer the questions, using a relative clause.

Example
> Where do you like to camp?
> → I like a place where there's a lake or a river.

1. What's the best time of the year?
2. Where do you like to go for a vacation?
3. Where do you like to study?
4. When did you have a frightening experience?
5. What's your favorite kind of restaurant?
6. What's your favorite time of day?
7. Where would you like to live in town?
8. What time do you remember as the happiest time in your life?

EXERCISE 5-18 Relative Pronouns — Review

Directions
Put the letter of the correct RELATIVE PRONOUN in the blank.
  a. who   d. which
  b. whom   e. who
  d. whose   f. which or that

1. The first people _____ immigrated to the United States came from Europe.
2. There aren't many Americans _____ ancestors were among the first settlers in the original thirteen states.
3. There were many regions in the west _____ were settled by Spanish, French, and even Russian people.
4. Louisiana, _____ is located at the mouth of the Mississippi River, was a center of French culture in the New World.
5. The names of towns, rivers, and mountains in the West came from the Spanish people _____ settled there.
6. Chinese and Japanese workers were very important in the completion of the Transcontinental Railroad, _____ they finished in the mid-1800s.

7. At the turn of the century the new wave of European immigrants, _____ settled in the eastern cities, provided labor for the large factories.

8. Many of the most recent immigrants _____ native language is Spanish live in the southern and western parts of the United States.

9. On the other hand, many people from Vietnam, _____ American sponsors supported on their arrival, live all over the United States.

10. Scientists speculate that the original Americans, _____ the European discoverers of America called "Indians," emigrated from someplace in Asia.

EXERCISE 5-19 Relative Clauses — Review

Directions

Complete the relative clauses below.

Example

Have you seen the movie that ___*is playing downtown*___ ?
___*the critics praised*___ ?

1. The subway which _____ has helped to relieve the traffic downtown.

2. I haven't heard anything about the trip _____ .

3. The soccer players whose _____ all received an extra $5,000.

4. Do you happen to know the people whom _____ ?

5. The Statue of Liberty, which _____ , was a gift from the people of France to the people of the United States.

6. The newspapers were full of stories about the fireman who _____ .

7. I need a couple of tickets to the game that _____ .

8. John Wayne, who _____ , died in 1979.

9. The concert to which _____ was the last one of the season.

10. Scientists say that the Sahara Desert, which _____ , is growing larger every year.

EXERCISE 5-20   Relative Clauses — Review

Directions
Combine the sentences below using RELATIVE CLAUSES. Use the appropriate punctuation. (Notice the continuing situation.)

Example
> The farmer couldn't harvest some of the crops.
> The tornado has destroyed some of the crops.
> → The farmer couldn't harvest some of the crops   that / which   the tornado had destroyed.

1. The tornado passed through several eastern states.
   The tornado destroyed buildings and private homes.
2. The people have to live with their friends and neighbors.
   The tornado had destroyed the people's houses.
3. The people were making plans to rebuild their houses.
   The reporters talked to the people.
4. The newspapers had many pictures of the damage.
   The tornado had caused the damage.
5. The reporters interviewed many victims.
   The victims were just happy to be alive and have their families safe.
6. The reporters were also very upset by the destruction.
   The reporters were used to seeing disasters.
7. The victims appreciated the help from their neighbors.
   The neighbors' property had not been damaged.
8. The reporters were impressed at the courage of the people.
   They interviewed the people.
9. Since many of the victims don't have the money, they will have to borrow it.
   They need the money to rebuild their houses.
10. There are special bank loan programs.
    The victims qualify for special bank loan programs.

Relative clauses   **145**

FINE POINTS FOR RECOGNITION

A. RELATIVE PRONOUN *which* REFERRING TO THE IDEA OF THE INDEPENDENT CLAUSE

Examples
1. Cindy has received the best grades of any accounting student, which makes Jim very proud.
2. Wiz flunked out of MIT, which disappointed his parents terribly.
3. At MIT, Wiz spent all of his time with the computers, which wasn't good for his other classes.
4. Wiz likes computers better than people, which Bill and Jim find strange.

Use *which* to refer to the entire idea of the preceding clause instead of just a one-word antecedent. Notice that *which* can be either a subject (Examples 1, 2, 3) or an object (Example 4) in the RELATIVE CLAUSE. There is always a comma before *which* in this type of RELATIVE CLAUSE construction.

B. DETERMINER + *of* + RELATIVE PRONOUN

DETERMINER	of	whom
		which

Examples
1. The students, all of whom had passed their final exams, went out to celebrate.
2. My bibliography contains over 100 books, many of which I borrowed from the public library.
3. After the performance they interviewed people in the audience, none of whom had enjoyed the new version of *MacBeth*.
4. He finally returned all of his library books, five of which were two weeks overdue.

Use DETERMINER + *of* + WHICH/WHOM when you want to give extra information about members of a group specified by the antecedent.

   a. *The students* went out to celebrate.
      All of *the students* had passed their final exams.
      The students, *all of whom had passed their final exams*, went out to celebrate.

146 GAINING GROUND

    b. My bibliography contains over 100 *books*.
       I borrowed many of *the books* from the public library.
       My bibliography contains over 100 books, *many of which I*
       borrowed from the public library.

In formal writing to give additional information about a specific part of an object, use the *of which* phrase.

  5. The critic couldn't recommend Bernard's latest book, the plot of which he found trite and boring.
  6. The Egyptian pyramids, the construction of which is still a mystery, are one of the wonders of the world.

In less formal English, the *of which* phrase is replaced by *whose*.

    c. The critic couldn't recommend Bernard's latest book, whose plot he found trite and boring.
    d. The Egyptian pyramids, whose construction is still a mystery, are one of the wonders of the world.

Note: All of these clauses are always nonrestrictive.

SUMMARY

  1. SUBJECT
    The department *which has the most students* is computer science.
    Sid, *who is from India*, lives next to Jim and Bill.
  2. OBJECT
    The hardest course *which Jim is taking* is math.
    Cindy, *whom Jim met in high school*, is majoring in accounting.
  3. POSSESSIVE
    The friend *whose notes Bill borrowed* called.
    Sid, *whose family lives in India*, is having financial difficulties.
  4. PREPOSITIONAL PHRASE
    Computer science is the department *for which HSU is best known*.
    Sid, *about whom everyone is worried*, still hasn't heard anything from his family.
  5. WHEN, WHERE, WHY
    Bad grades were the reason *why Wizard left MIT*.
    Midnight is the time *when Wizard usually returns home*.
    The library is the place *where Cindy studies*.

Conditionals 6

TYPE I: PRESENT/FUTURE REAL (*if*)

EXAMPLES
1. If Bill gets into MIT, he'll go there.
2. Sid won't go to graduate school if he doesn't have the money.
3. If Jim can find a job, he'll begin working right after graduation.

EXPLANATION

Form

If	PRESENT	,	will	VERB
	PRESENT PERFECT		MODAL*	
	PRESENT CONTINUOUS		IMPERATIVE	

If it rains, we'll postpone the picnic.
If they have finished, everyone can leave.
If you are having trouble, call us.

or:

will	VERB	if	PRESENT
MODAL*			PRESENT PERFECT
IMPERATIVE			PERFECT CONTINUOUS

We'll postpone the picnic if it rains.
Everyone can leave if they have finished.
Call us if you are having trouble.

*MODAL = can, should, ought to, may, might, must, could

147

Note: Put a comma after an if-CLAUSE that begins a sentence.

Meaning
The if-CLAUSE is possible and may occur in the future. The above forms can occur in any combination.

4. If you don't like big classes, you won't like Hoopersburg State University.
5. What can you do if you don't graduate?
6. You'll have to stand in a long line if you have waited till the last day to register.
7. If you fail the course, take it again.
8. If you haven't finished your paper by Monday, you'll have to ask for an extension.

EXERCISE 6-1 Type I

Directions
Based on the situation, complete the sentences with an if-clause or a main clause.

1. If Sid doesn't have enough money,
2. If Jim gets a good job,
3. If Jim can't get a student loan for his senior year,
4. If Cindy doesn't want to get married,
5. Bill will visit his parents this weekend
6. If Bill gets into MIT,
7. Bill and Jim will room together next year
8. Sid will go to graduate school in math

9. Sid will go home with Bill
10. Cindy won't marry Jim

EXERCISE 6-2   Type I

Directions
Complete the sentences with an if-clause or a main clause.

1. If I get a good grade in grammar,
2. I'll take the TOEFL again
3. I'll be able to go to the movies on Saturday
4. If you can't finish your composition by the end of class,
5. If you forget your homework,
6. If I don't eat breakfast,
7. I'll gain weight
8. I won't have time to eat breakfast tomorrow
9. If I need money before my check arrives,
10. If you don't pay your tuition bill on time,

EXERCISE 6-3   Type I

Directions
Make a comment in the form of a conditional sentence with an imperative as the second clause.

Example
Your classmate is having dinner with an American family tonight.
→ If you have enough money, take some flowers.

1. Your classmate isn't finished with his paper which is due this afternoon.
2. Your teacher is planning to visit your country next summer.
3. Your classmate wants to buy a used car.
4. Your classmate wants to go to the beach for the weekend.
5. Your classmate wants to find an American roommate.
6. Your teacher wants to study your native language.
7. Your classmate wants to apply to Harvard.
8. Your classmate wants to improve his score on the TOEFL.

EXERCISE 6-4   Type I

Directions
Ask questions with an if-clause.

1. (Student in class) can't afford his apartment any longer and is planning to move in with three roommates that he found in the university newspaper. He will probably have a variety of difficulties living with roommates. Ask him how he will deal with the potential problems.

   Example: What will you do if they are noisy?

2. (Student in class) can't afford to pay for any more English classes. He has only a 420 on the TOEFL, but he'll have to start academic classes in 2 weeks. Of course, he's going to have problems. Think of some problems he will have. Ask him how he will deal with these potential problems.

3. (Student in class) hurt his ankle yesterday. He's going to the hospital this afternoon because he's afraid it may be broken. He knows he'll have some problems at the hospital because his English is poor and he doesn't have insurance. Think of what problems he will have. Ask him how he will deal with these potential problems.

EXERCISE 6-5   Type I

Directions
Write "will" and an appropriate verb in the blanks below.

1. If he doesn't have enough money, Sid _____ _____ home.
2. If Sid's father sends him his tuition money for next term, the registrar _____ _____ him to register.
3. If Sid goes home to India, he _____ _____ a job.
4. If his family's financial situation improves, they _____ _____ him some money.
5. If Bill gets good grades in his engineering courses, he _____ _____ to MIT.
6. If MIT accepts him, he _____ _____ there.
7. If Jim has trouble with his homework tonight, he _____ _____ late at the library.

Conditionals **151**

8. If he gets back late, he _____ _____ enough sleep.

9. If he's sleepy tomorrow, he _____ _____ a bad grade on his quiz.

10. If Bill and Jim are hungry, they _____ _____ a pizza.

TYPE I: PRESENT/FUTURE REAL (*unless*)

EXAMPLES
1. Unless Sid gets financial aid, he won't go to graduate school.
2. Cindy won't have dinner with Jim unless she is able to finish her work on time.
3. Wiz will come to the party unless he's scheduled to work.

EXPLANATION

Form

	PRESENT		will	VERB
Unless	PRESENT CONTINUOUS	,	MODAL*	
	PRESENT PERFECT		IMPERATIVE	

Unless he's busy, he'll come to the picnic.
Unless you come home very late, call us.
Unless they have finished, no one can leave.

or:

will	VERB		PRESENT
MODAL*		unless	PRESENT CONTINUOUS
IMPERATIVE			PERFECT PERFECT

He'll come to the picnic unless he's busy.
Call us unless you come home very late.
No one can leave unless they have finished.

*MODAL = can, should, ought to, may, might, must, could

Note: Put a comma after an *unless*-CLAUSE that begins a sentence.

Meaning
The meaning of *unless* is equivalent to *if . . . not*.

The above forms can appear in any combination.

    a. *If* Sid *doesn't* get financial aid, he won't go to graduate school.
    b. Cindy won't have dinner with Jim *if* she *isn't* able to finish her work on time.
    c. Wiz will come to the party *if* he *isn't scheduled* to work.

4. Unless the snow stops, don't try to drive downtown.
5. You should pay your rent on time unless your landlord has given you an extension.
6. Unless he's arriving soon, we won't be able to see him.
7. We'll drive to the game unless our car isn't working.

EXERCISE 6-6 Type I (*unless*)

Directions
If the two sentences have the same meaning, circle S; if they have different meanings, circle D.

Example
    (S)/ D   Unless you like big classes, you won't like Hoopersburg State University.
               If you don't like big classes, you won't like Hoopersburg State University.

1. S/D   Unless you finish your paper by Monday, you'll have to ask for an extension.
          If you don't finish your paper by Monday, you'll have to ask for an extension.
2. S/D   Unless I get a good grade in grammar, I'll have to take the course again.
          If I get a good grade in grammar, I'll have to take the course again.
3. S/D   Unless I eat breakfast, I'm hungry all morning.
          If I don't eat breakfast, I'm hungry all morning.
4. S/D   I'll gain weight unless I stop eating so much.
          I'll gain weight if I don't stop eating so much.

Conditionals 153

5. S / D You can't register for classes unless you have paid your past bill.
You can't register for classes if you have paid your last bill.

6. S / D I won't stop by unless I have free time.
I won't stop by if I have free time.

EXERCISE 6-7 Type I (*unless*)

Directions

Complete the sentences with an unless-clause or a main clause.

1. Unless I get an A on the next test,
2. I'll visit my parents next summer
3. Unless the rain stops soon,
4. I'm going to buy a color TV
5. Unless the team wins the next game,
6. The miners will go on strike
7. The plane will arrive on time
8. Unless the workers at the airport end the strike soon,

TYPE II: PRESENT UNREAL

EXAMPLES

1. If Jim had all A's in his courses, any graduate program would accept him.
2. Could Sid apply for a bank loan for his tuition if he were from the United States?
3. If they attended a different university, their chances of gaining admission to graduate school would be better.

EXPLANATION

Form

If	PAST TENSE*	,	would	VERB
	PAST CONTINUOUS		could	
			might	

If he had the money, he'd take a vacation.
If he were making more money, he could take a vacation.

or:

would			PAST TENSE*
could	VERB	if	
might			PAST CONTINUOUS

He'd take a vacation if he had more money.
He could take a vacation if he were making more money.

*PAST TENSE: The verb *be* only appears as *were* in type II if-clauses.

Meaning

The if-CLAUSE signals an unreal condition *in the present time*. The above forms can appear in any combination.

4. If Bill didn't want a graduate degree, he could find a job in private industry easily.
5. Sid wouldn't send any applications if his financial situation were hopeless.
6. If Bill were making excellent grades, he wouldn't have to worry about his graduate admission.

EXERCISE 6-8   Type II

Directions

Read the following sentences. After each sentence is a statement that is either true or false. Circle the T if the statement is true; circle the F if the statement is false.

Example

If Sid were an American, he could get a scholarship.

(T)/ F   Sid is not an American.

1. Jim could live in an apartment off campus if he had more money.
   T / F   Jim has enough money for an apartment off campus.
2. If Bill were studying history, he wouldn't have laboratory classes.
   T / F   Bill is studying history.

3. Sid might not like Hoopersburg State University if he didn't have so many good friends there.

   T / F   Sid doesn't have many friends at Hoopersburg State University.
4. If Bill were on the football team, he wouldn't have so much time for studying.

   T / F   Bill is not a member of the football team.
5. Sid would have higher grades if he handed in his assignments on time.

   T / F   Sid hands in his homework on the day it is due.
6. If Jim and Cindy were married, they wouldn't live in dorms.

   T / F   Jim and Cindy are not married.

EXERCISE 6-9   Types I and II

Directions

Read the following sentences. After each sentence there is a statement that is either true or false. Circle the T if the statement is true; circle the F if the statement is false.

1. If a graduate program accepts Bill, he'll continue his studies.

   T / F   Bill may continue his studies.
2. If Bill's grades were higher, he wouldn't be so worried about graduate school.

   T / F   Bill isn't worried about graduate school.
3. Jim can pay back his student loan if he gets a job after graduation.

   T / F   Jim won't pay back the loan after graduation.
4. If the tuition rises next year, Jim will need a part-time job.

   T / F   Jim can't afford increased tuition on his present income.
5. If Sid had all A's, he might qualify for special financial assistance.

   T / F   Sid has not received A's in all his classes.
6. Bill could find a well-paying job if he didn't want to pursue a higher degree.

   T / F   Bill doesn't want to go on to graduate school.

EXERCISE 6-10   Type II

Directions

Complete the sentences. All the sentences refer to the Hoopersburg situation.

1. Cindy would study in her dormitory room
2. If she complained to her neighbors about the noise,
3. If Jim studied both computer science and business,

4. Sid could get a high-paying job in his country
5. If the university offered a special program combining computer science and business,
6. If the computer classes weren't so crowded,
7. Sid would not be so worried about his future
8. If the tuition were cheaper,

EXERCISE 6-11 Type II

Directions
    Complete the sentences.

1. If I had enough time,
2. I would get better grades
3. If my brother had one million dollars,
4. If I knew more English,
5. I would live with an American family
6. If I liked foreign food better,
7. If the teacher gave more homework,
8. I would be able to read faster in English
9. My classmates would have a party
10. I would live in the dormitory

EXERCISE 6-12 Types I and II — Review

Directions
    Fill in the blank with the correct form of the verb *be*.

1. If I _____ you, I'd apologize to her.
2. We _____ in London by 11:00 if the plane arrives on time.
3. They would release him from the hospital if he _____ in better condition.
4. If I _____ not there by 8:00, leave without me.
5. I'll give her your message if she _____ there.
6. If there _____ a thunderstorm, you shouldn't play golf.
7. If the car _____ bigger, we could all go together.
8. Our apartment _____ more comfortable if it _____ bigger.

TYPE III: PAST UNREAL

EXAMPLES
1. If Bill had studied harder in his freshman year, he would have received better grades.
2. Sid's father would have saved a lot of money if Sid had gone to a university in his country.
3. If Jim had moved off campus after freshman year, he would have missed dormitory life.

EXPLANATION

Form

If	PAST PERFECT / PAST PERFECT CONTINUOUS	,	would / could / might	have	VERB	-ed

If it had rained, we would not have gone to the picnic.
If it had been raining, we might not have gone to the picnic.

or:

would / could / might	have	VERB	-ed	if	PAST PERFECT / PAST PERFECT CONTINUOUS

We wouldn't have gone to the picnic if it had rained.
We might not have gone to the picnic if it had been raining.

Meaning
The if-CLAUSE signals an unreal condition *in the past time*.

Note: Listen to your teacher's pronunciation of *have* in this pattern. It is pronounced very similarly to *of*.

4. If Sid hadn't come to study in the United States, he wouldn't have met Jim and Bill.
5. Bill could have lived off campus if he had earned extra money during summer vacations.
6. If Bill had been working on his lab report all week, he would have finished it on time.

EXERCISE 6-13 Type III

Directions
Read the following sentences. After each sentence there is a statement that is either true or false. Circle the T if the statement is true; circle the F if the statement is false.

1. If Bill had submitted his application early, he might have heard from the university already.
   T / F   Bill did not submit his application early.
2. If Hoopersburg State University had not developed a good computer science department, the number of students would have decreased significantly.
   T / F   The university has developed a good computer science program.
3. Many students would have applied to other universities if Hoopersburg State University had not expanded its computer facilities.
   T / F   The university did not expand its computer facilities.
4. Bill would have gone to a different university if he had had better grades in high school.
   T / F   Bill didn't have good grades in secondary school.
5. If the rents for apartments had been lower, Sid would have found a room off campus.
   T / F   Sid moved into a room off campus.
6. If the university had offered evening courses, Bill would have registered for the evening program instead.
   T / F   The university only offered courses during the day.

EXERCISE 6-14 Type III

Directions
Complete the sentences.

1. Bill could have received a scholarship
2. If the graduate program had already sent him the application,
3. Jim could have changed his major
4. If Jim had changed his major,
5. Hoopersburg State University would have attracted more international students
6. If more foreign students had known about the university's good programs,
7. If Bill had not received a loan for his tuition,
8. Cindy might have gone to a different university

EXERCISE 6-15 Type III

Directions
Complete the sentences.

1. If I had studied more English in high school,
2. If the teacher hadn't given us a test last week,
3. I wouldn't have come here
4. The teacher wouldn't have been angry
5. If I hadn't come here to study,
6. If I hadn't spent so much money last month,
7. If he hadn't missed his bus yesterday,
8. If the university hadn't mailed my acceptance letter in time,
9. If I hadn't decided to come to this school,
10. The teacher would have spoken more loudly

EXERCISE 6-16 Type II

Directions
Answer the questions.

1. What would you do if your neighbors were very noisy?
2. What would you do if your hot water didn't work after you had moved into a new apartment?

3. What would you do if your friend didn't return some money that you had lent him?
4. What would you do if you were invited to dinner and a good friend came to visit you unexpectedly?
5. What would you do if your friend gave you a gift obviously much more expensive than the gift you had bought for him?
6. What would you do if your teacher gave you a lower grade than you thought you deserved?
7. What would you do if your classmate who had cheated on a test got a better grade than you did?
8. What would you do if you were arrested for a crime you hadn't committed?
9. What would you do if the friend who had driven you to the party got drunk?
10. What would you do if you forgot the name of a person whom you had just been introduced to?

EXERCISE 6-17   Type III

Directions
   Answer the questions.

1. What would you have done if you hadn't been able to come here?
2. What would you have done if you had arrived and your luggage had been lost?
3. What would you have done if you had received a scholarship for any country that you chose?
4. What would you have done if your parents hadn't wanted you to come here?
5. What would you have done if you hadn't decided to study _____?
6. What would you have done if your brother had married a girl you didn't like?
7. What would you have done if you had been the best student in your high school class?
8. What would you have done if you had been born into a very rich family?

EXERCISE 6-18   Types II and III

Directions
   Answer the questions.

1. What would you have done if your heater/radiator had broken last weekend?
2. What would you have done if you had won $1 million in the lottery?

Conditionals **161**

3. What would you do if you received a telephone bill for $1,000?
4. What would you do if you had a professor that you couldn't understand?
5. What would you do if someone stole your passport?
6. What would you do if your car broke down in the middle of the night in an unfamiliar place?
7. What would you have done if your parents had come to visit last week?
8. What would you do if you were on a plane that was being hijacked?
9. What would you do if you got stuck in an elevator?
10. What would you have done yesterday if you had arrived late to school?

MIXED TYPE: TYPES II AND III

EXAMPLES
1. If Bill had registered for fewer courses, he wouldn't have so many final examinations this week.
2. If Jim had received a scholarship, he wouldn't have any debts after graduation.
3. Bill's qualifications for graduate school would be much better if he had studied harder during his freshman year.

EXPLANATION

Form

If	PAST PERFECT	,	would could might	VERB

If we had bought less food, we wouldn't have so much left.

would could might	VERB	if	PAST PERFECT

We wouldn't have so much left if we had bought less food.

Meaning
There is a time contrast between the if-CLAUSE (past time + unreal condition) and the main clause (present time + unreal condition). Such sentences express speculation about the results of unfulfilled past actions in the present time.

4. You would be able to speak English without an accent if you had learned it as a child.
5. If you had qualified for a scholarship, you could study at a private university instead of a state university.
6. If you hadn't decided to study here, what would you be doing today?

EXERCISE 6-19   Mixed Type

Directions
Choose the correct form of the verb.

1. If I had bought a newspaper this morning, I _____ you the movie schedule.
   a. can tell   c. could have told
   b. could tell   d. will tell
2. The flight would be here by now if a storm _____ the departure from Los Angeles.
   a. had not delayed   c. had not delay
   b. would not delay   d. did not delay
3. If my mother had forced me to eat vegetables as a child, I _____ them now.
   a. like   c. would liked
   b. might like   d. liked
4. Our football team would be the champions this year if they _____ just one more game during the season.
   a. would have won   c. would win
   b. won   d. had won
5. If the government had supported different businesses in the past, the economy _____ more stable.
   a. was   c. can be
   b. would have been   d. were
6. You wouldn't need to go on a diet if you _____ more over the past few months.
   a. had exercised   c. would have exercised
   b. exercised   d. would exercise
7. If the city had built a subway system 10 years ago, the traffic _____ so bad today.
   a. weren't   c. wouldn't be
   b. won't be   d. isn't

8. I'd feel much better if I _____ 8 hours of sleep last night.
   a. had
   b. had had
   c. have had
   d. would have had

EXERCISE 6-20   Mixed Type

Directions
  There are many people who have been responsible for important historical events. Speculate on the course of history if such people had not lived or if they had acted differently.

Example
  If Columbus had sailed into New York harbor, we might be speaking Spanish today.
  If Oswald had not assassinated Kennedy, the United States would be very different today.

EXERCISE 6-21   Type I — Review

Directions
  Advertisements and TV commercials make many promises to the consumer. Use conditional sentences to express some of the promises made on TV, on the radio, and in magazines.

Example
  If you use our toothpaste, you will have whiter teeth.
  If you buy our tires, your car will perform better in all kinds of weather.

EXERCISE 6-22   Types I, II, and III — Review

Directions
  Complete the following sentences using type I, II, or III conditionals. The first six items refer to the Hoopersburg situation.

1. If Sid had more money,
2. If Bill's parents didn't live in Hoopersburg,
3. If Jim hadn't gotten a student loan for his junior year,
4. If Bill and Jim weren't roommates,
5. If Jim marries Cindy,
6. Sid will go to graduate school

164   GAINING GROUND

7. If I have enough money,
8. If I already had 600 on the TOEFL,
9. If I didn't want to study in the United States,
10. If I learn enough English this term,
11. If I had visited my family last Christmas,
12. My classmates would be happier
13. The teacher would have finished grading the tests

EXERCISE 6-23   Types I, II, and III — Review

Directions
    Write the correct form. Some of the sentences include negation.

1. If I had known the tuition, I _____ to such an expensive school.
    a - (not, apply)

2. He would need to take some extra courses if he _____ his major
    a - (change)
    now.

3. He wouldn't have passed the midterm exam if he _____ for
    a - (not, study)
    another week.

4. If he were a better student, his adviser _____ him to take a fifth
    a - (permit)
    course.

5. My adviser might have written me a better recommendation if I _____
    a - (not, be)
    late with so many assignments.

6. If I had taken fewer courses, I _____ so many assignments late.
    a - (not, hand in)

7. If I have time, I _____ my assignments early.
    a - (do)

8. I'll complain to the dean if the professor _____ me a bad grade.
    a - (give)

FINE POINTS FOR RECOGNITION

    A. TYPE I: *Should* in the if-CLAUSE

Form

If	should	VERB	,	will VERB
				IMPERATIVE

Meaning

When *should* appears in the if-CLAUSE of type I conditionals, it means "by chance."

Note: See the alternative word order below for this pattern.

Examples
1. If you should hear about an apartment near campus, let me know.
2. If anyone should call about the advertisement, please take a message.
3. The university will receive a lot of money if its football team should win the championship.

B. TYPE II: *Would* in the if-CLAUSE

Form

If	would	VERB	,	would / MODAL	VERB

Meaning

When *would* appears in the if-CLAUSE of type II conditionals, it means "be willing to."

Examples
1. If you would hold these books for me for a second, I could unlock the door.
2. If he would just listen to your arguments, he would change his mind about disarmament.
3. The landlord might lower the rent if we would agree to take care of the garden for him.

C. INVERTED WORD ORDER: Types I, II, III

Form

Type I:	Should*	VERB		will	VERB	
Type II:	Were*	to	VERB	,	IMPERATIVE	
Type III:	Had	VERB	-ed	would	VERB / have VERB -ed	

*Only *should* and *were* may be used in these sentences.

166   GAINING GROUND

Meaning
There is no change in meaning when the *if* is omitted and the first auxiliary begins the clause. Such sentences are used primarily in formal English.

Examples
1. Should the university expand its computer system, the students and faculty will benefit.
2. Were the university to increase tuition, many students would apply for additional student loans.
3. Had the university announced the tuition increase earlier, many parents would have complained to the chancellor.

SUMMARY

1. TYPE I: Present/Future Real
   If Bill *gets* into MIT, he*'ll go* there.
   If you *don't like* big classes, you *won't like* HSU.

2. TYPE I: Present/Future Real: *unless*
   Unless Sid *gets* financial aid, he *won't go* to graduate school.
   Cindy *won't have* dinner with Jim *unless* she *is able to finish* her work on time.

3. TYPE II: Present Unreal
   If Jim *had* all A's in his courses, any graduate program *would accept* him.
   If Sid *were* from the United States, he *could apply* for a bank loan.

4. TYPE III: Past Unreal
   If Bill *had studied* harder in his freshman year, he *would have received* better grades.

5. MIXED TYPES (II and III)
   If Bill *had registered* for fewer courses, he *wouldn't have* so many exams this week.

Passive 7

WITHOUT A *BY*-PHRASE

EXAMPLES
1. Wizard was thrown out of MIT.
2. Grades are not sent to the parents of Hoopersburg students; the students receive them.
3. Wizard's car was wrecked last week in the student parking lot.

EXPLANATION

Form

SUBJECT	BE*	VERB	-ed	(...)

The house was destroyed.

SUBJECT - affected person or thing
*Be must agree in number with the subject and in tense with the situation.

Meaning
In most English sentences, the doer of the action is the subject of the verb. Such sentences are called ACTIVE.

a. Wizard left MIT.
b. Bill lives in the dorm.
c. Sid wrote his family a letter.

167

168 GAINING GROUND

In some sentences, however, the doer of the action is not as important as the affected person or thing (see Examples 1, 2, 3). In such cases, where the doer of the action doesn't need to be mentioned, the PASSIVE can be used (inclusion of the *doer* in a *by phrase* will be discussed in the next section).

4. Sid's dreams of graduate school were crushed when his family's financial problems began.
5. Is he registered to take the course for credit?
6. In this experiment the liquid is heated to 90°C.

You may think of PASSIVE sentences as being related to corresponding ACTIVE sentences:

Example 1: (University officials) threw Wiz out of MIT.
Example 2: (The office) does not send grades to the parents of Hoopersburg students.
Example 3: (Someone) wrecked Wizard's car last week in the student parking lot.

Note that the subjects in these ACTIVE sentences don't give much information: they are obvious from the situation (Examples 1 and 2) or unknown (Example 3). Therefore, the PASSIVE forms of these sentences are more appropriate to the situation.

Use the PASSIVE when the doer (subject) of an action is:

    a. unknown, or
    b. obvious from the situation, or
    c. not important

Also use the PASSIVE if you want to avoid placing blame or to hide the doer (subject).

7. Coffee was spilled on my homework.

EXERCISE 7-1   Passive

Directions
Circle the letter of the correct explanation of the sentence.

Example
Grades are sent to the parents of Hoopersburg students.
a. The parents send the grades.
b. Someone sends the grades to the parents.

1. Bill's calculator was stolen in the library yesterday.
   a. A thief stole Bill's calculator.
   b. Bill stole his calculator.
2. That course was canceled after the first day.
   a. The first day canceled the class.
   b. The school canceled that class after the first day.
3. The dorms are decorated for Christmas every year.
   a. Someone decorates the dorms each year for Christmas.
   b. Christmas decorates the dorms each year.
4. ID cards are given to students at the beginning of the school year.
   a. The students receive ID cards.
   b. The students distribute ID cards.
5. Grades are sent to the students at the end of every term.
   a. The university sends the grades.
   b. The students send the grades.

6. The students in science classes are provided with lab equipment.
   a. The university provides equipment.
   b. The students provide equipment.

EXERCISE 7-2 Passive

Directions
   Situation: Yesterday a tornado hit a small town in Ohio. Use the passive to describe the problems caused by the tornado. Give passive sentences about the tragedy, using the subjects given.

Example
   Many cars (wreck).
   → Many cars were wrecked.

1. Two people (kill)
2. Twenty homes (destroy)
3. One family (trap) in cellar
4. Many windows (break)
5. Several cars (move) more than 100 feet
6. Many trees (pull) out of the ground
7. Several stores (damage)
8. Thirty people (hurt)
9. The electric current (cut)

EXERCISE 7-3 Passive

Directions
   Last year a chemist performed an experiment. Give passive sentences about this experiment, using the subjects given. Add articles where appropriate.

Example
   Two liquids (mix)
   → Two liquids were mixed.

1. mixture (boil)
2. several chemicals (add)
3. mixture (stir)

4. liquid (pour into container)
5. container (put in refrigerator overnight)
6. temperature (set at 40°F)
7. container (remove from refrigerator)
8. liquid (heat to 90°F)

EXERCISE 7-4   Passive

Directions
Last week a charity organization had a party to raise money for an orphanage. What happened at the party? Use your imagination. Write at least five passive sentences.

Example
→ Twenty-five dollars was charged for admission.

WITH A *BY*-PHRASE

EXAMPLES
1. Sid's paper had already been corrected by the teaching assistant.
2. Bill and Jim's dorm room was robbed by a masked man.
3. Seniors were interviewed last week on campus by corporation officials.

EXPLANATION

Form

SUBJECT	BE	VERB	-ed	(...)	by	AGENT

The house was destroyed by a hurricane.

Meaning
In most PASSIVE sentences, the agent (doer) of the action is not mentioned. However, if the agent is known and you want to mention it, you may use a *by*-phrase.

4. Was the graduation speaker introduced by the Dean or by the Chancellor?

5. The witnesses to the robbery were interviewed by both the police and the press.
6. The prize money was donated to a hospital by the winner.

Use the PASSIVE with *by + phrase* when you want to de-emphasize the agent. If you want to emphasize the agent, use an ACTIVE sentence with the agent as the subject.

1a. Sid's paper had already been corrected by the teaching assistant.
(The teaching assistant's involvement is not emphasized.)
1b. The teaching assistant had already corrected Sid's paper.
(The role of the teaching assistant is emphasized.)

EXERCISE 7-5 Passive with a *by-phrase*

Directions
Circle the letter of the correct explanation of the sentence.

Example
Wizard was thrown out of MIT by the dean.
a. The dean threw Wizard out of MIT.
b. Wizard threw the dean out of MIT.

1. The stolen money was found by three children playing in the park.
   a. Three children playing in the park found the stolen money.
   b. Three children were playing in the park and stole the money.
2. John's stereo was repaired by another student.
   a. John and another student repaired his stereo.
   b. Another student repaired John's stereo.
3. Food is collected for the poor by community organizations.
   a. The poor collect the food.
   b. The community organizations collect the food.
4. Mail is delivered daily to the residents by a private company.
   a. A private company delivers the mail daily.
   b. The residents deliver the mail daily.
5. As we approached, the garage door was opened by an electronic device.
   a. We approached the garage door and opened it.
   b. An electronic device opened the garage door as we approached.

6. Prizes were distributed to the winners by the sponsors.
   a. The winners distributed the prizes.
   b. The sponsors distributed the prizes.

EXERCISE 7-6   Passive with a *by-phrase*

Directions
Make statements concerning each topic, using the passive with a *by-phrase*.

Example
   tuition — pay/provide
   → My tuition was paid by my government.
   → My tuition is provided by my parents.

1. apartment — find / clean / paint / choose
2. car — wash / buy / wreck / choose
3. friend — injure / select / arrest
4. class — praise / reprimand / visit
5. passport — steal / examine
6. grammar book — read / buy / publish
7. hometown — visit / establish / praise
8. leader of my country — choose / visit / criticize
9. national university — establish / praise / attend
10. grandfather — employ / help

EXERCISE 7-7   Passive with a *by-phrase*

Directions
Choose an annual celebration in your country. Explain what happens using the passive (with *by-phrases* when necessary).

Example
   → Christmas trees are sold in many locations all over town. One tree is bought and taken home by each family. It is decorated by the whole family during the week before Christmas.

INDIRECT OBJECT AS THE PASSIVE SUBJECT

EXAMPLES
1. Wizard was given a car by his father.
2. Bill was assigned a lab partner in his first lab class.
3. Cindy was sent two valentines by Jim.

EXPLANATION

Form

SUBJECT	BE	VERB	-ed	DIRECT OBJECT	(by AGENT)

The driver was given a ticket by the policeman.

Meaning
In these sentences the indirect object in the corresponding ACTIVE sentence is functioning as the subject of the PASSIVE sentence.

4. U.S. citizens are mailed tax forms each January.
5. Children are sometimes told ghost stories that frighten them.
6. Why was he refused a visa last year?

Note that there are alternative PASSIVE sentences, using the direct object as the subject of the PASSIVE sentence in each case:

a. A car was given *to Wizard* by his father.
b. A lab partner was assigned *to Bill* in his first class.
c. Two valentines were sent *to Cindy* by Jim.

Note that in the case of these sentences, *to* must be used before the indirect object. Some verbs require *for* instead of *to*.

Compare:

d. A favor was done for Bill by Jim.
e. A present was bought for Jim by Cindy.

EXERCISE 7-8 Indirect Object as the Passive Subject

Directions
Circle the letter of the correct explanation of the sentence.

Example
>Wizard was given a car by his father.
>a. Wizard gave his father a car.
>(b.) Wizard's father gave him a car.

1. Mary was sent a $100 check by her mother.
   a. Mary's $100 check was sent to her mother.
   b. Mary's mother sent her a $100 check.
2. Jim was assigned a lab partner by Professor Smith.
   a. Professor Smith assigned Jim a lab partner.
   b. A lab partner assigned Jim to Professor Smith.
3. Parents are shown their children's work when they visit the school.
   a. The school shows the work.
   b. The parents show the work.
4. The winner is awarded a gold medal by the committee at the annual picnic.
   a. The winner receives a gold medal.
   b. The committee receives a gold medal.
5. Bill was handed a note during Professor Smith's lecture.
   a. Professor Smith handed Bill a note during his lecture.
   b. Someone handed Bill a note during Professor Smith's lecture.
6. We were told a lie by our government.
   a. The government told us a lie.
   b. We told the government a lie.

EXERCISE 7-9 Indirect Object as the Passive Subject

Directions
>Answer each question using a passive sentence with the indirect object as the subject of the passive verb.

Example
>Who was given a car by his father?
>→ Wizard was given a car by his father.

1. Who was paid your tuition money?
2. Who is given presents at Christmas?
3. Who is sent the report on your English progress?
4. Who is usually sent cards on Valentine's Day?

176 GAINING GROUND

5. Who is usually given a diamond ring at the beginning of their engagement?
6. Who is usually refused a loan?
7. When are you mailed your phone bill?
8. When are you assigned your class?
9. In schools in your country, when are you first taught the writing system?
10. Why are some people denied a visa to enter the United States?
11. How were you told the news about your admission to college?
12. How often are you given grades in this school?

PASSIVE WITH OTHER TENSES

EXAMPLES
1. Sid's major had been decided before he arrived in the United States.
2. Hoopersburg University has often been chosen by middle-class families for their sons' and daughters' educations.
3. Nowadays, less money is being contributed to Hoopersburg by the alumni.

EXPLANATION

Form

CONTINUOUS

BE	being	VERB	-ed

The room is being painted.

PERFECT

has			
have	been	VERB	-ed
had			

The room has been painted.

FUTURE

BE going to	be	VERB	-ed
will			

The room is going to be painted.

Meaning
The PASSIVE may be in any verb tense which the time situation of the sentence requires. The normal rules for the use of the CONTINUOUS and the PERFECT also apply to the PASSIVE sentences.

4. The election won't be held until November.
5. Over 200 people have been arrested since the demonstration began this morning.
6. This week a movie is being filmed downtown near Market Square.

EXERCISE 7-10 Passive with Other Tenses

Directions
Give the correct passive form of the verb.

Example

The election __won't be held__ until November.
(NEGATIVE, hold)

1. The project _____ this week.
   a - (complete)
2. The construction site _____ next month.
   a - (choose)
3. The roof _____ already.
   a - (repair)
4. That work _____ yet.
   a - (NEGATIVE, do)
5. The road _____ when I left for work this morning.
   a - (fix)
6. I can't wear my suit today. It _____ today.
   a - (clean)
7. The car _____ before we left on our vacation.
   a - (check)
8. At this moment the winners _____ .
   a - (select)

EXERCISE 7-11 Passive with Other Tenses

Directions
Give a passive sentence, using the following verb phrases.

Example

had been elected
→ After the president had been elected, he received congratulations from around the world.

1. have been criticized
2. is being improved

178 GAINING GROUND

3. had been polluted
4. will be painted
5. was being built
6. has been neglected
7. are being harvested
8. will be arrested
9. were being repaired
10. is going to be installed

PASSIVE FORMS WITH MODALS

EXAMPLES
1. Registration can be done by mail.
2. The application should be filled out with a No. 2 pencil.
3. Wizard's car may have been wrecked by another student.

EXPLANATION

Form

MODAL	be	VERB	-ed

The book has to be read by
     Friday.

MODAL	have	been	VERB	-ed

The work should have been finished
     already.

Meaning
When used with the PASSIVE, the MODALS have their usual meanings.
(See Chapter 2.)

4. The application should have been mailed no later than June 1.
5. Wizard's car might not be repaired until next month.
6. Your registration could have been done by mail, but now you may
   register in person in room 318.

EXERCISE 7-12 Passive with Modals

Directions
Choose the correct form of the modal.

Example
Registration can (be done)/ have been done   by mail.

1. All of the papers should   typed. / have been typed.
2. Accurate records must   be kept. / keep.
3. The passengers had to   rescue / be rescued   from the airplane.
4. You could   be hurt / have been hurt   in that accident.
5. The books should   be ordered / have been ordered   by last week.
6. The jewels might   be found / found   soon.
7. The plants must   be watered / watered   once a week.
8. The plans could   be made / have been made   before this.

EXERCISE 7-13 Passive with Modals

Directions
Give a sentence using the verb phrases below. Give a context if necessary.

Example
  should be written
  → Your compositions should be written in pen.

1. must be finished
2. might be elected
3. can be seen
4. must have been damaged
5. should have been typed
6. has to be fixed
7. should be fed
8. could have been written
9. can be arrested
10. should be punished

PASSIVE CAUSATIVES

EXAMPLES
1. Sid had his research paper typed a week ago.
2. Wiz has his car washed twice a month.
3. Bill had his grades sent to several graduate schools.

EXPLANATION

Form

SUBJECT	have / get*	OBJECT	VERB	-ed

He had the house painted last year.

Get is used in this structure only in informal English.

Note: Do not confuse the PRESENT PERFECT with this pattern.

Compare:
> a. Mr. Brown *has cut* his son's hair several times.
> b. Mr. Brown *has* his own hair *cut* (by a barber).

Meaning
In Chapter 4 the use of causative *have* is presented.

> c. Mr. Brown had his wife cut his hair last night.
> d. Old Mrs. O'Connor has Jimmy Thomas mow her grass every week.
> e. We got them to paint the house for $850.
> f. I had someone repair the TV at a store on 6th Street.

In sentences with PASSIVE CAUSATIVES the doer of the second action is not important and is usually not mentioned. In Example c "his wife" is important, but in Example 4 the person is not important. (We assume that a barber cut his hair.)

> 4. Mr. Brown had his hair cut last week.
> 5. Old Mrs. O'Connor has her grass mowed by Jimmy Thomas every week.
> 6. We got the house painted for $850.
> 7. I had the TV repaired at a store on 6th Street.

EXERCISE 7-14   Passive Causative

Directions
Identify the person who does the main action in each sentence.

Example
>Mr. Brown has cut his son's hair several times.
>Mr. Brown ___X___ unknown person _____

1. We had the car washed last weekend.
   we _____ unknown person _____
2. Mrs. Blackmoor has all her clothes dry-cleaned.
   Mrs. Blackmoor _____ unknown person _____
3. The carpenter has repaired the Jacksons' roof.
   the carpenter _____ unknown person _____
4. The nurse had the patient moved to another room.
   the nurse _____ unknown person _____

5. The doctor has X-rayed Jimmy's foot.
   the doctor _____ unknown person _____
6. Mrs. McDonald had the morning newspaper delivered to her house.
   Mrs. McDonald _____ unknown person _____

EXERCISE 7-15   Passive Causatives

Directions
   Answer the questions.

1. When did you have your hair cut last?
2. How often does your landlord have your apartment painted?
3. What do you have done to your car?
4. What did you have done to your clothes?
5. What did you have done to your bad tooth?
6. What did your landlord have done to your apartment last year?
7. What did you have repaired in the last month?
8. What did you have delivered to your house last week?

EXERCISE 7-16   Passive Causatives

Directions
   Give five things you do yourself and five things you have done for you by others.

Example
   I wash my own clothes.
   I have my sweaters dry-cleaned.

EXERCISE 7-17   Review

Directions
   Fill in the blank with the correct passive verb tense.

1. Last week flight 93 to London _____ .

a - (hijack)
2. He _____ by IBM since 1962.

a - (employ)

3. After the luggage _____ a - (inspect), the passenger _____ b - (permit) to leave the customs area.
4. The disease _____ a - (spread) rapidly now by travelers who are visiting the region.
5. The ship _____ a - (unload) when it sunk during a sudden storm.
6. All the applicants for the position _____ a - (already interview), and the decision _____ b - (announce) by the end of the week.
7. I can't drive to work today. My car _____ a - (repair) this morning.
8. Donations _____ a - (collect) every year during the holiday season to provide clothing for the needy.
9. An interview with the Secretary-General of the UN _____ a - (televise) on last night's news.
10. A concert to raise money for the refugees _____ a - (hold) next Saturday night.

EXERCISE 7-18   Review

Directions

Describe some disaster that occurred in your country using the passive. Use *by-phrases* only when necessary.

Example

In 1972, Hurricane Agnes hit Norristown, Pennsylvania, and caused a large flood in the area. The two halves of the town were cut off for a week by the water. Many people's homes were destroyed. Much of the flood damage could have been prevented, but many people didn't pay attention to the warnings which were broadcasted on the radio.

EXERCISE 7-19   Review

Directions

Using the passive, describe the process involved in (1) getting a driver's license, (2) getting admitted to a university, (3) getting a visa to come to the United States to study.

FINE POINTS FOR RECOGNITION

A. PASSIVE INFINITIVES:

EXAMPLES
1. He hates to be criticized.
2. His goal is to be elected president.
3. The children don't appear to have been injured in this crash.
4. It was unfair for him to have been chosen.

Form

to	be	VERB	-ed
	have been		

Meaning
PASSIVE INFINITIVES have the same range of functions as ACTIVE INFINITIVES.

B. PASSIVE GERUNDS

EXAMPLES
1. Being frightened makes my palms sweat.
2. He hates being criticized.
3. He denied having been arrested previously.

Form

being	VERB	-ed
having been		

Meaning
PASSIVE GERUNDS have the same range of functions as ACTIVE GERUNDS.

Passive   185

SUMMARY

1. WITHOUT AGENT
   Grades *are not sent* to the parents.
   Coffee *was spilled* on my homework.

2. WITH AGENT
   Sid's paper *was corrected by the teaching assistant*.

3. INDIRECT OBJECT as PASSIVE SUBJECT
   Wizard was given a car by his father.
   U.S. citizens are mailed tax forms every January.

4. WITH OTHER TENSES
   The room *is being painted*.
   The room *has been painted*.
   The room *is going to be painted*.

5. MODALS
   Registration *can be done* by mail.
   The application *should be filled out* with a No. 2 pencil.
   Wiz's car *may have been wrecked* by another student.

6. PASSIVE CAUSATIVES
   Sid *had* his research paper *typed* a week ago.

Logical Connectors   8

Part I   Coordination

COORDINATING CONJUNCTIONS TO CONNECT CLAUSES

EXAMPLES
1. Bill and Jim are thinking about getting an apartment, but Sid wants to stay in the dorm next year.
2. The deadline for registering for a dorm room is the end of this month, so Bill and Jim will have to decide soon.
3. Cindy might audit a computer science course, or she may decide to take it for credit.
4. Wizard doesn't have much time for socializing, nor does he feel comfortable in large groups.

EXPLANATION

Form

INDEPENDENT CLAUSE	,	and	INDEPENDENT CLAUSE
		but	
		or	
		nor	
		for	
		so	
		yet	

He is a student, and he has a part-time job.

186

A comma must be used when you connect two independent clauses with a COORDINATING CONJUNCTION.

Meaning

The COORDINATING CONJUNCTIONS have the following meanings.

MEANING	COORDINATING CONJUNCTION
Addition	and
Contrast	but, yet
Choice	or, nor
Cause	for
Result	so

Note: *Yet* and *for* are rarely used in informal English.

5. They would like to be more independent, yet they enjoy the convenience of dormitory life.
6. Hoopersburg State University is recruiting more international students, for the number of U.S. students is decreasing.

Note: Avoid *so* in formal English. Refer to page 209 for alternative connectors that are more appropriate for formal English.

EXERCISE 8-1 Coordinating Conjunctions

Directions

Connect the second clause with the first clause using an appropriate coordinating conjunction (and, but, for, so)

1. There's going to be a party in Bill and Jim's dorm,
   a. __and__ everyone's invited.
   b. _____ they can't go.
   c. _____ everyone's contributing $5.
   d. _____ the semester is almost over.
2. A special committee is responsible for the refreshments,
   a. _____ no one has to bring anything.
   b. _____ another committee is arranging entertainment.
   c. _____ no one on the committee has time to go shopping.
   d. _____ at the last party there wasn't enough to eat.
3. The entertainment committee hired a band,
   a. _____ they can't start playing until 11:00.
   b. _____ the committee asked some students to bring their guitars.
   c. _____ everyone is tired of listening only to stereos.
   d. _____ everyone may need to contribute more money.

POSITIVE CORRELATIVES AS COORDINATING CONJUNCTIONS

EXAMPLES
1. Both Jim and Bill need 30 more credits to graduate.
2. Wizard spends most of his time either at the computer center or in the library.
3. Either Sid gets enough money to cover his expenses, or he will have to return to his country.

EXPLANATION

Form

both ... and ...
either ... or ...
He wants either a motorcycle or a car.

These pairs of words are called CORRELATIVE CONJUNCTIONS. They join two words or phrases that function the same way grammatically.

In Example 1 two nouns are joined:

    a. Both *Jim* and *Bill* ...

In Example 2 two prepositional phrases are joined:

    b. ... either *at the computer center* or *in the library*.

In Example 3 two independent clauses are joined and a comma is necessary:

    c. Either *Sid gets enough money to cover his expenses*, or *he will have to return to his country*.

4. I either *jog* or *swim* every day for exercise.
5. The tourists visited both *the Smithsonian Institution* and *the National Gallery* while they were in Washington, D.C.
6. You can be responsible either *for buying the food for the picnic* or *for cooking the food on the barbecue*.

Meaning
Use *both ... and* to express addition. Use *either ... or* to express a choice or an alternative.

EXERCISE 8-2   Positive Correlatives

Directions
    Underline the words or phrases joined by the correlative conjunctions.

Example
    Both <u>Jim</u> and <u>Bill</u> need 30 more credits to graduate.

1. You should visit either Boston or Washington during your semester break.
2. While I was vacationing at the beach, I enjoyed both lying in the sun and walking along the shore.
3. Either start exercising or stop eating so much!
4. To get to Washington you can take either the plane, which takes about 1 hour, or the bus, which takes about 5 hours.
5. I took pictures of our vacation spot both during the day and at night.
6. We either forgot to pack our umbrella or lost it in the airport.

EXERCISE 8-3 Postive Correlatives

Directions
Answer the questions with *either . . . or*.

Example

What do you do every day for exercise?
→ I either jog or swim every day.

1. Who are you going to eat lunch with tomorrow?
2. What do you enjoy doing on the weekend?
3. Where do you go grocery shopping?
4. What kinds of movies do you enjoy watching?
5. How can you get to the bank/library/cafeteria from here?
6. What do you usually eat for breakfast?
7. Where do you like to go for vacations?
8. How do you spend your free time?
9. Where do you like to take a walk?
10. How can you come to school?

EXERCISE 8-4 Positive Correlatives

Directions
Combine the following pairs of sentences using *both . . . and*.

Example

The tourists visited the Smithsonian Institution. The tourists visited the National Gallery.
→ The tourists visited both the Smithsonian Institution and the National Gallery.

1. Jim is majoring in computer science. Wiz is majoring in computer science.
2. Bill participates in intramural basketball. Bill participates in a local baseball league.
3. In order to pay his tuition Bill works in the summer. Bill has a student loan.
4. Cindy enjoys working with numbers. Cindy enjoys having contact with people.
5. Wiz has decided to pursue his interest in computers. He has also decided to apply himself to his other course work.

Logical connectors   **191**

6. Wiz has an appointment to see Dr. Watson tomorrow. Jim has an appointment to see Dr. Watson tomorrow.
7. Cindy writes to her mother fairly frequently. Cindy calls her mother fairly frequently, too.
8. Jim and Cindy will probably invite Wiz to the wedding. They'll probably invite Sid, too.
9. Sid's goal is to finish his degree in the United States. Another goal is to start his own business in India.
10. Sid's adviser suggested applying for a special scholarship. His adviser also suggested applying for an extension on his tuition payment.

NEGATIVE CORRELATIVES AS COORDINATING CONJUNCTIONS

EXAMPLES
1. Cindy not only works hard but also makes good grades.
2. Neither Bill nor Jim owns a car.
3. Hoopersburg State University offers not only day classes for full-time students but also evening courses for people who work during the day.
4. Wiz has neither called nor seen his parents in a long time.

EXPLANATION

Form

neither ... nor ...
not only ... but also ...
He speaks not only English but also Hindi and Tamil.
He speaks neither Russian nor Chinese.

These pairs are also **CORRELATIVE CONJUNCTIONS**. They join words, phrases, or clauses that function the same way grammatically.

192   GAINING GROUND

Note: When these negative CORRELATIVE CONJUNCTIONS introduce clauses, the clauses have question word order, including *do/does/did.*

5. Not only *does Cindy want to graduate*, but *she* also *wants to work as an accountant.*
6. Neither *has Jim registered for next term*, nor *has he talked with his adviser.*

(See "Fine Points for Recognition" for other cases of question word order in clauses beginning with negatives.)

Meaning
Use *neither . . . nor* to express exclusion (in other words, not A and not B).

Use *not only . . . but also* to express emphatic addition.

EXERCISE 8-5   Negative Correlatives

Directions
Complete the sentences.

Example
→ Cindy not only works hard but also *makes good grades* .
                                      is a member of the volleyball team.

1. When Wiz needs a break from his work, he either plays pool or
2. When Jim is angry at Cindy, he not only shouts at her but also
3. When Cindy is angry at Jim, she either refuses to talk to him or
4. When Jim sits in math class, neither can he understand the lectures nor
5. When Bill relaxes after classes, either he goes to the gym or
6. When Sid is in the mood to write letters, he writes both to his parents and
7. When Jim and Cindy want to spend some time together, they take a walk either in the park or
8. When Cindy is studying she neither takes a break to eat nor
9. When Wiz is in a bad mood he avoids not only talking to people but also
10. When Wiz was at MIT not only did he not study hard but also

EXERCISE 8-6   Negative Correlatives

Directions

Combine the following pairs of sentences, using *not only . . . but also* or *neither . . . nor*.

Example

Bill doesn't own a car. Jim doesn't own a car.
→ Neither Bill nor Jim owns a car.

Cindy wants to graduate. She wants to work as an accountant.
→ Cindy not only wants to graduate but also wants to work as an accountant.

1. Sid doesn't have the time to travel around the United States.
   Sid doesn't have the money to travel around the United States.
2. Before he came to the United States, Sid traveled extensively in India.
   He traveled extensively in the Middle East, too.
3. Sid enjoys listening to traditional Indian music.
   He enjoys playing traditional Indian music.
4. Sid has never taken music lessons.
   Sid doesn't even read music.
5. Sid played for his family.
   He played for local weddings and parties.
6. He didn't bring his instruments.
   He didn't bring his records of Indian music.
7. Sid's friends want him to play for them.
   They asked him to teach them some songs.
8. Bill had never heard Indian music before.
   Jim had never heard Indian music before.

COORDINATING CONJUNCTIONS: SUBJECT-VERB AGREEMENT

EXAMPLES
1. Either Bill or Jim is going to register for their dorm room next term.
2. Neither Sid nor the two Americans want to move out of the dorm now.
3. Either the Americans or Sid is going to have first choice of rooms since the three of them have lived there the longest.

EXPLANATION

Form

The verb following *either ... or / neither ... nor* agrees with the subject which is closer to it. In Example 1 the closer subject "Jim" is singular, so the verb is also singular. In Example 2 the closer subject "the two Americans" is plural, so the verb is plural.

4. Neither they nor he is willing to live on the first floor.
5. Either he or they are going to choose the big room at the end of the hall.
6. Neither you nor I am satisfied with our current apartments.

Note: Many English speakers do not follow this rule or they avoid such sentences by using modal verbs:

3a. Either the Americans or Sid is going to have first choice of rooms since the three of them have lived there the longest.
3b. Either the Americans or Sid will have the first choice of rooms since the three of them have lived there the longest.

EXERCISE 8-7   Subject-Verb Agreement

Directions

There's a mistake in subject-verb agreement in some of the sentences. Underline the mistakes and then rewrite the sentences in their correct forms.

Example

Neither they nor he <u>are</u> willing to live on the first floor.
→ Neither they nor he is willing to live on the first floor.

1. Both my friend and I thought the movie was too violent.
2. In the film neither the hero nor his friends are able to fight the men from another planet.
3. Either the aliens or the hero kill someone in every scene.
4. Not only the men from outer space but also the humans want to control the universe.
5. Neither the alien commander nor the hero have the power to gain total control.
6. As a result, both the humans and the aliens dies in great numbers.

Logical connectors   **195**

7. In order to increase their armies, either the hero or the men from outer space goes from planet to planet to find soldiers.
8. By the end of the movie, not only the humans but also the aliens has died.
9. Neither your roommate nor you are going to enjoy this movie.

Part II   Subordination

SUBORDINATING CONJUNCTIONS INDICATING TIME SEQUENCE
(after, before, until, by the time, when)

EXAMPLES
1. After / When   Bill graduates from Hoopersburg, he wants to go to graduate school.
2. Cindy wants to establish her career before she gets married.
3. Until Jim gets a job, he won't have any extra money.
4. Jim hopes Cindy will marry him by the time they graduate.

EXPLANATION

Form

After		
Before		
Until	DEPENDENT CLAUSE	INDEPENDENT CLAUSE
By the time		
When		

By the time he finished his homework, it was midnight.
Until he finished his homework, he couldn't go to bed.

	after	
	before	
INDEPENDENT CLAUSE	until	DEPENDENT CLAUSE
	by the time	
	when	

It was midnight by the time he finished his homework.
It was midnight when he finished his homework.

Note: Use a comma after an introductory DEPENDENT CLAUSE.

Note: When the clauses introduced by SUBORDINATING CONJUNCTIONS refer to the future, the verb is in the present tense.

5. I can't watch TV until I finish my homework.
6. We'll have to continue driving until we reach the next town.

Note: See Chapter 1 for the use of *while* and for the use of these SUBORDINATING CONJUNCTIONS with past actions.

Meaning
These SUBORDINATING CONJUNCTIONS are used to show the time sequence of two clauses. *After* and *when* introduce the first action in a sequence; *before, until,* and *by the time* introduce the second action (see page 11).

Use *until* to indicate an action that specifies the end point of a continuing action.

7. I'll take English classes until I get a good TOEFL score.

Use *by the time* to indicate an action that specifies the end point of the time during which a single action occurs.

8. You'll get a good TOEFL score by the time this term is over.
9. By the time they arrived, the party had ended.

EXERCISE 8-8 Subordinating Conjunctions
              Indicating Time Sequence

Directions
   Circle the correct conjunction.

Example
   →(Until) / After   Jim gets a job, he won't have any extra money.

1. Bill hopes Jim will be his roommate   by the time / until   they graduate.
2. Cindy and Jim went to the same high school   before / after   they came to Hoopersburg.
3. Bill wants his parents to continue paying his tuition   by the time / until   he graduates.
4. Cindy hopes to have a scholarship   by the time / until   she graduates.
5. Sid expects that his family's financial problems will be over   by the time / until   he graduates.

6. Jim and Cindy were living in New York City   by the time / when   they were accepted at Hoopersburg.
7. Wiz may have completed enough courses to graduate   by the time / until   Jim and Bill gradaute.
8. Cindy doesn't want to marry Jim   before / after   they graduate.

EXERCISE 8-9   Subordinating Conjunctions
               Indicating Time Sequence

Directions
  Answer the questions with a sentence containing *before, after, until,* or *by the time.*

Example
   When did you come to the United States?
   → I came to the United States after I had graduated from high school.

1. How long will you study English?
2. When will you get married?
3. When will you see your family again?
4. How long will you stay where you are living now?
5. When did you decide on your major?
6. When did you first travel outside your country?
7. How long will you stay in this city?
8. When did you learn how to drive?
9. When will you feel comfortable in this city?
10. How long will you keep your car?

EXERCISE 8-10   Subordinating Conjunctions
                Indicating Time Sequence

Directions
  Complete the sentences according to the information in the Hoopersburg situation. (*Guess about what will happen in the future.)

Example
   Cindy wants to establish her career before...
   → Cindy wants to establish her career before she gets married.

1. Jim wants to get a job after...
2. Sid wants to stay in the United States until...
3. Cindy and Jim had been sweethearts before...

198   GAINING GROUND

4. Wizard had been studying at MIT before . . .
5. Wiz moved into Bill and Jim's dorm after . . .
*6. Wizard will work at the computer center until . . .
*7. Cindy will marry Jim when . . .
*8. Bill and Jim will room together until . . .
*9. Wizard will leave Hoopersburg when . . .
*10. Jim will get a job before . . .

SUBORDINATING CONJUNCTIONS
INDICATING CAUSE (*because, since*) AND PURPOSE (*so that*)

EXAMPLES
1. Sid may have to go back to India because his family has financial problems.
2. Since Wizard got bad grades, he had to leave MIT.
3. Cindy got a scholarship so that she could continue at Hoopersburg.

EXPLANATION

Form

INDEPENDENT CLAUSE (result or effect)	because / since	DEPENDENT CLAUSE (cause)

He never eats eggs since he's allergic to them.

Because* / Since	DEPENDENT CLAUSE (cause)	,	INDEPENDENT CLAUSE (result or effect)

Since he is allergic to eggs, he never eats them.

*The first pattern is traditionally more acceptable for *because* (i.e., put the *because/since* clause second).

INDEPENDENT CLAUSE	so that	DEPENDENT CLAUSE (purpose)

She eats eggs every day so that she can save money.

Note: Use a MODAL verb in the DEPENDENT CLAUSE. The most common MODALS are *can, could, will,* and *would.*

Meaning
Because, since, and *so that* are SUBORDINATING CONJUNCTIONS. *Because* and *since* show a relationship of a cause leading to an effect or result.

4. Cindy doesn't want to marry Jim now since she wants to have a career.
5. Because her grades were good freshman year, she received a scholarship.

So that indicates the purpose of the previous action.

6. She wants to finish her degree so that she can be an accountant.

It is different from the COORDINATING CONJUNCTION *so* which indicates result.

a. He broke the window, so he had to pay for it. (result)
b. He broke the window so that he could get into the house. (purpose)
c. She goes jogging every evening at 6:00, so she misses the evening news on TV. (result)
d. She goes jogging every evening at 6:00 so that she can stay in shape. (purpose)

EXERCISE 8-11 Subordinating Conjunctions Indicating Purpose

Directions
Choose the correct clause to complete the sentence.

Example
He broke the window so that   he had to pay for it.
                                        (he could get into the house.)

1. He parked the car on the sidewalk so that   he got a ticket.
                                                             he could load it easily.
2. He opened the window before the meeting began so that   the room would stay cool.
                                                                               the rain came in.
3. He kept the library books past the due date so that   he had to pay a fine.
                                                                    he could finish reading them.

4. She turned on the TV so that   she could see the weather forecast.
                                          I couldn't concentrate on my work.
5. Classes were canceled so that   the teachers could attend a conference.
                                          the students didn't learn anything.
6. She started exercising at the gymnasium so that   she hurt her knee.
                                                            she could lose weight.

EXERCISE 8-12   Subordinating Conjunctions
                              Indicating Cause and Purpose

Directions
      Complete each sentence by adding a cause, an effect, or a purpose.

Example
      I'm studying English because . . .
     → I'm studying English because I want to study engineering in the United States.

1. Since my handwriting is poor, . . .
2. I'm reading a book on agriculture now because . . .
3. He took a drivers' training course so that . . .
4. I don't know how to play the piano since . . .
5. They bought their airline tickets in advance so that . . .
6. We moved into a new apartment because . . .
7. He's at the library now so that . . .
8. Since the phone bill was so high, . . .
9. Since the heat in my apartment was working last night, . . .
10. We ate lunch early so that . . .

EXERCISE 8-13   Subordinating Conjunctions
                              Indicating Cause and Purpose

Directions
      Think about the Hoopersburg situation. Ask your partner *Why* questions. Your partner should answer using *because, since,* or *so that.*

Example
   → Why did Wiz leave MIT?
   → He left because he had gotten poor grades.

EXERCISE 8-14 Subordinating Conjunctions Indicating Cause and Purpose

Directions
Answer the questions, using *because, since*, or *so that*.

Example
Why are you studying English?
→ I'm studying English so that I can study engineering next year.

1. Why did you wear sneakers to school yesterday?
2. Why are they going grocery shopping?
3. Why did he call the police last night?
4. Why is she moving into the dorm?
5. Why did they buy an air conditioner?
6. Why don't we have class on July 4th?
7. Why did he buy her a present?
8. Why were you absent?
9. Why do you walk (take the bus/drive) to school?
10. Why do you live in the dorms (an apartment/with a family)?

PREPOSITION OF CAUSE (*because of*)

Form

because of	NOUN

She had to lie down because of her headache.

Meaning
The preposition *because of* can also be used to show cause.
1. Because of his poor grades, Wizard left MIT.
2. Cindy was able to continue her studies because of her scholarship.
3. Because of his family's problems, Sid may have to return to India.

EXERCISE 8-15 *Because* vs. *because of*

Directions
Give a paraphrase, using either *because* or *because of*.

Example
> He stayed home because he was sick.
> → He stayed home because of his sickness.

1. The picnic was canceled because it was raining.
2. His family is proud of him because he got good grades.
3. He couldn't go to the dance because of his homework.
4. She couldn't sleep because of the thunder.
5. They couldn't buy the house because it was too expensive.
6. The teacher marked him absent because of his lateness.
7. He's a good teacher because he's patient.
8. He couldn't enter the bar because of his age.

SUBORDINATING CONJUNCTIONS INDICATING CONTRAST
(*while, although, even though, though*)

EXAMPLES
1. (Al)though Wizard got poor grades at MIT, he's been doing well at Hoopersburg.
2. While Cindy is in love with Jim, she doesn't want to get married now.
3. Wizard has plenty of free time even though he works at the computer center.

EXPLANATION

Form

Although / Even though / Though / While	DEPENDENT CLAUSE	,	INDEPENDENT CLAUSE

Although he doesn't get good grades, he studies hard.

| INDEPENDENT CLAUSE | although
even though
though
while | DEPENDENT CLAUSE |

He studies hard although he doesn't get good grades.

Note: In spoken English, *though* can appear at the end of the sentence.

Sid: Can you help me with this computer assignment?
Wiz: Sure. I don't have much time now, though. How about later?

Meaning
While, although, even though, and *though* are SUBORDINATING CONJUNCTIONS used to show a contrast.

4. Although the sun is bright today, it's cold.
5. The patient felt much better though he still couldn't get out of bed.
6. Even though the team keeps losing, a lot of fans still attend the games.

EXERCISE 8-16 Subordinating Conjunctions Indicating Contrast

Directions
Give a paraphrase of the sentences using another of the contrast subordinating conjunctions.

Example
Although Wizard got poor grades at MIT, he's been doing well at Hoopersburg.
→ While Wizard got poor grades at MIT, he's been doing well at Hoopersburg.

1. My grandmother still works even though she's 80 years old.
2. Though he seldom studies, his grades are good.
3. While I traveled with my parents when I was a child, I've never lived in another country until now.
4. Even though Carlos has spent many years studying here, he wants to return home soon.
5. Though the streets were icy, we had no problems on the road.
6. Although she was out, I left a message on her phone machine.

7. While he didn't want to, he was forced to drop out because of financial problems.
8. She paid the bill even though she believed it was wrong.
9. He opened the door although there was smoke coming out from under it.
10. Although she heard a strange noise, she didn't turn on the light.

EXERCISE 8-17 Subordinating Conjunctions Indicating Contrast

Directions
Complete the following statements of contrast.

Example
> Even though I prefer to study engineering, ...
> → Even though I prefer to study engineering, I have to study English now.

1. While American food is different from the food in my country,
2. Although his grammar is good,
3. Though he likes to party,
4. Even though I'm studying English,
5. Though she needs the exercise,
6. While she enjoys cooking,
7. Although the dentist is expensive,
8. Even though I have next Monday off,
9. While my professor agreed to give me an extension,
10. Even though he has a beautiful apartment,

EXERCISE 8-18 Subordinating Conjunctions Indicating Contrast

Directions
Contrast your country with a neighboring country. Write one sentence of contrast on each of the following topics using *while, although, even though*, or *though*.

Example
> climate Although both the United States and Canada have four seasons, Canada's winters are much colder.
> language While Canadian high school students usually study French in school, U.S. high school students generally study Spanish.

1. food
2. weather
3. prices
4. natural resources
5. education
6. clothing
7. crime
8. transportation

PREPOSITIONS OF CONTRAST (*despite, in spite of*)

Form

despite / in spite of	NOUN

We went on a picnic
despite the weather.
We went on a picnic in
spite of the weather.

Meaning
The prepositions *despite* and *in spite of* can also be used to show contrast.

1. Despite his poor grades at MIT, Wizard has been doing well at Hoopersburg.
2. Wizard has plenty of free time in spite of his job at the Computer Center.
3. It's cold today despite the bright sun.

EXERCISE 8-19 Prepositions of Contrast

Directions
Give a paraphrase using *despite* or *in spite of*.

Example
Wizard got poor grades at MIT, but he's doing well at Hoopersburg.
→ Despite / In spite of   his poor grades at MIT, Wizard has been doing well at Hoopersburg.

1. This apartment is nice but the rent is inexpensive.
2. Although he ate a big lunch, he's already hungry.
3. While he's wealthy, he's not very happy.
4. She loves cats even though she is allergic to them.
5. We're enjoying our vacation even though we've had some problems.
6. Although that car was expensive, it doesn't run well.
7. He slept for eight hours, but he's still tired.
8. She failed the test although she studied for hours.

EXERCISE 8-20 Prepositions of Contrast

Directions
Complete the following sentences.

1. He graduated in spite of
2. They want to buy a car despite
3. They took a trip to London in spite of
4. The class planned a picnic despite
5. The tourists stayed at the Hilton Hotel in spite of
6. They enjoyed the meal despite
7. He continues to go jogging in spite of
8. The children are playing in the street despite

Logical connectors 207

Part III Transition

TRANSITIONS INDICATING SEQUENCE: TIME SEQUENCE OR LOGICAL SEQUENCE

Beginning: First, first of all
Continuation: Second, third, next, then, afterward (time only)
End: Lastly (logical), finally, at last (time)
Summation: In conclusion, in summary (both logical only)

EXAMPLES
1. First of all, Wiz went to MIT; afterward, he entered Hoopersburg.
2. Cindy tried to obtain a variety of types of financial aid; at last /finally , she was given a scholarship in her sophomore year.
3. Adviser to Jim: "We have discussed some career options for you; lastly, you could consider graduate school."

208   GAINING GROUND

EXPLANATION

Form

First		
First of all		
Next		
Then		
Afterward	,	INDEPENDENT CLAUSE
Finally		
At last		
Lastly		
In conclusion		
In summary		

First, he studied the situation carefully.

		at last		
		next		
INDEPENDENT CLAUSE (first in time)	;	afterward	,	INDEPENDENT CLAUSE (second in time)
		then		
		finally		

He studied the situation carefully; then, he made some
    suggestions.

A transition is always followed by a comma. When a transition joins
two clauses, a semicolon marks the end of the first clause.

Meaning

These TRANSITION words and phrases are used to show a sequence,
either in time or in logical reasoning. Note that most can be used for
either type of sequence, but *afterward* and *at last* are limited to time
sequences, and *lastly, in conclusion*, and *in summary* are used only in
logical sequences.

EXERCISE 8-21 Transitions Indicating Sequence

Directions
Explain the educational system in your country, using the transition indicating time sequence. Use modals.

Example
→ First, five-year-olds can go to kindergarten.
→ Finally, you can do postdoctoral work at many universities.

EXERCISE 8-22 Transitions Indicating Sequence

Directions
Explain the reasons why you feel the educational system in your country is either good or bad, using the transitions indicating logical sequence.

Begin with the following sentence:
There are three / four reasons why the educational / university system in _____ is bad / good .

TRANSITIONS INDICATING CAUSE/EFFECT
(*consequently, therefore, thus*)

EXAMPLES
1. Sid's family has financial problems; therefore, he may have to go back to India.
2. Wizard got bad grades at MIT; consequently, he had to leave.
3. Cindy got a scholarship; thus, she could continue at Hoopersburg.

EXPLANATION

Form

INDEPENDENT CLAUSE (cause)	;	consequently / therefore / thus	,	INDEPENDENT CLAUSE (effect)

There was heavy traffic; consequently, they missed their plane.

| INDEPENDENT CLAUSE (cause) | . | Consequently
Therefore
Thus | , | INDEPENDENT CLAUSE (effect) |

There was heavy traffic. Consequently, they missed their plane.

Meaning
These TRANSITION words introduce the effect of a previously stated cause.

4. The rent was very high; therefore, we didn't take the apartment.
5. His visa expired. Consequently, he had to leave the country.
6. The oil supply increased; thus, the price dropped.

EXERCISE 8-23 Transitions Indicating Cause/Effect

Directions
Add an *effect* introduced by a transition to each of the following *causes*.

Example
    Hoopersburg is a state university.
→ Hoopersburg is a state university; thus, the tuition is low.

1. Sid has financial problems.
2. Jim wants to marry Cindy.
3. Wiz is good at computers.
4. Bill and Jim live in the dorms.
5. Jim is majoring in computer science.
6. Bill wants to go to graduate school.
7. Jim is from out of state.
8. Bill's parents live near the campus.
9. Hoopersburg is a big school.
10. Wizard got poor grades at MIT.

EXERCISE 8-24 Transitions Indicating Cause/Effect

Directions
Write eight sentences about your country, using causal transitions.

Example
→ India's population is very large; thus, the cities are quite crowded.

TRANSITIONS INDICATING CONTRAST
(*however, in contrast, on the other hand, nevertheless*)

EXAMPLES
1. Professor Smith gives a lot of homework; however, his exams are rather easy.
2. Cindy is in love with Jim; nevertheless, she doesn't want to get married now.
3. Wiz works at the computer center; however, he has plenty of free time.

EXPLANATION

Form

INDEPENDENT CLAUSE	;	however / nevertheless / in contrast / on the other hand	,	INDEPENDENT CLAUSE

The traffic was heavy; nevertheless, they arrived on time.

INDEPENDENT CLAUSE	.	However / Nevertheless / In contrast / On the other hand	,	INDEPENDENT CLAUSE

The traffic was heavy. Nevertheless, they arrived on time.

Meaning
These TRANSITIONS are used to show a relationship of contrast between two independent clauses.

4. The drinking age in that state is eighteen; however, many young teenagers drink.

Use *in contrast* only when the two clauses deal with different situations.

5. The Department of Computer Science often accepts foreign students; in contrast, the Philosophy Department rarely does.

Use *on the other hand* only when the contrast is one of total opposites.

6. Wizard got poor grades at MIT; on the other hand, he's been doing well at Hoopersburg.

Use *nevertheless* to express an unexpected contrast.

7. The president is attempting to stimulate the economy; nevertheless, unemployment is still high.

EXERCISE 8-25 Transitions Indicating Contrast

Directions
Give a paraphrase of the sentences, using *however* or *nevertheless*.

Example
My grandmother still works even though she's 80 years old.
→ My grandmother is 80 years old; nevertheless, she still works.

1. Although Wizard got poor grades at MIT, he's been doing well at Hoopersburg.
2. Though he seldom studies, his grades are good.
3. While I traveled with my parents when I was a child, I've never lived in another country until now.
4. Even though Carlos has spent many years studying here, he wants to return home soon.
5. Though the streets were icy, we had no problems on the road.
6. Although she was out, I left a message on her phone machine.
7. While he didn't want to, he was forced to drop out because of financial problems.
8. She paid the bill even though she believed it was wrong.
9. He opened the door although there was smoke coming out from under it.
10. Although she heard a strange noise, she didn't turn on the light.

EXERCISE 8-26   Transitions Indicating Contrast

Directions

Give five statements of contrast concerning the Hoopersburg situation, using *however, in contrast, on the other hand*, or *nevertheless* in each statement.

Example

→ Wiz has passesd all his courses at Hoopersburg State University; nevertheless, he may not be able to graduate with his class.

EXERCISE 8-27   Transitions Indicating Contrast

Directions

Give eight statements of contrast concerning the past and the present in your country, using *however, in contrast, on the other hand*, or *nevertheless* in each statement.

Example

→ There were very few black Americans who held political office before the 1960s; however, by 1984 there were a number of black governors as well as black mayors of major cities.

Possible topics: transportation
　　　　　　　　　imports
　　　　　　　　　entertainment
　　　　　　　　　tourism
　　　　　　　　　politics

TRANSITIONS INDICATING SIMILARITY (*similarly, likewise*)

EXAMPLES
1. Cindy is paying for her education with a scholarship; similarly, Jim is using student loans.
2. Jim's family lives in New York City; likewise, Wizard is an out-of-state student at Hoopersburg State.
3. Jim is majoring in computer science because it's a practical field; similarly, Cindy is majoring in accounting.

EXPLANATION

Form

| INDEPENDENT CLAUSE | ; | similarly / likewise | , | INDEPENDENT CLAUSE |

The body of the car was damaged; likewise, its motor didn't run well.

| INDEPENDENT CLAUSE | . | Similarly / Likewise | , | INDEPENDENT CLAUSE |

The body of the car was damaged. Likewise, its motor didn't run well.

Meaning
These TRANSITIONS are used to show a relationship of similarity between two sentences. Note the position and typical punctuation of the transitions.

4. The heat in our apartment doesn't work dependably. Similarly, our neighbors complain about having inadequate heat.
5. The landlord told us not to worry about the heat; likewise, he promised our neighbors to adjust the furnace.

EXERCISE 8-28 Transitions Indicating Similarity

Directions
Think of the similarities between your country and some other country. Comment on each of the following topics, using a transition word or phrase in each comment.

Example
food → Beef is the most popular meat in the United States; similarly, beef is prized as a food for honored guests in Japan.

1. industry
2. agriculture
3. weather
4. transportation
5. clothing
6. homes
7. pets
8. education

Logical connectors   **215**

TRANSITIONS INDICATING EMPHATIC RESTATEMENT
(actually, indeed, in fact)

EXAMPLES
1. Hoopersburg is a large university; in fact, it has more than 20,000 students.
2. Sid's family is having financial problems; indeed, for the past 4 months he hasn't received any money from them.
3. Cindy usually gets good grades; actually, she's never received any grade below A.

EXPLANATION

Form

INDEPENDENT CLAUSE	;	actually	,	INDEPENDENT CLAUSE
		indeed		
		in fact		

He's a good athlete; in fact, he has just won another marathon.

INDEPENDENT CLAUSE	.	Actually	,	INDEPENDENT CLAUSE
		Indeed		
		In fact		

He's a good athlete. In fact, he has just won another marathon.

Meaning
These TRANSITION words and phrases are used to introduce an emphatic restatement of the preceding statement.

4. Much of the real work of teaching occurs outside of the classroom; indeed, many teachers estimate that they spend more time on preparation and grading than on teaching.
5. Small babies produce a large variety of speech sounds before they learn to talk. In fact, linguists assert that babies produce all possible language sounds before their "speech" becomes limited to the sounds of their native language.

Use *actually* only when the restatement includes a minor correction of some information in the first statement.

6. The colors surrounding a person can affect his moods; actually, red has been shown to produce tension and blue and green to produce a calming effect.

EXERCISE 8-29 Transitions Indicating Emphatic Restatement

Directions
For each of the following topics, give a statement about your country and then an emphatic restatement, using *actually, indeed,* or *in fact*.

Example
→ Americans eat a lot of fast food; in fact, some surveys have indicated that more than half of all meals eaten in restaurants are fast food.

1. food
2. universities
3. employment
4. public transportation
5. clothing
6. postal system
7. finding a husband or wife
8. housing

TRANSITIONS INDICATING EXEMPLIFICATION
(*for example, for instance*)

EXAMPLES
1. Cindy gets good grades; for example, last term she received all A's.
2. Wizard likes to travel on his vacations; for instance, right now he's planning a trip to Hawaii.
3. Bill is taking some difficult courses this term, for example, computer science and vector analysis.

EXPLANATION

Form

INDEPENDENT CLAUSE (statement)	;	for example for instance	,	INDEPENDENT CLAUSE (supporting example)

He's a serious athlete; for example, he trains every day for three hours.

| INDEPENDENT CLAUSE (statement) | . | For example / For instance | , | INDEPENDENT CLAUSE (supporting example) |

He's a serious athlete. For example, he trains every day for three hours.

| ... NOUN | , | for example / for instance | , | NOUN (and NOUN) | , | ... |

He does a variety of exercises every day, for example, sit-ups and push-ups.

Meaning
These TRANSITION phrases are used to introduce examples that support the preceding statement.

4. Japan imports most of its food; for example, most of the soybeans used in Japan come from the United States.
5. Many national holidays in the United States are not religious holidays; for instance, Thanksgiving has no religious origin.

EXERCISE 8-30 Transitions Indicating Exemplification

Directions
Give a statement from your field of study or about your country. Then add one or more examples to support your statement, introduced by one of these transitions.

Example
→ Many Asian languages use tone to distinguish words; for example, Mandarin and Vietnamese are tone languages.

EXERCISE 8-31 Transitions Indicating Exemplification

Directions
Give five statements about your country or hometown. Then add one or more examples to support your statement, introduced by one of these transitions.

Example
→ My hometown is a very historic place; for instance, several buildings, which are still standing, were built before the Revolutionary War.

TRANSITIONS: ADVERBS OF EXEMPLIFICATION

Simple: such as
Emphatic: especially, particularly

EXAMPLES
1. State universities, such as Hoopersburg, tend to be less expensive than private schools.
2. Sid thinks that Americans, especially / particularly Bill and Jim, are friendly.

EXPLANATION
Form

...	NOUN	,	such as / especially / particularly	NOUN	(and NOUN)	,	...

Athletes, such as basketball players and gymnasts,

Note: The noun that precedes these expressions is plural if it is countable.

Meaning
These expressions are used to introduce examples of a class of nouns mentioned in the sentence. Note that *such as* introduces any member(s) of that class.

3. Carbohydrates, such as rice and bread, form the basis of the diets of most people of the world.

Especially and *particularly* give very emphatic (or strong) examples.

4. Many Americans, especially / particularly those living in the West, do not want stronger gun control laws.

EXERCISE 8-32 Transitions: Adverbs of Exemplification

Directions
Answer the questions, using *such as, especially*, or *particularly*.

Example
Which universities are less expensive in the United States?
→ State universities, such as Hoopersburg, tend to have lower tuition.

Logical connectors　**219**

1. Which kind of cars are the most economical to drive?
2. Which kind of American universities are the most difficult to get into?
3. Which countries have the spiciest foods?
4. What kinds of things are your country's main exports?
5. What is your favorite kind of TV show?
6. What are your favorite kinds of music?
7. What kind of things do you find relaxing?
8. What is your favorite kind of food?
9. What are the hardest things to learn in the English language?
10. What kinds of problems are most serious in your country?

TRANSITIONS INDICATING ADDITION
(*moreover, in addition, furthermore, also, besides*)

EXAMPLES
1. Cindy got high grades in high school; moreover, her college grades have been excellent.
2. Financial problems may prevent Sid from going to graduate school; furthermore, his parents may want him to return home.
3. Wiz works at the computer center. In addition, he tutors students who have difficulty with their computer courses.

EXPLANATION

Form

INDEPENDENT CLAUSE	;	also	,	INDEPENDENT CLAUSE
		furthermore		
		moreover		
		in addition		
		besides		

Athletes must train hard; also, they have to watch their diets.

INDEPENDENT CLAUSE	.	Also	,	INDEPENDENT CLAUSE
		Furthermore		
		Moreover		
		In addition		
		Besides		

Athletes must train hard. Also, they have to watch their diets.

Meaning
These TRANSITION words and phrases are used to connect two statements containing very similar information. They function to add the second piece of information to the first one.

4. The car's exterior was in poor condition; in addition, its engine wasn't functioning.
5. The new tax proposal lowers taxes for the wealthy; moreover, corporations will pay fewer taxes.

Also is slightly less formal than the others.

6. His new girlfriend is beautiful; also, she is rich.

Besides shows that the second statement is emphasized.

7. Wiz partied too much at MIT; besides, he rarely studied.

EXERCISE 8-33 Transitions Indicating Addition

Directions
Give two true reasons for each of the following statements. Connect the reasons with a transition of addition.

Example
> I didn't do my homework for today.
> → I forgot to take my books home; also, I wasn't feeling well last night.

1. I like living in _____.
2. My favorite author is _____.
3. Learning a second language is difficult.
4. Getting a visa takes time.
5. Health care is expensive/inexpensive in _____.
6. My favorite type of music is _____.
7. There are several requirements for obtaining a driver's license.
8. My hobby is _____.
9. My favorite vacation spot is _____.
10. The worst problem my country faces is _____.

PREPOSITIONS INDICATING ADDITION (*besides, in addition to*)

EXPLANATION

Form

Besides / In addition to	NOUN	INDEPENDENT CLAUSE

Besides his regular job he has a part-time job.

INDEPENDENT CLAUSE	besides / in addition to	NOUN

He has a part-time job besides his regular job.

Meaning
These prepositions are used to add similar information to a statement.

1. Besides his poor grades Wizard had disciplinary problems at MIT.
2. In addition to a scholarship, Cindy uses the money from her part-time job to pay her expenses.
3. In addition to exporting wheat, the United States supplies many countries with soybeans.

EXERCISE 8-34 Prepositions Indicating Addition

Directions
Give a paraphrase of the statement, using *besides* or *in addition to*.

Example
Cindy got high grades in high school; moreover, her college grades have been excellent.
→ In addition to her high grades in high school, Cindy's college grades have been excellent.

1. He has studied German for 3 years; furthermore, he has studied Russian for 2 years.
2. Bob is an excellent cook; in addition, he enjoys entertaining.
3. There was a lot of rain yesterday; moreover, there were high winds all day.
4. The patient has a high fever; furthermore, she is having difficulty breathing.

5. The vocabulary in that reading selection is difficult; in addition, the grammar is quite complex.
6. Her pronunciation is good; moreover, she speaks very fluently.
7. The United States exports more wheat than any other country; in addition, they lead the world in soybean exports.
8. Wearing seat belts can save your life; furthermore, it will lower your chance of serious injury.

EXERCISE 8-35 Review

Directions
Explain the plot of a movie you have seen recently. Be sure to use appropriate logical connectors in order to make the events and the reasons they occurred clear.

EXERCISE 8-36 Review

Directions
Read the following list of sentences concerning coming to the United States to study. Make a paragraph, using these sentences and adding appropriate logical connectors.

1. Ali wanted to come to the United States.
2. He wanted to study engineering.
3. He talked to some friends.
4. Those friends had studied in the United States.
5. He chose a university.
6. He applied to the university.
7. The university accepted him.
8. The university sent him an I-20.
9. He took his passport and I-20 to the American Embassy.
10. They gave him a visa.

EXERCISE 8-37 Review

Directions
There are punctuation mistakes in some of the sentences. Circle the mistake and add the correct punctuation.

Example
→ Until Jim gets a job(,) he won't have any extra money.
→ Wiz works at the computer center(;) however(,) he has plenty of free time.

1. Karen and Sue decided to drive to Washington for the weekend, because they had Monday off.
2. They didn't have any trouble finding a motel in fact, they took a room at the first place they stopped.
3. After they had unpacked the car Karen and Sue drove downtown.
4. Since it was already after 5:00, most of the historical buildings were closed so they went out to dinner.
5. Sunday they spent all morning touring the area around the Capitol. For example, they saw the Washington Monument and Smithsonian Institution in addition to the Capitol.
6. They drove to other famous monuments, before they met some friends for dinner.
7. They ate at a Korean restaurant, then, all four of them went to a show.
8. Karen and Sue felt that they had seen a lot; even though, they had only been there 2 days.

EXERCISE 8-38 Prepositions Indicating Addition — Review

Directions
Choose the appropriate logical connector.

Example
Bill and Jim are thinking about getting an apartment, _____ Sid wants to stay in the dorm next year.
(a.) but   b. however   c. while

1. Hoopersburg State University received a gift of $100 from a former student; _____, more books will be added to the library.
   a. so   b. so that   c. consequently
2. The science departments wanted the money to be used for laboratory equipment, _____ the Chancellor decided in favor of the library.
   a. but   b. although   c. however
3. The library has a large collection of books on technical subjects _____ the humanities collection is rather small.
   a. yet   b. while   c. in contrast
4. The Chancellor wanted to help balance the University's collection; _____, he hoped to interest more students in the humanities.
   a. and   b. in addition to   c. moreover
5. Most of the students at Hoopersburg State University major in the natural sciences; _____, they study chemistry or physics.
   a. for example   b. such as   c. especially
6. The students are worried about getting jobs after graduation, _____ they avoid the social sciences.
   a. so   b. since   c. as a result
7. Engineering has been a popular major for many years _____ computer science is gaining steadily in popularity.
   a. but   b. though   c. however
8. Most students at Hoopersburg State University are interested in finding good jobs _____ they have spent 4 years studying.
   a. after   b. afterward   c. finally

Logical connectors 225

FINE POINTS FOR RECOGNITION

A. NEGATIVE WORDS AT THE BEGINNING OF THE SENTENCE

In addition to *neither . . . nor* and *not only . . . but also*, there are other negative words which may appear at the beginning of the sentence. Use question word order including the addition of *do/does/did*.

Other words with a negative meaning: *never, hardly, scarcely, few, little, seldom, rarely*.

EXAMPLES
1. Not only did he fail the test, but he also failed the course.
2. Not a word did the student say to explain his failure.
3. Seldom has a student at Hoopersburg State University known as much about computers as Wiz does.

Note: Sentences like 2 and 3 are rare in informal English.

B. PRESENT PERFECT IN TIME CLAUSES

The PRESENT PERFECT may also be used for future time in TIME clauses. Choose this form of the verb to emphasize the completion of the action in the future.

EXAMPLES
1. I'm going to take pictures today until I   have used / use   up this roll of film.
2. By the time you   have done / do   your homework, we will be home from the movie.
3. When you   have decided / decide   on your research topic, you should consult with your professor.

SUMMARY

	COORDINATION	SUBORDINATION	TRANSITION	PREPOSITIONS/ ADVERBS
Addition	and		also furthermore moreover in addition besides	besides in addition to
Contrast	but yet	although even though though while	however nevertheless in contrast on the other hand	in spite of despite
Choice	or no			
Cause	for	because since		because of
Purpose		so that		
Result/Effect	so		consequently therefore thus	

	COORDINATION	SUBORDINATION	TRANSITION	PREPOSITIONS/ADVERBS
Time		after before until by the time when	first second then afterward . . . at last	
Similarity			similarly likewise	
Restatement			actually indeed in fact	
Exemplification			for example for instance	such as especially particularly

PUNCTUATION

COORDINATION: A comma must be used when you connect two independent clauses with COORDINATING CONJUNCTIONS.

SUBORDINATION: A comma must be used after an introductory DEPENDENT CLAUSE. Do not use a comma before a DEPENDENT CLAUSE in second position.

TRANSITIONS: A comma must be used after a TRANSITION. When a TRANSITION joins two clauses, a semicolon (;) marks the end of the first clause.

Noun Clauses 9

Part I Statements

NOUN CLAUSES AS DIRECT OBJECTS (*that*)

EXAMPLES
1. Jim doesn't realize that Cindy is serious about getting a job after graduation.
2. Cindy thinks that Jim understands her attitudes about marriage and work.
3. When they got engaged, both Jim and Cindy thought that they had discussed everything.

EXPLANATION

Form

VERB	(that)	CLAUSE
I think that he is crazy.		

Note: Don't use a comma between a verb and direct object.

229

230 GAINING GROUND

The tense of the main verb determines the possible tenses of the verb in the noun clause:

MAIN VERB   VERB in the NOUN CLAUSE

time of action	before action of main verb	same time as action of main verb	after action of main verb
present	past present perfect past perfect	present	will + VERB
past	past perfect	past	would + VERB

Note: When the main verb is in the past tense, some tense differences are lost. Compare a and b with c and d.

    a. I think that he has been sick since last week.
    b. I think that he went to the doctor last week.
    c. I thought that he had been sick since last week.
    d. I thought that he had gone to the doctor last week.

Meaning
The *that*-CLAUSE functions as a direct object in these sentences. In simple sentences, nouns function as direct objects, so a clause that can replace a noun is called a NOUN CLAUSE.

    e. Jim doesn't realize *Cindy's intention.*
    f. Jim doesn't realize *that Cindy is serious about getting a job.*

4. I doubt that she has actually applied for any jobs yet.
5. Did you forget that we had to mail the rent to our landlord by the fifth of the month?
6. The landlord decided he would buy a new refrigerator for our apartment.

EXERCISE 9-1 Noun Clauses as Direct Objects (*that*)

Directions
  Circle the correct verb.

Example
  Jim doesn't realize that Cindy (is) / was serious about getting a job after graduation.

1. I heard that the Arts Festival   opens / opened   today.
2. We didn't notice that the door   was / had been   left open.
3. I guess that we   will / would   all meet at the park around 2:00.
4. He remembered that he   has / had   an appointment with the career counselor.
5. Can you prove that someone   is / has been   opening your mail since January?
6. He doesn't believe that men actually   walked / had walked   on the moon.
7. He found out that he and his roommate   were / had been   born in the same small town.
8. Do you think that the store   will / would   be open by 10 a.m.?

EXERCISE 9-2   Noun Clauses as Direct Objects (*that*)

Directions
Use the verbs below to tell about your first week here.

Example
    see   → I saw that most of the streets were very wide.
    think → I thought that the cars looked very big.

1. discover
2. notice
3. observe
4. figure out
5. realize
6. think
7. learn
8. find out
9. assume
10. decide

EXERCISE 9-3   Noun Clauses as Direct Objects (*that*)

Directions
Complete the sentences. (Notice that the object pronoun is obligatory with these verbs.)

1. When I left this morning, my roommate reminded me that
2. Before I came here, my family warned me that
3. Although I didn't believe it at first, a friend convinced me that
4. When I came to class the first day, our teacher informed us that
5. When I received my latest bill, the phone company notified me that
6. During my physical examination the doctor assured me that
7. While she was campaigning for office, the candidate told the voters that
8. While I was looking for a new car, the salesman persuaded me that

NOUN CLAUSES AS DIRECT OBJECTS (*if*, *wh*-words)

EXAMPLES
1. Jim doesn't know   if / whether   he wants to move back to the city after graduation.
2. He doesn't understand why Cindy insists on finishing her degree before their wedding.
3. Cindy and Jim even discussed whom they would invite to the wedding.

EXPLANATION

Form

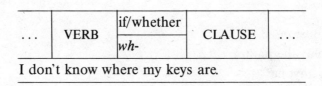

Meaning
Wh-words and *if* also introduce NOUN CLAUSES. The *wh*-words have the same meanings as they do in questions. However, the word order is different because these clauses are not questions.

    a. What time is it?
    b. I don't know what time it is.   (*wh*—SUBJECT—VERB)
    c. Where did he go?
    d. I don't remember where he went.   (*wh*—SUBJECT—VERB)

If and *whether* introduce NOUN CLAUSES that are related in meaning to YES/NO questions. Notice the change in word order.

    e. Is he coming with us?
    f. I don't know   if / whether   he is coming with us.
      (If / Whether—SUBJECT—VERB)

Use the sequence of verb tenses presented on page 230.

Note: Do not write a question mark at the end of the sentence unless the main clause is a question.

4. I didn't ask him how much the car tire cost.
5. The man couldn't say when he would have time to repair my brakes.
6. He didn't know   if / whether   the car needed new shock absorbers, too.

Note: See Part II of this chapter for the special case of indirect speech, which is a further example of NOUN CLAUSES as direct objects.

EXERCISE 9-4   Noun Clauses as Direct Objects (*if/whether*)

Directions
Give statements with the questions. Use "I can't remember" to begin each statement.

Example
Does Jim want to move back to the city?
→ I can't remember   if / whether   Jim wants to move back to the city.

1. Is Jim from Boston?
2. Can Cindy play the piano?
3. Is Sid dating anyone?
4. Has Wiz ever been to Europe?
5. Does Bill have to pay back his loans immediately?
6. Are Bill and Wiz good friends?
7. Have Wiz and Cindy ever met?
8. Should Wiz reapply to MIT for graduate school?
9. Do Bill and Cindy like each other?
10. Could Wiz graduate at the same time as Bill and Jim?

EXERCISE 9-5   Noun Clauses as Direct Objects (*wh*-words)

Directions
Make questions beginning with "Can you tell me...?"

Example
What time is it?
→ Can you tell me what time it is?

1. How do you pronounce the word "r-e-c-e-i-p-t"?
2. What's the teacher's name?
3. How do I get to the post office?
4. What's the date today?
5. When does the bank open?

6. What does "actual" mean in English?
7. How do you use the bank machine?
8. Where can I buy some film?
9. Why do I need a social security number?
10. How can I find out the address of my university?
11. Where do I register?
12. Who can translate for me at the doctor's office?

EXERCISE 9-6   Noun Clauses as Direct Objects (*if/wh*-words)

Directions

Ask a classmate about his or her country. Begin your question with "Do you know..." (Possible subjects: population, geographical features, government system, imports, exports, film stars.)

Example

→ Do you know what the tallest mountain in (your country) is?
→ I don't know. / It's Mt. McKinley.

EXERCISE 9-7   Noun Clauses as Direct Objects (*if/wh*-words)

Directions
Complete the following sentences with a noun clause.

Example
   I forgot my watch yesterday. I didn't know what *time it was*   .

1. I was introduced to Mr. and Mrs. Peterson at the reception. Later on I couldn't remember what _____.
2. While we were driving to Butler, the car broke down. We didn't know how _____.
3. Liz and John invited me to a party tonight, I don't recall when _____.
4. Today's registration. I need to find out where _____.
5. My cousin has been staying with me for one month. I wonder when _____.
6. My composition is due Monday, but I'm not finished. I have to find out if_____.
7. Louis and I were going to go to the movies tomorrow, but he got sick. He called and wanted to know whether _____.

236   GAINING GROUND

8. Someone sent me flowers anonymously. I never discovered who _____ .
9. Last summer I bought an electric fan, which works very well. I don't remember how
   much _____ or where _____ .

NOUN CLAUSES AS SUBJECT COMPLEMENTS

EXAMPLES
1. The truth is that Sid may have to return to India soon.
2. Sid's suspicion is that his father is sick and hasn't been able to work.
3. His adviser's comment was that he should consider finishing his degree in India.
4. The question is whether he will continue to study at Hoopersburg.

EXPLANATION

Form

SUBJECT	BE	that if/whether *wh*-ever	CLAUSE

The problem is that the road is under construction.

Meaning
The subject may be completed by three main types of NOUN CLAUSES:
that clauses, *if/whether* clauses, and *wh*-clauses that are introduced by
the special *wh*-words below.

whoever	(anyone who)	whenever	(any time that)
whomever	(anyone whom)	whichever	(anything that)
whatever	(anything that)	however*	(any way that)
wherever	(any place that)		

5. The winner will be whoever submits the funniest black-and-white photograph.
6. The prize is whatever you choose from the store's catalog.

Notice that all these *wh*-words are indefinite in meaning. They also may be used as direct objects.

    a. You can invite whomever you wish.
    b. I didn't hear whatever they said.

*Don't confuse *however* with the transition word that is spelled the same way. Compare the sentences below.

    c. The woman tolerates *however her children behave*, but her husband is much stricter.
    d. The woman tolerates any kind of behavior from her children; *however*, her husband is much stricter.

EXERCISE 9-8   Noun Clauses as Subject Complements
                  (*wh* + *ever* words)

Directions
    Match the two columns in order to make complete sentences.

Column A
1. Choose _____
2. Do _____
3. Try to help _____
4. Invite _____
5. Home is _____
6. Elect _____
7. The best time to travel is _____
8. Copy _____

Column B
a. whomever you like.
b. wherever you feel comfortable.
c. whenever we have a long vacation.
d. whoever is weak or needy.
e. however that antique cabinet was made.
f. whichever film interests you the most.
g. whatever you think is right.
h. whoever is the best qualified.

EXERCISE 9-9   Noun Clauses as Subject Complements

Directions
    Complete the *that*-CLAUSES, based on the situation.

Situation
    The writing teacher returns your composition with a grade and corrections.
1. His general opinion was that
2. His criticism was that
3. Another point was that
4. His final comment was that

238   GAINING GROUND

Situation

Lee Williams, who is 18 years old, wants to borrow his father's car to take his girlfriend to the movies.

5. Mr. Williams' answer is that

6. Mr. Williams' concern is that

7. Mr. Williams' fear is that

7. Lee's feeling is that

Situation

Becky has just come home from the hospital after a serious operation.

9. The doctor's assumption is that

10. The doctor's hope is that

11. The doctor's fear is that

12. Becky's attitude is that

NOUN CLAUSES AS SUBJECTS

EXAMPLES

1. That Wiz had flunked out of MIT did not influence his admission to Hoopersburg State University.
2. If Wiz will graduate next year is not yet certain.
3. How Wiz will feel about staying at Hoopersburg State University an extra term worries his parents.
4. However the university wants to handle the parking problem will be an improvement over the current situation.

EXPLANATION

Form

that			
if/whether	CLAUSE	VERB	. . .
wh-/ wh-ever			

That you are always late annoys me.

Noun clauses **239**

NOUN CLAUSES with *that, if,* and all *wh*-words may function as subjects. NOUN CLAUSES often function as subjects with verbs expressing emotional reactions (group I below) and with BE + adjective (group II below).

Group I		Group II (BE + adjective)		
amaze	disturb	clear	certain	amazing
astonish	irritate	curious	lucky	astonishing
bother	shock	evident	odd	disgusting
disgust	surprise	important	possible	irritating
		obvious	sad	surprising
		true	etc.	etc.

5. *What the student said in class* didn't shock the teacher.
6. *That the final exam was so soon* surprised most of the class.
7. *Whether the car uses regular gasoline or diesel fuel* is important.

IT	VERB	(...)	that	CLAUSE
			wh-	
			*if/whether	

It annoys me that you are always late.

It usually replaces the *that*-CLAUSE in subject position. *It* may replace *wh*-word CLAUSES and *if/whether* CLAUSES only in sentences with BE + *evident/obvious/clear.*

Note: It cannot replace *wh-ever* CLAUSES.

8. It did not influence Wiz's acceptance to Hoopersburg State University *that he had flunked out of MIT.*
9. It surprised most of the class *that the final exam was so soon.*
10. It's not clear *how they actually got here.*
11. It surprised me *that the university doesn't have more parking facilities for students.*
12. It isn't clear *whether (or not) the university has any land available for additional facilities.*

Note: The main verb is always singular with a NOUN CLAUSE subject.

Note: The verbs in group III below require *that*-CLAUSE subjects with *it* in subject position.

> *Group III*
> appear
> happen
> seem
> turn out

13. It turned out *that there were two lottery winners.*
14. It doesn't often happen *that two people win the lottery.*
15. It seems *that parking places are becoming harder to find on campus.*

Meaning
There is no change in meaning when *it* replaces a *that*-CLAUSE or *wh*-CLAUSE in subject position.

EXERCISE 9-10 Noun Clauses as Subjects

Directions
Indicate which sentences below can be changed to begin with *it*, then make those new sentences.

Example
> That the final exam was so soon surprised us.
> → Yes.
> → It surprised us that the final exam was so soon.

1. Whether the defendant actually committed the robbery is not clear.
2. How the defendant behaved in court surprised the jury.
3. That the defendant looked like an honest man impressed the jury.
4. Whether he spoke convincingly or not is another question.
5. What he said sounded like the truth.
6. That the defendant had an alibi will influence the jury.
7. Why the defendant is the main suspect in the case is the next part of the lawyer's presentation.
8. That the police think he is guilty is quite apparent.
9. What the jury decides is certain to influence the judge.
10. Whatever the judge says determines the fate of the defendant.

Noun clauses 241

EXERCISE 9-11   Noun Clauses as Subjects

Directions
   Give a paraphrase of the sentences, using a *that*-clause.

Example
   My colleague's whistling all the time annoys me.
   → It annoys me that my colleague whistles all the time.

1. His driving so quickly frightens us.
2. The baby's crying at night bothers the downstairs neighbors.
3. Mr. White's working for the CIA amazed Mrs. White.
4. Ellen's leaving home without saying "good-bye" upset her mother.
5. Her participating in the Olympics thrilled the family.
6. Armstrong's walking on the moon astonished the public.
7. His wasting so much time and money disgusts all his colleagues.
8. Our flying with a hot-air balloon scared our parents.
9. The students' progressing so rapidly delights the teacher.
10. The patient's refusing to continue the treatment frustrated the doctor.

EXERCISE 9-12   Noun Clauses as Subjects

Directions
   Complete the sentence, using *wh-ever* words at the beginning of the noun clause.

Example
   However *the university wants to handle the parking problem* will be an improvement.

1. Whatever _____ surprises me.
2. Whenever _____ is fine with me.
3. Whoever _____ is sure to win the election.
4. However _____ is okay with us.
5. _____ shocked me.
6. _____ will be a good teacher.
7. _____ was enjoyable for us.
8. _____ will be convenient for me.
9. _____ is a mystery to us.
10. _____ can become a U.S. citizen.

NOUN CLAUSES AS ADJECTIVE COMPLEMENTS

EXAMPLES
1. Wiz's parents were disappointed that he flunked out of MIT.
2. Cindy is often angry that Jim doesn't take her seriously.
3. Cindy's parents are very proud that she's doing so well in school.

EXPLANATION

Form

SUBJECT	BE*	ADJECTIVE	that	CLAUSE
I was angry that you were late.				

*seem or appear can also function as the main verb.

Meaning
Most of these sentences can be paraphrased using the adjective + preposition with gerunds.

  a. Wiz's parents were disappointed at his flunking out of MIT.
  b. Cindy is often angry at Jim's not taking her seriously.
  c. Cindy's parents are very proud of her doing so well in school.

4. You don't seem very pleased that you got a promotion.
5. I'm confident that you can do the job.
6. Are you sure that you locked the door when you left this morning?

EXERCISE 9-13 Noun Clauses as Adjective Complements

Directions
Give a paraphrase of the sentences, using a *that*-CLAUSE. Be careful of the verb tense in the *that*-CLAUSE.

Example
  You don't seem very pleased about getting a promotion.
  → You don't seem very pleased that you got a promotion.

1. The passenger was afraid of missing his connecting flight.
2. She wasn't aware of our winning the lottery.
3. The editor was very critical of the mayor's spending so much money.
4. I am very glad about my brother's getting married.

5. The tourists were impressed about Edison's working night and day in the laboratory.
6. Mrs. Layton was envious of her sister's moving to the big city.
7. Penny always gets mad about her boyfriend's coming late.
8. The police are positive about her participating in the robbery.
9. Mr. Chandler is proud of his daughter's playing in the school orchestra.
10. How can you be sure of winning the competition?

EXERCISE 9-14 Noun Clauses as Adjective Complements

Directions
Answer the questions, using a *that*-CLAUSE.

Example
What were you annoyed about lately?
→ I was annoyed that the bank had made a mistake in my account.

1. What were you angry about last week?
2. With regard to your children's education, what are you concerned about?
3. What are you confident about in your country's future?
4. What were you disappointed about lately?
5. What has your son or daughter been excited about in the last month?
6. With regard to your upbringing, what are you grateful about?
7. With regard to your progress in English, what are you pleased about?
8. With regard to your education, what are you sorry about?
9. What are you worried about?
10. What are you happy about?

NOUN CLAUSES AS OBJECTS OF PREPOSITIONS

EXAMPLES
1. Jim doesn't always pay close attention to what Cindy says.
2. The director of the computer center is critical of whoever works for him.
3. Isn't Sid sure about how he will pay the tuition for next term?

EXPLANATION

Form

(. . .)	PREPOSITION	wh- / wh-ever	CLAUSE

You can get the information from whoever works there.
You can get the information from what you read.
You can get the information from whichever source you find.

Meaning

The *wh*-CLAUSES function as the object of a preposition in these sentences.

4. Attitudes about marriage nowadays are very different from when our parents were young.
5. Companies can't export high technology products to wherever they want.
6. We're not positive about why our proposal was rejected.

EXERCISE 9-15 Noun Clauses as Objects of Prepositions

Directions

Match the two columns in order to make complete sentences. Find all the possible sentences.

Column A
1. I'm not sure about _____
2. I'm thinking about _____
3. She always asks me about _____
4. I'm not responsible for _____
5. I'm tired of _____
6. I'm grateful to _____
7. I'm in favor of _____

Column B
a. what he said.
b. who's coming to the party.
c. where we always go on vacation.
d. how my parents are.
e. whatever she writes.
f. whichever candidate supports gun control.
g. whoever can help me.

EXERCISE 9-16 Noun Clauses as Objects of Prepositions

Directions
Complete the following sentences.

Example
The director is critical of whoever *works for him*   .

1. An adviser should be willing to listen to whatever _____.
2. I don't have any faith in what _____.
3. The United States exports rice to whichever _____.
4. I feel a lot of respect for whoever _____.
5. The secretary didn't pay any attention to who _____.
6. Parents often worry about when _____.
7. The painting by Picasso is typical of how _____.
8. The teacher wasn't sure about why _____.
9. Our neighbors were very interested in where _____.
10. Her boyfriend seems jealous of whomever _____.

EXERCISE 9-17 Noun Clauses as Objects of Prepositions

Directions
Give three sentences with each of the phrases below. Try to use a variety of noun clauses.

Example
critical of → My mother is critical of what I do.
            → My mother is critical of whomever I speak to.
            → My mother is critical of how I spend my time.

1. be interested in
2. disapprove of
3. be aware of
4. be tolerant of
5. boast about

246 GAINING GROUND

NOUN CLAUSES WITH UNINFLECTED VERBS*

EXAMPLES
1. The Director of the Computer Center requires that Wiz work a minimum of 10 hours per week.
2. It's essential that each machine be monitored regularly.
3. The Director suggested that Wiz keep a list of the students who use the Center regularly.

EXPLANATION

Form

...	that	SUBJECT	(not)	VERB*

It is essential that he be on time.

*The VERB has no ending: no -s for third person singular, no -ed for past tense.

4. It is imperative that the Ambassador speak with the President immediately.

Use *be* instead of *are, am*, or *is* (see Example 2).

5. The recommendation of the State Department is that the U.S. Embassy be closed until conditions stabilize in the capital.

Use *not* without an auxiliary in the NOUN CLAUSE (see Example 6).

6. The Ambassador proposed that he not return to Washington so that he could participate in negotiations.

Meaning
When a NOUN CLAUSE follows one of the words below, the verb in the NOUN CLAUSE has no endings, as indicated above. These words express urgency and necessity, or they express the will of a knowledgeable or powerful person.

VERB	NOUN	ADJECTIVE
advise	advice	advisable
ask (= request)		
command	command	
demand	demand	
desire	desire	desirable
direct		
		essential
		imperative
		indispensable
insist		
order	order	
		necessary
		obligatory
prefer		
propose	proposal	
recommend	recommendation	
request	request	
require	requirement	
suggest	suggestion	
urge		urgent

This structure is formal, and many Americans avoid it, especially in speaking. *Should* + VERB is used as an alternative form in speech.

7. The Director suggested that Wiz should keep a list of the students who use the Center regularly.

EXERCISE 9-18 Noun Clauses with Uninflected Verbs

Directions
There are mistakes in some of the sentences. Circle any mistakes and write the correct form above them.

Example

→ It's imperative that the ambassador (spoke) with the president.
  speak

1. It was the doctor's suggestion that Sam stays in bed for 2 weeks after the operation.
2. She also recommended that he follow a diet high in protein.
3. It's advisable that he has physical therapy 2 to 4 hours per day.
4. Another piece of advice was that he bought a special bicycle for indoor exercise.
5. The doctor prefers that he is examined again before returning to work.
6. It's essential that Sam doesn't use his legs too strenuously for 2 to 3 months.

7. The doctor's recommendation was that he begin swimming as part of his therapy program.
8. She urged that Sam not be impatient.
9. It's necessary that he makes a gradual recovery.
10. She insisted that he call her before making any changes in his therapy program.

EXERCISE 9-19 Noun Clauses with Uninflected Verbs

Directions
Give sentences with the following words using a noun clause. Use current events as the topic for your sentences and use countries as the subjects of the noun clauses.

Example
suggest → The UN suggested that Norway supply 2,000 men for a peace-keeping force.

1. essential
2. recommendation
3. propose
4. ask
5. advise
6. necessary
7. suggestion
8. request
9. imperative
10. prefer

Noun clauses **249**

Part II Indirect Speech

1. NOUN CLAUSES AS STATEMENTS IN INDIRECT SPEECH

EXAMPLES
1. Sid says that a letter from home has not arrived in about 6 months.
2. He said that they had sent his last check in the letter.
3. He added that the Indian Embassy wasn't very helpful in resolving the problem.

EXPLANATION

Form

"	CLAUSE	"	→	SUBJECT	VERB	(that)	CLAUSE

"John is late."	She said that John was late.

When the main clause verb is in the past tense, change the tense of the verb in the NOUN CLAUSE; for example, PRESENT becomes PAST, PAST becomes PAST PERFECT, and *will* becomes *would*.

Note: MODAL verbs also follow the rule of verb tense change if the main verb is past. The past tenses of the modals in NOUN CLAUSES are as follows:

CHANGES		NO CHANGES
may	→ might	should/ought to
will	→ would	must
can	→ could	might
has to ⎱	→ had to	could
have to ⎰		would
		had better

Note: Might, would, and *could* are not normally regarded as past tense modals, but in NOUN CLAUSES they are considered to be the past forms of *may, will,* and *can.*

4. The flight attendant said the flight would take about 5 hours.
5. She also announced that all passengers should keep their seat belts fastened while seated.
6. Later, the pilot said that it was turbulent over Chicago and that everyone had better stay seated.

Note: That is optional as in other NOUN CLAUSES that function as direct objects (see page 229). Comma and quotation marks are omitted.

Meaning
A direct quotation can be restated as a NOUN CLAUSE when the speaker or writer reports the speech of another person. This is known as INDIRECT SPEECH or REPORTED SPEECH. The meaning does not change in spite of some obligatory grammatical changes (see next section, too).

Example 1. Sid says, "A letter from home hasn't arrived in about 6 months."
Example 2. He said, "They sent the last check in the letter."
Example 3. He added, "The Indian Embassy isn't very helpful in resolving this problem."
Example 4. The flight attendant said, "The flight will take about 5 hours."
Example 5. She also announced, "All passengers should keep their seat belts fastened while seated."
Example 6. Later, the pilot said, "It's turbulent over Chicago. Everyone had better stay seated.

EXERCISE 9-20 Statements in Indirect Speech

Directions
Circle the letter of the quotation that was the source of the indirect speech.

Example
Sid said that a letter from home had not arrived in 6 months.
a. "A letter from home doesn't arrive in 6 months."
b. "A letter from didn't arrive in 6 months."
ⓒ "A letter from home hasn't arrived in 6 months."

1. Cindy said that Jim would come to the library at 2:00.
   a. "Jim would come to the library at 2:00."
   b. "Jim will come to the library at 2:00."
   c. "Jim shall come to the library at 2:00."
2. She says that Jim could bring his brother who's visiting.
   a. "Jim could bring his brother who is visiting."
   b. "Jim can bring his brother who was visiting."
   c. "Jim can bring his brother who is visiting."
3. Cindy added that Jim's brother Harry had arrived unexpectedly on Monday.
   a. "Jim's brother Harry is arriving unexpectedly on Monday."
   b. "Jim's brother Harry could arrive unexpectedly on Monday."
   c. "Jim's brother Harry arrived unexpectedly on Monday."
4. She explained Harry was going to stay for a few days.
   a. "Harry was going to stay for a few days."
   b. "Harry is going to stay for a few days."
   c. "Harry will stay for a few days."
5. Cindy commented that he should have called to tell Jim about his plans.
   a. "He should call to tell Jim about his plans."
   b. "He shall call to tell Jim about his plans."
   c. "He should have called to tell Jim about his plans."
6. Cindy added that Harry had better be more thoughtful in the future.
   a. "Harry have better be more thoughtful in the future."
   b. "Harry had better be more thoughtful in the future."
   c. "Harry should be more thoughtful in the future."

EXERCISE 9-21 Statements in Indirect Speech

Directions
   Change the following sentences into indirect speech.

Example
   "The flight will take about 5 hours."
   → The flight attendant said that the flight would take about 5 hours.

1. "The exits are located over the wings and at the front of the plane."
2. "Lunch will be served about one hour after departure."
3. "The weather forecast predicted clear skies all the way to Houston."
4. "Passengers should refrain from smoking in the aisles."

5. "The forecast has just changed, and thunderstorms are expected over St. Louis."
6. "The local time is 4:35 and it's 85°."
7. "Ticket agents can provide transit passengers with up-to-date flight information."
8. "Passengers who are staying in Houston can claim their baggage on the ground floor."
9. "Passengers continuing on flight 96 to Dallas may stay on board."
10. "Wright Air Lines hopes that the trip was a pleasant one."

EXERCISE 9-22   Statements in Indirect Speech

Directions
What did people tell *you* about this place before you came here? Tell your classmates what you heard.

Example
→ My brother-in-law told me that the policemen in the United States were surprisingly fat.

EXERCISE 9-23   Statements in Indirect Speech

Directions
Select a topic in the news. Tell your classmates what you heard about the topic on the TV or radio news or what you read in the newspaper.

Example
[A journalist on CBS said
  An article in the *L.A. Times* reported]   that fighting had broken out again along the border.

---

2. NOUN CLAUSES AS STATEMENTS IN INDIRECT SPEECH

EXAMPLES
1. Cindy's adviser said that she should start applying for jobs at the beginning of her senior year.
2. She said she would have a chance to get some experience that summer.
3. She explained that she had been accepted as a summer intern at a local accounting firm starting the next month.

4. Jim and Bill told Wiz that they were having a party in their room that night and they wanted him to come.
5. Wiz said that the room was rather small for a party.
6. Jim said that they could move their beds over against the wall to get more room.

EXPLANATION

Form

In addition to changes in verb tense, the following changes are also necessary when you change DIRECT SPEECH to INDIRECT SPEECH. (Compare Examples 7 to 12 with 1 to 6.)

DIRECT SPEECH	INDIRECT SPEECH
I, you	→ he/she
my, your	→ his/her
we, you	→ they
our, your	→ their

Note: These changes take place when a third person reports a conversation in which he or she was not involved. However, notice the changes below:

   a. "*You* look tired."
   b. My wife told *me* that *I* looked tired.
   a. "*You* missed a good movie."
   b. She said that *we* had missed a good movie.

254 GAINING GROUND

TIME EXPRESSIONS
Change the expression to one which is relative in time to the speaker's statement.

today	→	that day
tomorrow	→	the next day, the day after
yesterday	→	the previous day, the day before
now	→	then, at that time
next month	→	the next month

Another possible change is to mention the exact day or time which the speaker meant.

tomorrow	→	Tuesday (if the original statement was made on Monday)

PLACE EXPRESSIONS
Change the expression to one that clarifies the location.

here	→	there; on the desk, at the library, downtown, etc.

DEMONSTRATIVES
Change demonstratives to the definite article unless the referent is obvious to the listener/reader.

this/these	→	that/those
this/these	→	the

Meaning
The changes from the original statement to REPORTED SPEECH increase the listener/reader's understanding of the entire conversation. Some words in a direct quotation are only clear to the participants in the conversation. Specific information must be added to the statements in INDIRECT SPEECH. (Compare Examples 7 to 12 with 1 to 6.)

7. "*You* should start applying for jobs at the beginning of *your* senior year."
8. "*I*'ll have a chance to get some experience *this* summer."
9. "*I* have been accepted as a summer intern at a local accounting firm *next month*."
10. "*We*'re having a party *here tonight*, and *we* want *you* to come."
11. "*This* room is rather small for a party."
12. "*We* can move our beds *over there* to get more room."

EXERCISE 9-24 Statements in Indirect Speech

Directions
Change the following statements into reported speech.

Note
Avoid using the same pronoun (e.g., *he*) to refer to two different people. Use the pronoun for the speaker and the noun "motorist" or name for the other people mentioned in the sentence.

Example
Jim: "We're having a party tonight."
→ Jim said that they were having a party that night.

1. Policeman to motorist: "You were driving 15 m.p.h. over the speed limit."
2. Motorist to policeman: "I'm a doctor and I have to get to the hospital immediately."
3. Policeman: "I'll escort you the rest of the way to the hospital."
4. Teacher: "You made too many spelling mistakes in this composition."
5. Student: "I left my dictionary in my locker yesterday afternoon so I couldn't check anything."
6. Teacher: "Maybe you should keep a dictionary here and at home."
7. Mechanic: "Your car needs two new tires."
8. Motorist: "I'm not surprised. Those tires must be 3 years old."
9. Mechanic: "We carry Goodyear and Firestone tires."
10. Motorist: "I'll take the medium-priced Goodyear radials if you can put them on now."
11. Bank employee: "Your account is overdrawn."
12. Customer: "I deposited a check just yesterday. I should have $350 in that account."
13. Bank employee: "According to the computer there is still a deficit. All deposits appear on the computer by the end of the day."
14. Customer: "I want to speak to your supervisor."

EXERCISE 9-25 Statements in Indirect Speech

Directions
What did your teachers or adviser tell you about your classes or your program during the first week?

Example
→ The teacher said that we would have laboratory class every day.
→ They told us that we couldn't wear shorts to class.

EXERCISE 9-26 Statements in Indirect Speech

Directions

Ask an American how he or she celebrates either Thanksgiving or Christmas. Tell the class what that person told you.

Example

→ One friend said that he always went to his parents' for Thanksgiving and ate turkey.

MAIN VERBS IN INDIRECT SPEECH

EXAMPLES
1. Cindy told her mother that she had no intention of getting married for at least another year.
2. Cindy explained she intended to be a working wife.
3. Her mother admitted that she understood Cindy's point of view.

EXPLANATION

Form

VERB		
VERB*	Object	(that) Object

She said that she was happy.
She told them that she was happy.

*Very few verbs have an obligatory object. (See group III verbs in the list below.) In order to specify an object with other verbs, you may add a prepositional phrase with *to*. (See group I.)

    a. The President announced (to the cabinet) that he would be visiting France and West Germany in the fall.
    b. The cabinet members pointed out (to him) that he could also arrange a meeting with the British Prime Minister.

Note: Be especially careful when you use *say* and *tell*. *Tell* must have a direct object. Study the examples below.

4a. They told *me* that I should be careful.
4b. They said that I should be careful.

5a. We always tell *new students* that this city is dangerous.

5b. We always say that this city is dangerous.

6a. The President told *the reporters* that he would visit Canada next month.

6b. The President said that he would visit Canada next month.

Meaning

There are a variety of verbs that can be used as main verbs in INDIRECT SPEECH. Very few of them are exact synonyms of *say*.

GROUP I (optional "*to* + OBJECT)		GROUP II (no OBJECT)	GROUP III (obligatory OBJECT)	GROUP IV (optional OBJECT)
acknowledge	protest	add	inform	answer
admit	remark	assert	remind	promise
announce	repeat	claim	tell	
comment	reply	deny		
declare	report	maintain		
emphasize	reveal			
explain	say			
indicate	state			
mention	swear			
point out				

7. Dr. Johnson asserted that she had found the cure for cancer.

8. The Food and Drug Administration announced that it would begin testing Dr. Johnson's drug immediately.

9. Dr. Johnson pointed out that her success rate had been remarkably high in all her test cases.

10. She denied that she had used the drug only on monkeys and rabbits.

11. She reported that the drug was now being used under strict supervision in selected hospitals around the country.

12a. Dr. Johnson promised the Food and Drug Administration that she would report her results every 6 months.

12b. Dr. Johnson promised that she would report her results every 6 months.

EXERCISE 9-27 Main Verbs in Indirect Speech

Directions
Circle the letter of the correct answer(s). Both may be correct *or* both may be wrong.

Example
Cindy told
a. her mother that she intended to be a working wife.
b. that she intended to be a working wife.

1. The mayor acknowledged
   a. the reporters that crime was up in the city.
   b. to the reporters that crime was up in the city.
2. He told
   a. that he was hiring 20 additional policemen.
   b. to them that he was hiring 20 additional policemen.
3. He also said
   a. that the current economic situation contributed to the higher crime rate.
   b. to them that the current economic situation contributed to the higher crime rate.
4. The mayor explained
   a. them that the city would try to create some extra jobs.
   b. to them that the city would try to create some extra jobs.
5. He announced
   a. to them that the city would also receive federal money for the job program.
   b. that the city would also receive federal money for the job program.
6. The mayor told
   a. that most big cities were experiencing the same problem.
   b. them that most big cities were experiencing the same problem.
7. He said
   a. that things would be better the next year.
   b. them that things would be better the next year.
8. He emphasized
   a. to them that it was only a temporary situation.
   b. that it was only a temporary situation.

EXERCISE 9-28 Main Verbs in Indirect Speech

Directions
Turn back to Exercise 9-21 and give a new version of the sentence using a different main verb to replace *say*.

Example
"The flight will take about 5 hours."
→ The flight attendant stated that the flight would take about 5 hours.

YES/NO QUESTIONS AS NOUN CLAUSES IN INDIRECT SPEECH

EXAMPLES
1. Bill asked Jim if he wanted to go jogging.
2. Jim asked Bill whether they would be back by 6:00.
3. Bill asked Jim if he had a date with Cindy that night.

EXPLANATION

Form

" Yes/No Question? "	→	SUBJECT	VERB	if / whether	CLAUSE
"Were they late?"		She asked if they had been late.			

Sometimes *whether or not* is also used:

a. Jim asked Bill ⎡whether or not they would be back by 6:00.⎤
⎣whether they would be back by 6:00 or not.⎦

Use all the rules about changing tenses, pronouns, time, and place expressions for these sentences, too.

Use statement word order, the same as in any noun clause.

Note: Ask has an optional object. Compare Examples 1 to 3 with 4 and 5.

4. When I get home, I always ask if the mail has come yet.
5. I asked if he was going to take anything to the party.

Meaning

Use this form to report Yes/No questions in INDIRECT SPEECH.

    b. Bill asked, "Do you want to go jogging?"
    c. Jim said, "Will we be back by 6:00?"
    d. Bill said, "Do you have a date with Cindy tonight?"
    e. I always ask, "Has the mail come yet?"
    f. I said, "Are you going to take anything to the party?"
    g. They said, "Should we bring anything to the party?"

Other main verbs: *inquire, want to know, wonder*

6. They wanted to know if they should bring something to the party.

EXERCISE 9-29   Yes/No Questions in Indirect Speech

Directions

Change the following questions into indirect speech. Use different main verbs. Notice the continuing situation.

Example

    Bill said, "Has the mail arrived yet?"
→ Bill asked if the mail had arrived yet.

1. Jim said, "Am I supposed to pick you up at 6:00 or 6:30?"
2. Jim said, "Is it OK with you for me to come a little later?"
3. Cindy said to Jim, "Can you call me before you come over?"
4. Cindy said, "Did you have to stay late in the laboratory?"
5. Jim said, "Could you loan me $20 till tomorrow?"
6. Cindy said, "Have you forgotten that you already owe me $35?"
7. Jim said, "Did you have to mention that?"
8. Cindy said, "Can't you stop at the money machine on your way over here?"
9. Jim said, "Do you have any other suggestions?"
10. Cindy said, "Can we go out another night instead?"

EXERCISE 9-30   Yes/No Questions in Indirect Speech

Directions

Change the following questions into indirect speech.

1. "Is there a bus stop nearby?"
2. "Can you tell me the way to the post office?"

3. "Will you be around later on?"
4. "Should I lock the door?"
5. "Have you ever eaten dinner with an American family?"
6. "Did you happen to see the 6:00 news last night?"
7. "Aren't you the new student from Nigeria?"
8. "Don't you live a few blocks from here?"
9. "Are there any nice parks in town?"
10. "Do I have to send these papers to Immigration?"
11. "Can I borrow a pen?"
12. "Have you noticed any drugstores close by?"

EXERCISE 9-31 Yes/No Questions in Indirect Speech

Directions
What do foreigners often ask you about your country? (For this exercise only mention the yes/no questions which people ask.)

Example
→ They usually ask if people in Saudi Arabia all have camels.

EXERCISE 9-32 Yes/No Questions in Indirect Speech

Directions
What yes/no questions did you ask about this school when you first arrived here?

Example
→ I asked a teacher if I always had to carry my ID card.

WH-QUESTIONS AS NOUN CLAUSES IN INDIRECT SPEECH

EXAMPLES
1. Jim asked Cindy what she would like to do that evening.
2. Cindy asked where he wanted to go.
3. Jim asked why he always had to decide.

EXPLANATION

Form

"	wh-Question?	"	→	SUBJECT	VERB	wh-	CLAUSE
Why were they late?				She asked why they had been late.			

Use all the previous rules about changing tenses, pronouns, time, and place expressions. Use statement word order.

4. The passerby wanted to know what time it was.
5. She also wanted to know which bus she should take to get downtown.
6. The teacher asks who needs more time for the test.

Meaning
Use this form to report *wh*-questions in INDIRECT SPEECH.

 a. Jim asked Cindy, "What would you like to do this evening?"
 b. Cindy said, "Where do you want to go?"
 c. Jim said, "Why do I always have to decide?"
 d. The passerby asked, "What time is it?"
 e. She also asked, "Which bus should I take to get downtown?"
 f. The teacher asks, "Who needs more time for the test?"

EXERCISE 9-33 WH-questions in Indirect Speech

Directions
Change the following questions into indirect speech.

Example
 Cindy said to Jim, "Where do you want to go?"
→ Cindy asked Jim where he wanted to go.

Situation
 Wiz is a student at MIT and telephones his father, Mr. Whitney.

1. Mr. Whitney said, "Why are you failing your courses?"
2. Mr. Whitney said, "How do you spend your time?"
3. Wiz said, "Why do I need to take anything but computer science?"
4. Mr. Whitney said, "Why don't you ask your adviser that question?"
5. Wiz said, "What should I do?"
6. Mr. Whitney said, "Where do you think you can get accepted?"

7. Wiz said, "How much money are you willing to spend?"
8. Mr. Whitney said, "Why are you worried about money?"
9. Wiz said, "Which university will accept a student who flunks out of MIT?"
10. Mr. Whitney said, "Why didn't you think about that before?"

EXERCISE 9-34   *wh*-Questions in Indirect Speech

Directions
Change the questions into indirect speech.

1. "What's the temperature?"
2. "How much does that blue bicycle cost?"
3. "Where's the wedding going to be?"
4. "When was the house sold?"
5. "Why has the weather been so cold this year?"
6. "Whose glasses are these?"
7. "Whom did they elect?"
8. "How many inches are in a yard?"
9. "What's his name?"
10. "Who won the tennis match?"
11. "Which part of the chapter should they omit?"
12. "When can the flowers be planted outside?"
13. "How cold does it get here in the winter?"
14. "Where can you go camping close by?"
15. "Who left all the windows open?"

EXERCISE 9-35   *wh*-Questions in Indirect Speech

Directions
When you went abroad what did the immigration officials ask you? What did the customs officials ask you?

Example
→ He asked how long I intended to stay in the country.

EXERCISE 9-36 *wh*-Questions in Indirect Speech

Directions
When you speak with or write to your family, what do they ask you?

Example
→ My mother always asks when I'm coming home.

COMMANDS AND REQUESTS AS NOUN CLAUSES IN INDIRECT SPEECH

EXAMPLES
1. Sid asked his neighbors not to play their stereo so loud.
2. They told him to mind his own business.
3. He asked the dorm counselor to talk to his neighbors about the noise.

EXPLANATION

Form

" IMPERATIVE! "	→	SUBJECT	VERB	OBJECT	INFINITIVE
					that CLAUSE
"Be on time!"		He told us that we should be on time.			

Note: The verb in the clause contains *should*.

A command, which is usually in the form of an IMPERATIVE, may be reported in two ways; however, the INFINITIVE pattern is much more common.

4. The bank robbers told their victims to put up their hands.

The main verb *tell* is normally used to report commands. Other main verbs: *warn, command, order*.

5. The robbers warned them that they shouldn't try to call for help.

" REQUEST "	→	SUBJECT	VERB	(OBJECT)	INFINITIVE
Please come on time.		They asked (us) to come on time.			

Requests are usually made with MODALS or "Please + IMPERATIVE." These sentences are rephrased in the INFINITIVE pattern shown above. *Ask* with or without an object is normally used to report requests. Other main verb: *request*.

6. The police asked the witnesses to look through their mug files.

Meaning
Compare these direct commands and requests with the example sentences.

a. "Please, turn down your stereo."
b. "Mind your own business!"
c. "Could you please talk to my neighbors about the noise?"
d. "Don't try to call for help!"
e. "Put your hands up!"
f. "Would you mind looking through our mug files?"
(mug files = a collection of photos of known criminals)

Ask may be used without an object. In this case, the request contains "I."

g. "Can I borrow your calculator?"
He asked to borrow his classmate's calculator.

EXERCISE 9-37   Commands and Requests in Indirect Speech

Directions
Change the following sentences to indirect speech. Remember that the main verbs are different for requests and commands.

Example
"Please wait for me."
→ My classmate asked me to wait for her.

"Hand in your papers by Friday."
→ The professor told us to hand in our papers by Friday.

1. "Hold the elevator, please."
2. "Turn right at the next traffic light."
3. "Pass the salt and pepper, please."
4. "Could you hand me a napkin?"
5. "Take everything out of your suitcase and put it on the table."
6. "Fasten your seat belts and make sure your seat is in an upright position."

7. "Pass your tests to the front of the room."
8. "Would you mind not sitting in the first two rows?"
9. "Be quiet!"
10. "Don't waste so much time!"
11. "Can you help me with my homework?"
12. "Don't be late!"

EXERCISE 9-38   Imperatives in Indirect Speech

Directions
    Answer the following question.
      What did your family tell you to do when you came here?
    → My father told me to study hard.
    → My friends told me not to forget them.

EXERCISE 9-39   Requests in Indirect Speech

Directions
    Change the requests to indirect speech using the infinitive pattern.

Example
    "Please turn down your stereo."
    → He asked them to turn down their stereo.

1. "Could I have another glass of water?"
2. "Would you mind opening the window?"
3. "Please give another example."
4. "Can I make an appointment for next week?"
5. "May I read your summary of the article?"
6. "Could you hand me the phone?"
7. "Would you spell that word for me?"
8. "Repeat the last sentence, please."
9. "Could I talk to Suzanne?"
10. "Put your litter in the trash cans."

Noun clauses

EXERCISE 9-40 Commands and Requests in Indirect Speech

Directions
Complete the sentences, using the infinitive pattern.

Example
→ The teacher told *us not to plagiarize*.

1. My neighbor asked
2. The policeman told
3. The doctor warned
4. One of my classmates asked
5. My brother asked
6. The judge ordered
7. My landlord told
8. The passenger asked
9. The dentist told
10. My roommate asked

EXERCISE 9-41 Review

Directions
Underline the noun clauses in the sentences.

Example
I knew that he was lying.

1. Penny told me she had gotten a job with a local law firm.
2. Whichever team wins the championship will win $10,000.
3. We weren't sure if you wanted to come.
4. It's just not possible that the phone bill could be so high.
5. I'm still angry about what you said the other day.
6. Dr. Stafford insisted his patient be operated on immediately.
7. The nurse asked why the patient hadn't eaten all her dinner.
8. The winner will be whoever identifies the name of the song the fastest.
9. They wanted to know if we ever felt homesick.
10. That the world was round was not a known fact in the time of Columbus.

EXERCISE 9-42 Indirect Speech — Review

Directions
Relate a conversation that you have had lately with your landlord or neighbor.

Example
I called my landlord and asked him if he would paint my apartment.

EXERCISE 9-43 Noun Clauses — Review

Directions
Tell the class what you have heard or read about your country lately.

Example
Dan Rather on the CBS news said that workers in X had been striking for 4 days for more pay.

EXERCISE 9-44 Indirect Speech — Review

Directions
There's at least one mistake in each sentence. Underline it and write the correct word(s) above.

Example
                    could
He said that he <u>can</u> not come to the party on Friday.

1. The woman said whether she could help us.
2. Gail told her brother that I had a date with my boyfriend this Thursday night.
3. Mrs. Stapleton said that we could borrow her lawn mower today.
4. She told not to cut the grass too short.
5. He asked what is my name.
6. The President announced that he and the Mexican ambassador had met here and had had a useful discussion.
7. People often ask why Americans liked such big cars.
8. She asked me to not sit on the antique furniture.
9. My friend said that she has been studying English for 6 years.
10. My roommate told me that the party last night had been a lot of fun.

EXERCISE 9-45 Noun Clauses — Review

Directions
Use the noun clauses below as *at least* two different grammatical functions.

Example
What you said
→ I don't remember what you said.
→ I didn't listen to what you said.
→ What you said shouldn't be repeated.

1. how I make a collect call
2. what time it is
3. why Americans are so conscious of time
4. who wants to go to the picnic
5. whatever you want to do

FINE POINTS FOR RECOGNITION

A. PASSIVE

EXAMPLES
1. It is said that this winter will be a hard one.
2. It was claimed that some American wines are now superior to French wines.
3. It has been reported that the United States will expand its space program over the next 10 years.

These PASSIVE constructions are paraphrases of the following sentences:

a. People say that ...
b. People claimed that ...
c. People have reported that ...

Notice that these sentences have *it* as the grammatical subject.

270 GAINING GROUND

B. NOUN COMPLEMENT

EXAMPLES
1. The committee approved the suggestion that Mr. Owens be nominated for the directorship.
2. The request that the informer's identity not be revealed was honored.
3. In spite of the fact that his identity was not revealed, the organization found the informer.
4. The organization didn't even consider the possibility that the informer had not given the FBI valuable information.

A small group of nouns may have *that*-CLAUSE complements. These clauses are different from RELATIVE CLAUSES because *that* does not replace the noun with the clause.

5. The suggestion that Mr. Owens made was rejected.
   The suggestion was rejected.
   Mr. Owens made the *suggestion*.

However, in Example 1, *that* does not refer to "suggestion." The noun clause specifies the suggestion ("Mr. Owens should be nominated for the directorship").

Note that the nouns in Examples 1 and 2 belong to the special group of words on page 246 that require the noninflected verb form. Other nouns like *fact* and *possibility* have complements with the usual verb forms.

SUMMARY

1. DIRECT OBJECT
   I doubt *that she has actually applied for any jobs yet.*
   I didn't ask *how much the car tire cost.*
   He didn't know *if the car needed new shock absorbers, too.*

2. SUBJECT COMPLEMENT
   The truth is *that Sid may have to return to India soon.*
   The winner will be *whoever submits the funniest photograph.*

3. SUBJECT
   If Wiz will graduate next year is not yet certain.
   It surprised the class *that the final exam was so soon.*
   Whatever he said was not clear to me.

Noun clauses 271

4. ADJECTIVE COMPLEMENT
   I'm confident *that you can do the job.*

5. OBJECT OF PREPOSITION
   We're not positive about *why our proposal was rejected.*

6. UNINFLECTED VERB
   It's essential *that each machine be monitored regularly.*
   He requires *that Wiz work a minimum of 10 hours per week.*

7. INDIRECT SPEECH: Statements
   He said *that they had sent his last check in the letter.*
   She told him *she would have a chance to get some experience that summer.*

8. INDIRECT SPEECH: Yes/No Questions
   Bill asked Jim *if he wanted to go jogging.*

9. INDIRECT SPEECH: WH-Questions
   Cindy asked *where he wanted to go.*
   The teacher asks *who needs more time for the test.*

10. INDIRECT SPEECH: Commands and Requests
    Sid *asked his neighbors not to play their stereo so loud.*
    They *told him to mind his own business.*

Participles 10

PARTICIPLES AS ADJECTIVES

EXAMPLES
1. Wiz is often bored in his math class because of the professor's lecture style.
2. Dr. Atlas, who is a very boring lecturer, never calls on Wiz for any answers.
3. In contrast to his classes, his term paper projects seem fascinating.

EXPLANATION

Form

DETERMINER	VERB	-ing / -ed	NOUN

an interesting speaker

or:

SUBJECT	BE*	VERB	-ing / -ed

The audience was interested.

*Other verbs used with adjective complements are *seem, appear, look, smell, taste, feel.*

PARTICIPLES function similarly to other adjectives.

Meaning

Verbs of emotion, such as *surprise, shock, irritate*, and *embarrass*, are often a source of PARTICIPLES. To determine the correct ending on the PARTICIPLE, you have to analyze if you are talking about:

    a. the person who feels the emotion, or   (= -ed)
    b. the person or thing that caused the emotion.   (= -ing)

4. Dr. Tomberlin is interesting.
   (She causes students to feel interest.)
5. Dr. Tomberlin is interested in computer languages.
   (She feels interest in computer languages.)

Note: PARTICIPLES from other verbs may also be used as adjectives. To choose the correct ending on the PARTICIPLE, you must analyze the verb as you did for emotion verbs.

6. The business executives had a tiring trip.
   (The trip caused the people to feel exhaustion.)
7. The tired business people reported on the success of their trip.
   (The people feel exhaustion.)

Note: Another way to choose the correct ending on the PARTICIPLE is to think about the meaning of ACTIVE and PASSIVE:

    a. the person/thing that does the action: -ing
    b. the person/thing that is affected by the action of the verb: -ed

8. Sid reacted quickly and put out the burning papers with the fire extinguisher. (The papers burned.)
9. Bill and Jim noticed the blackened curtains and smell of smoke in the corridor. (The fire blackened the curtains.)
10. They felt relieved to see Sid's smiling face. (Sid smiled.)
11. The scientists revised the experiment because of the previous disappointing results. (The results disappointed the scientists.)
12. The injured passengers waited for help. (Something injured the passengers.)

Note: Remember that some verbs will never be passive, such as *arrive* or *rain*. Consequently, these verbs will never appear as -ed PARTICIPLES.

EXERCISE 10-1 Participles as Adjectives

Directions
   Give the correct adjective.

Example
   Wiz is often (bored)/ boring   in his math class because of the professor's lecture style.

1. We saw an   excited / exciting   movie last weekend.
2. The news story about the plane crash was   shocked. / shocking.   I still haven't gotten over it.
3. Walking around museums is   tired. / tiring.
4. We have invited a   fascinated / fascinating   speaker to our next meeting.
5. The   surprised / surprising   customers thought the advertisement was very effective.
6. Jill is so   bored / boring   I try not to spend too much time with her.
7. From the   confused / confusing   look on your face I can see that you need help.
8. The   interested / interesting   students attended extra lectures to learn more about acupuncture.
9. After seeing the horror movie Dick was so   frightened / frightening   that he couldn't fall asleep.
10. The scores of their tests were   disappointed. / disappointing.

Participles 275

EXERCISE 10-2   Participles as Adjectives

Directions
Answer the questions with phrases that include participles.

Example
What can you see at the beach?
→ playing children, sunburned people

1. What can you hear in the forest?
2. What can you see downtown?
3. What can you see in a harbor?
4. What can you see in a park?
5. What can you see on a farm?

EXERCISE 10-3   Participles as Adjectives

Directions
There is a participle mistake in some of the sentences. Underline the mistakes and write the correct participle above the word.

Example
They were glad to see Sid's <u>smiled</u> face.   *(smiling)*

1. In the winter most people eat freezing vegetables instead of fresh ones.
2. It's necessary to have a validated ticket to leave the parking lot.
3. A shining coin attracted the child's attention.
4. All arrived passengers should report to Customs before leaving this area.
5. Many oil-imported countries have difficulty paying for the oil.
6. The wounded soldiers were visited by their commanding officer.
7. The farmers loaded the harvesting wheat into the train cars.
8. The striking workers would not permit anyone to enter the factory.

EXERCISE 10-4 Participles as Adjectives

Directions
Make sentences, using the participles as adjectives.

Example
burning   → I like the smell of burning leaves.

1. excited
2. entertaining
3. manufactured
4. educated
5. ticking
6. embarrassing
7. imported
8. amazing
9. damaged
10. smiling
11. qualified
12. worried
13. dripping
14. depressed
15. changing

EXERCISE 10-5 Participles as Adjectives

Directions
Identify the participles functioning as adjectives in one of your reading passages from another class. Choose a selection that is a fiction narrative. Make a list of the adjectives and nouns.

Participles   **277**

PARTICIPLES AS ADJECTIVE PHRASES

EXAMPLES
1. The letter sent from India arrived in Hoopersburg on Monday morning.
2. The students living next to Sid noticed the letter in his mailbox.
3. The envelope, containing one little sheet of paper, had already been opened.

EXPLANATION

Form

NOUN	RELATIVE PRONOUN	VERB ACTIVE
the flight that arrives at 8 p.m.		

→

NOUN	VERB	-ing
the flight arriving at 8 p.m.		

NOUN	RELATIVE PRONOUN	VERB PASSIVE
the flight that is scheduled at 8 p.m.		

→

NOUN	VERB	-ed
the flight scheduled at 8 p.m.		

All verbs, even stative verbs (verbs that are not normally used in the VERB-ing form) can be used as VERB-ing participles.

4. Next week Judge Montgomery will hear the case involving the FBI.

Note: Participles used as adjective phrases do not always express the time differences that are possible with verb tenses in RELATIVE CLAUSES.

    a. ... the flight that   arrives / arrived / has arrived   at 8 p.m.
      → the flight arriving at 8 p.m.
    b. ... the flight that   is scheduled / was scheduled / has been scheduled   at 8 p.m.
      → the flight scheduled at 8 p.m.

Note: PARTICIPIAL PHRASES, like RELATIVE CLAUSES, always follow the noun which is modified. They may be restrictive or nonrestrictive.

Note: Negation is possible in participial phrases. *Not* precedes the participle.

5. Students not attending class regularly are required to take an extra examination.
   (Students who do not attend class regularly . . .)
6. The teacher put an F on any paper not handed in on time.
   (any paper that had not been handed in on time)

Meaning
PARTICIPIAL PHRASES can also modify nouns. These phrases are related to relative clauses.

7a. The business executives made reservations on the flight leaving at 5:30.
7b. The business executives made reservations on the flight that leaves / is leaving / will leave / left   at 5:30.

8a. Do you know anything about the merchandise delivered here last week?
8b. Do you know anything about the merchandise that was delivered here last week?

EXERCISE 10-6   Participles as Adjective Phrases

Directions
Underline the participial phrase(s).

Example
The letter <u>sent from India</u> arrived in Hoopersburg on Monday morning.

1. The book lying on the floor belongs to the student sitting next to the window.
2. The cars manufactured by Ford cost very little in those days.
3. Have you ever read a book written by Mark Twain?
4. The woman wearing the navy blue jacket is working with us on the project commissioned by General Motors.
5. I can't pay attention to anyone speaking in such a low voice.
6. Birds flying south for the winter usually stop here to rest.
7. The United States, interested in keeping an oil reserve, has a lot of storage areas made from caverns in some southern states.
8. The space shuttle launched on Friday is supposed to return to earth next week.

EXERCISE 10-7 Participles as Adjective Phrases

Directions
Give a paraphrase, using a participial phrase.

Example
The students who live next to Sid noticed the letter.
→ The students living next to Sid noticed the letter.

1. The letter that was sent yesterday should arrive by the end of the week.
2. The President, who leaves on a trip to the Far East tomorrow, spent the day preparing himself for his visit.
3. Ships that sail into the harbor have to pass by the Statue of Liberty.
4. The company is considering hiring four of the people who were interviewed for the job.
5. The government, which is concerned about decreasing agricultural productivity, rewards farmers who produce additional grain.
6. State universities are supported by the taxes that are paid by residents of the state.
7. All of the factories that are located along the river used to pour the waste materials that were produced in the factory into the water.
8. Anyone who parks near a fire hydrant will get a ticket.
9. All the streets that run east to west have presidents' names.
10. The race promoters gave a T-shirt to the runners who participated in the competition.

EXERCISE 10-8 Participles as Adjective Phrases

Directions
Describe students in your class, using participial phrases.

Example
→ Maria is the student wearing the light blue sweater.
→ The man sitting by the window is from Indonesia.

280   GAINING GROUND

PARTICIPLES AS VERBAL COMPLEMENTS

EXAMPLES
1. Jim found Cindy crying when he arrived early at her place.
2. Cindy heard him coming up the front stairs, and she ran into the kitchen.
3. Jim couldn't remember Cindy ever acting like that before.

EXPLANATION

Form

SUBJECT	VERB	OBJECT	VERB	-ing
We felt the ground moving during the earthquake.				

Meaning

Sense Perception	*Others*
feel	catch
hear	discover
notice	find
observe	imagine
overhear	recall
see	remember
smell	
watch	

The action expressed by the PARTICIPLE is either incomplete or repeated.

4. On the bus I overheard someone talking about my roommate and her boyfriend.
5. Have you ever noticed any ants walking around in the kitchen?
6. Mr. Hawkins discovered his son and some friends smoking behind the garage.

The verbs of sense perception may also be used with a bare (without *to*) INFINITIVE (see page 93), which expresses a completed action or one that is not repeated.

    a. I heard Judy sing.
      (She sang for a while and then stopped.)
    b. I heard Judy singing.
      (While I was listening to her, Judy was singing. = ongoing)

Participles   281

    c. The coach was watching the players kicking the balls.
       (The players kicked the balls again and again.)
    d. The crowd watched the player kick the ball into the goal.
       (The player made one kick and scored.)

Note: This structure looks very similar to the GERUND as direct object.

    e. The audience appreciated Judy's singing.
    f. I remember his putting the keys in his pocket.

The list of verbs with a GERUND as direct object is on page 107. Only *remember, recall,* and *imagine* belong on both lists. The PARTICIPIAL PHRASE emphasizes the doer of the action while the GERUND emphasizes the action.

EXERCISE 10-9   Participles as Verb Complements

Directions
    Answer the questions, using a participial phrase.

Example
       How did you know when to get up this morning?
    → I heard the birds singing. I heard the alarm clock ringing.

1. How can you tell when children have summer vacation?
2. How did you know that the plane ride was rough?
3. How did you know that there was a fire in your neighborhood?
4. How can you tell that someone is fixing dinner?
5. How can you tell if your neighbors bought a new car?
6. How can you tell if there's an earthquake?
7. How would children know if their school were on fire?
8. How can you tell when you should leave a party?
9. How can you tell when winter is coming?
10. How did you know that it rained last night?

EXERCISE 10-10   Participles as Verbal Complements

Directions
Complete the sentences, using a participial phrase.

Example
→ One witness remembered him *sitting in the park every afternoon*.

1. The police caught two young men _____.
2. They also discovered friends of the two men _____.
3. Some people in the neighborhood recall them _____.
4. In fact, somebody even observed them _____.
5. The police told everyone in the neighborhood to call if anyone noticed the young men _____.
6. While we were swimming in the lake, I felt _____.
7. As I was walking back to the picnic area I could smell _____.
8. When I got there, I found _____.
9. While we were eating, I noticed _____.
10. We weren't very far from the lake, so we could hear _____.
11. Can you imagine _____?
12. Did your father ever catch _____?
13. Have you ever watched _____?
14. Do you remember _____?

Participles   283

PARTICIPLES AS ADVERBIAL PHRASES OF TIME, REASON, AND CONTRAST

EXAMPLES

1. Opening the letter from India, Sid was almost afraid to read the message.
2. Prepared to receive bad news, Sid still felt nervous about reading the letter.
3. Finding out about the arrival of the letter, Jim and Bill were anxious to hear the news.

EXPLANATION

Form

Time clause		
Reason clause	,	CLAUSE
Contrast clause		

After she opened her book, she
    turned to the correct page.
Since she did not hear the page
    number, she turned to the wrong
    page.
Although she was looking at the
    wrong page, she could still
    answer correctly.

VERB	-ing*	(...),	CLAUSE
	-ed		

Opening her book, she turned to the
    correct page.
Not having the page number, she turn-
    ed to the wrong page.
Looking at the wrong page, she could
    still answer correctly.

*The choice of -ing or -ed PARTICIPLE
depends on the verb in the subordinate
clause. Choose -ing for ACTIVE verbs and
-ed for PASSIVE verbs.

Note: The subject of the CLAUSE must be the same as the understood
subject of the PARTICIPLE. (See Exercises 10-12 and 10-13.)

4. Compiling a list of complaints, the representatives of the labor union planned to present their demands to the corporation.
5. Forced out of business by this competition, Mr. Larsen sold the store and left town.

Meaning
Participial phrases can paraphrase conjunctions of time (after, while), reason (because, since), and contrast (although).

6a. Flying by himself, the child received special treatment from the flight attendant.
6b. Since he was flying by himself, the child received special treatment from the flight attendant.

7a. Vacationing in the Caribbean, Jane got sunburned.
7b. While she was vacationing in the Caribbean, Jane got sunburned.

8a. Burned in the accident, the woman made a swift recovery.
8b. Although she had been burned in the accident, the woman made a swift recovery.

EXERCISE 10-11 Participles as Adverbial Phrases of Time, Reason, and Contrast

Directions
Give a paraphrase, using a participial phrase.

Example
> While he was opening the letter from India, Sid was almost afraid to read it.
> → Opening the letter from India, Sid was almost afraid to read it.

1. While she warned Bob about late payment, the Registrar agreed to wait until the end of the week.
2. Because he hoped to graduate that semester, Bob was worried about the deadline.
3. While she looked through the course catalog, Trudy decided to change her major.
4. Although he agreed with Trudy's motives, her adviser told her not to make any hasty decisions.
5. Because he was disappointed by his low grade on the composition, Tim made an appointment to talk to his teacher.
6. While they were walking around campus, Alice and Trudy noticed an art class drawing university buildings.
7. While they were speaking with the president of the company, the labor leaders presented the demands of the workers.

8. Although they were satisfied with most of the agreement, the workers still wanted more vacation days.
9. While they were driving across the country, the O'Connors stopped and saw a lot of famous places.
10. Because they drove so many hours each day, they were ready to get out of the car and walk around.

EXERCISE 10-12 Participles as Adverbial Phrases of Time, Reason, and Contrast

Directions
  Choose the correct clause to complete the sentence.

Example
  Lying all over the table,
  a. you should put all the magazines in a pile.
  (b.) the magazines should be put in a pile.

1. Totally confused by the problems,
   a. my grade on the test was very low.
   b. I got a low grade on the test.
2. Burned in the oven,
   a. the rolls were inedible.
   b. we couldn't eat the rolls.
3. Walking to school,
   a. an accident surprised us.
   b. we saw an accident.
4. Watering the plants,
   a. water spilled all over the rug.
   b. I spilled water all over the rug.
5. Stunned by the explosion,
   a. the man was found wandering aimlessly.
   b. the police found the man wandering aimlessly.
6. Watching a movie on TV,
   a. the electricity went off.
   b. we were surprised by a blackout.
7. Turning out the light,
   a. it became pitch black.
   b. we found ourselves in the pitch dark.

8. Arrested for stealing cars,
   a. he confessed to a variety of other crimes.
   b. the police questioned him for hours.

EXERCISE 10-13 Participles as Adverbial Phrases of Time, Reason, and Contrast

Directions
  The subjects in some of the sentences are incorrect. Rewrite the sentences in their correct forms. (Remember that the subject of the sentence must also be the subject of the participial action.)

Example
  Lying all over the table, you should put all the magazines in a pile.
  → Lying all over the table, the magazines should be put in a pile.

1. Swimming out in the lake, a sudden thunderstorm forced the people to go quickly back to shore.
2. Caught between two rocks, the animal could not free itself.
3. Elected for 6 years, the people trusted Mayor Frost.
4. Walking down the shady path, the trees hid the people from view.
5. Hearing the siren, the people looked around to see what was happening.
6. Driving down the highway, a black car overtook us.
7. Surprised by the loud noise, the little child started to cry.
8. Made fresh every day, the bakery sells delicious bread and rolls.
9. Sitting in the sun, the teenagers got sunburned.
10. Interviewed for the position, the applicant felt confident about her chances.

PARTICIPLES AS ADVERBIAL PHRASES OF MANNER

EXAMPLES
1. Wiz was busy at the computer center, writing a new program for one of his classes.
2. Bill stood in the long line at registration, disgusted with himself for waiting till the last minute.
3. Cindy has been typing Jim's research paper all afternoon, trying to correct the grammar as she goes along.

EXPLANATION

Form

| CLAUSE | , | VERB | -ing* / -ed | (...) |

He sat on the bus, studying his notes.

*The choice of -ing or -ed PARTICIPLE depends on whether the meaning is ACTIVE or PASSIVE.

Meaning

The participial phrase expresses *how* the subject performs the action of the main verb. It elaborates the manner of the subject's action.

In Example 1 the phrase explains how Wiz is busy.
In Example 2 the phrase describes how Bill stood in line.
In Example 3 the phrase elaborates the way that Cindy is typing.

4. The prisoners sat in individual cells, tied to their beds.
5. For three days the flood waters rose, causing heavy damage in several communities.
6. The drunk driver drove down the street, ignoring the traffic lights.

EXERCISE 10-14 Participles as Adverbial Phrases of Manner

Directions

Match the main clause in column A with a participial phrase in column B. The phrases express *how* the action of the main verb is performed. Find all the possible sentences.

Column A
1. He lay on his bed _____ ,
2. The women sat in the park _____ ,
3. Bob walked down the street _____ ,
4. Mrs. Williams went to the meeting _____ ,
5. She stood at the window _____ ,
6. Mr. Green talked on the public phone _____ ,
7. The Bates built their own home _____ ,
8. I planted the tomatoes _____ ,
9. He cut all the wood _____ ,

Column B
a. watching their children playing.
b. looking at her new neighborhood.
c. ignoring all the people waiting.
d. measuring very carefully.
e. wearing her jogging shoes.
f. leaving one foot between each one.
g. listening to his stereo.
h. whistling.
i. following the architect's drawings.

EXERCISE 10-15 Participles as Adverbial Phrases of Manner

Directions
Complete the sentences below using a participial phrase that expresses how the action is performed.

Example
The old men sat in the park, _____*playing chess*_____.

1. The girls sat on the beach, _____.
2. The patient lay in the hospital, _____.
3. The football player stood on the sidelines, _____.
4. The police car drove quickly down the street, _____.
5. The athlete ran around the park, _____.
6. Old Mr. Atkins walks up and down the street, _____.
7. He planted the flowers, _____.
8. He painted her a picture, _____.
9. They lit a big fire, _____.
10. Keith and John paddled their canoe around the lake, _____.

EXERCISE 10-16 Review

Directions
Make sentences, using participles made from the pairs of nouns and verbs.

Example
  letter — send
  → The letter sent last week still hasn't arrived yet.

1. man — sleep
2. box — contain
3. clock — tick
4. money — contribute
5. plant — grow
6. sign — paint
7. parent — worry
8. product — manufacture
9. film — interest
10. faucet — drip
11. child — kidnap
12. bookshelf — hold

EXERCISE 10-17 Review

Directions
Answer the questions, using participles.

Example
> What did the woman notice out her window?
> → She noticed a neighbor walking her dog.
>
> How did you spend your time sitting in the park?
> → I sat there watching the students playing frisbee.

1. What did you overhear on the bus lately?
2. How did you spend your time sitting in the library?
3. What did you smell cooking last night?
4. How do patients spend their time in the hospital?
5. What do you remember your family doing on weekends when you were younger?
6. What have you observed children doing in your neighborhood?
7. How do old people spend their time?
8. What do you remember your teacher doing on the first day of class this term?
9. How can you tell when someone's very cold?
10. What do you recall your family doing during vacations when you were a child?

FINE POINTS FOR RECOGNITION

A. PARTICIPLES: Adjectives

Form

DETERMINER	NOUN	VERB	-ing / -ed

Meaning
A participial adjective that is related to a restrictive RELATIVE CLAUSE may follow the NOUN that it modifies. This pattern is used more commonly in formal English.

EXAMPLES
1. Of all the applications submitted, only three candidates have the proper qualifications.

2. The people protesting think that all chemical weapons should be destroyed.
3. The man singing is my brother-in-law.
4. The last applicant interviewed will probably get the job.
5. The plane hijacked has not yet been identified.

The more common phrases, corresponding to the above examples, are:

   a. ... the applications that were submitted ...
   b. The people who are protesting ...
   c. The man who is singing ...
   d. ... applicant who was interviewed ...
   e. The plane that was hijacked ...

B. PERFECT PARTICIPLES

Form

having	been	VERB	-ed

Note: Use *having been* when the meaning is PASSIVE.

Meaning

PERFECT PARTICIPLES are used to indicate a time contrast between the action of the main verb and the action of the participle. PERFECT PARTICIPLES may be used in adjective phrases or adverbial phrases.

EXAMPLES
1. Any student having taken the course previously is not allowed to register for it again. (Adjective phrase)
2. Only the students having been awarded a scholarship are required to attend the meeting. (Adjective phrase)
3. Having negotiated the peace treaty, the prime minister submitted it to Parliament for its approval. (Adverbial phrase)
4. Having been mistakenly arrested, Mr. Katz decided to sue the police department. (Adverbial phrase)

C. ABSOLUTE CONSTRUCTION

Form

SUBJECT	VERB	-ing / -ed	...	,	CLAUSE

CLAUSE	,	SUBJECT	VERB	-ing / -ed	. . .

There are two subjects in sentences with absolute constructions: the subject of the main verb and the "subject" of the participle.

This construction is not commonly used in informal English.

Meaning
The meaning of absolute construction is the same as that for the participial phrases on page 283.

EXAMPLES
1. The driver suddenly stopped at the side of the road, his engine steaming.
2. Dinner cooking in the oven, she decided to take a quick shower before the guests arrived.
3. His plants destroyed by the hail, the farmer realized that he would make no profit that year.
4. The first prize having been awarded to someone else, George still felt proud of his paintings.

SUMMARY

1. ADJECTIVES
   Wiz is often *bored* in his vector analysis class.
   Dr. Atlas is a *boring* lecturer.

2. ADJECTIVE PHRASES
   The letter *sent from India* arrived in Hoopersburg Monday.
   The students *living next to Sid* noticed the letter.

3. VERBAL COMPLEMENT
   Cindy heard him *coming up the front stairs*.
   Mr. Hawkins discovered his son *smoking*.

4. ADVERBIAL PHRASES
   Opening the letter from India, Sid was almost afraid to read the message.
   Prepared to receive bad news, Sid still felt nervous about reading the letter.

5. ADVERBIAL PHRASES
   The drunk driver drove down the street, *ignoring the traffic lights*.
   The prisoners sat in individual cells, *tied to their beds*.

Appendix I

IRREGULAR VERBS

awake	awoke	awaked	draw	drew	drawn
be	was/were	been	drink	drank	drunk
beat	beat	beaten	drive	drove	driven
become	became	become	eat	ate	eaten
begin	began	begun	fall	fell	fallen
bend	bent	bent	feed	fed	fed
bet	bet	bet	feel	felt	felt
bite	bit	bitten	fight	fought	fought
bleed	bled	bled	find	found	found
blow	blew	blown	fly	flew	flown
break	broke	broken	forget	forgot	forgotten
bring	brought	brought	freeze	froze	frozen
build	built	built	get	got	gotten
burn	burned/	burned/	give	gave	given
	burnt	burnt	go	went	gone
buy	bought	bought	hang	hung	hung
catch	caught	caught	have/has	had	had
choose	chose	chosen	hear	heard	heard
come	came	come	hide	hid	hidden
cost	cost	cost	hit	hit	hit
creep	crept	crept	hold	held	held
cut	cut	cut	hurt	hurt	hurt
deal	dealt	dealt	keep	kept	kept
dig	dug	dug	kneel	knelt	knelt
do	did	done	know	knew	known

293

lay	laid	laid	sit	sat	sat
lead	led	led	sleep	slept	slept
leave	left	left	slide	slid	slid
lend	lent	lent	speak	spoke	spoken
let	let	let	spend	spent	spent
lie	lay	lain	spin	spun	spun
lose	lost	lost	spread	spread	spread
make	made	made	spring	sprang	sprung
mean	meant	meant	stand	stood	stood
meet	met	met	steal	stole	stolen
pay	paid	paid	stick	stuck	stuck
prove	proved	proven	sting	stung	stung
put	put	put	stink	stank	stunk
quit	quit	quit	strike	struck	struck
read	read	read	swear	swore	sworn
ride	rode	ridden	sweep	swept	swept
ring	rang	rung	swim	swam	swum
rise	rose	risen	swing	swung	swung
run	ran	run	take	took	taken
say	said	said	teach	taught	taught
see	saw	seen	tear	tore	torn
seek	sought	sought	tell	told	told
sell	sold	sold	think	thought	thought
send	sent	sent	throw	threw	thrown
set	set	set	understand	understood	understood
shake	shook	shaken	undertake	undertook	undertaken
shine	shone	shone	wake	woke	woken
shoot	shot	shot	wear	wore	worn
show	showed	shown	weep	wept	wept
shrink	shrank	shrunk	win	won	won
shut	shut	shut	wind	wound	wound
sing	sang	sung	wring	wrung	wrung
sink	sank	sunk	write	wrote	written

Appendix II

ADJECTIVES, NOUNS, AND VERBS + PREPOSITIONS

Adjective + Preposition

acquainted with
adequate for
afraid of
ahead of
angry at someone about
appropriate for
ashamed of
aware of
capable of
certain of/about
composed of
conscious of
critical of
different from
difficult for
disgusted with
doubtful about
eager for
enthusiastic about

equal to
essential to
familiar with
famous for
fond of
generous about/with
glad about
good at
grateful to/for
happy about/over
hopeful of
identical to/with
incapable of
independent of
inferior to
instead of
jealous of
known for
lazy about

loyal to
mad at someone about
perfect for
positive of/about
proud of
responsible for
rich in
successful in
suitable for
superior to
sure of/about
suspicious of
tired from
tired of
tolerant of
typical of
upset about/over
useful for

Noun + Preposition

in agreement with	difficulty in	on the point of
attention to	in exchange for	in the process of
attraction to	faith in	profit from
for the benefit of	in favor of	for the purpose of
in charge of	in hope of/in the hope of	reason for
confidence in	impression of	respect for
in connection with	for lack of	result of
in contrast to	in the middle of	in return for
in the course of	need for	for the sake of
in danger of	in heed of	talent for
a great deal of	in payment for	in terms of
in debt to/for	in place of	

Verb + Preposition

adapt to	depend on	persist in
adjust to	devote to	prefer to
agree with someone on	discourage from	prepare for
apologize to someone for	distinguish from	profit from
approve of	encourage in	prohibit from
argue with someone about	engage in	protect from
blame for	faith in	provide with
bring about	forgive for	put up with
bring up	get away with	quarrel about
care about	help with	refer to
care for	impose on	remind of
complain to someone about	inquire about	result from
concentrate on	insist on	result in
be concerned with	interfere with	succeed in
confuse with	judge between	suffer from
connect with	keep on	tell from
consist of	laugh at	think about
consult about	limit to	think of
contribute to	look forward to	transform into
convince of	object to	warn about
decide on	participate in	worry about

Appendix   III

DETERMINERS

Form

DETERMINER	(ADJECTIVE)	NOUN

Meaning

DETERMINERS give information about NOUNS and answer the following general questions:

a. Is the person or thing definite or indefinite? (*a/an* vs. *the*)
b. Is the person or thing near the speaker or far? (*this/these* vs. *that/those*)
c. How many persons or things are important? (*all, some, every, few*, etc.)

The meaning of the NOUN is important for choosing the correct DETERMINER. A count NOUN requires some different DETERMINERS from those of a noncount NOUN.

Some Noncount NOUNS:

1. Certain kinds of food: bread, meat, butter, rice, sugar
2. Liquids: coffee, tea, milk, oil
3. Metals and materials: steel, iron, wood, cotton, wool
4. Abstract nouns: beauty, happiness, importance
5. Others — often used as count nouns   advice, baggage, equipment, furniture,
   in other languages: information, luggage, news, weather

297

298   GAINING GROUND

ARTICLES (*a/an, the*)

NOUN	ARTICLE
count singular	a/an the
count plural	the
noncount	the

Indefinite Article: a/an
Use *a/an* to introduce a person or thing that is new in conversation or writing.
1. I saw *an interesting program* on TV last night.
2. *A person* stopped me on the street and asked directions.

Use *a/an* to describe one member or item of a group. (You can paraphrase with "any" or "every.")
3. You can often recognize *an American tourist* overseas.
4. *A Japanese car* is often more economical than *an American car*.
5. *A cardinal* is *a red bird* which lives in the eastern part of the United States.

Use *a/an* to replace "one."
6. We'd like three hamburgers, two iced teas, and *a coke*.
7. He walked *a block* and then turned left.

Use *a/an* to replace "per."
8. Some people are paid *twice a month*, and others are paid *once a month*.
9. The concert wasn't too expensive—only $7.50 *a ticket*.

Definite Article: the
Use *the* to refer to a person or thing that has been introduced into conversation or your writing.
10. I saw an interesting program on TV. *The program* was a documentary about changes in the earth's climate. *The show* was filmed in Europe.

Use *the* to refer to a familiar or well-known person or object.
11. *The moon* revolves around *the earth*.
12. *The front door* was not locked last night.
13. A reporter asked to interview *the President*.

Use *the* to refer to a member or members of a group. (This is similar to items 3 to 5.)
14. *The redwood tree* is native to California.
15. *The typewriter* was important in the history of women's employment outside the home.

Appendix III   **299**

16. *The Scandinavians* settled in the north central part of the United States.
17. *The Democrats* won by a large margin.

Note: A singular noun is used most frequently for plants, animals, or mechanical devices. A plural noun is used for a specific group of people.

Use *the* with the superlative form of adjectives and adverbs.
18. *The tallest member* of the basketball team is 6 feet 8 inches.
19. Of all the players, John can jump *the highest*.

Use *the* with some geographical names:

the United States	the Rocky Mountains	the Pacific Ocean
the U.S.S.R.	the Andes	the Atlantic Ocean
the United Kingdom	the Alps	the Red Sea
the Soviet Union	the Urals	the Amazon River
the Philippines	the Sahara Desert	the Mississippi River
the Azores	the Mojave Desert	

Note: Do not use *the* for individual mountains (Mount Everest), individual islands (Greenland); use *the* for groups of mountains, islands, and lakes (the Great Lakes).

Use *the* to refer to a person or thing that will be further identified by modifiers after the noun.
20. *The milk on the table* is for your cereal.
21. He could not express *the happiness that he felt*.
22. Their goal is *the equality of men and women*.
23. *The reading of Shakespeare's tragedies* was his assignment for the term.

No article
Do not use an article with mass nouns (air, sugar, iron, food, money, gas, etc.)
24. It's healthy to drink *milk*. (Contrast this sentence with 20.)
25. No living creature can live without *oxygen*.

Do not use an article with abstract nouns (art, beauty, truth, peace, freedom, etc.)
26. *Happiness* is difficult to define. (Contrast this sentence with 21.)
27. Don't talk about *politics* or *religion* with them!

Do not use an article to refer to all members or items in a group.
28. For *Hindus cows* are holy.
29. *Computers* are a necessity in the modern business world.

Do not use an article to refer to activities or places associated with activities.
30. Her youngest son is attending *college* this year.
31. He usually goes to *bed* around 11:00.
32. I'd like to invite you to *dinner* this Tuesday.

DEMONSTRATIVES (*this/these; that/those*)

this that	NOUN – singular count	this pen that pencil
this that	NOUN – noncount	this information that news
these those	NOUN – plural count	these pens those pencils

QUANTIFIERS

all both half	(of)	the these those	NOUN – plural	all (of) the books both (of) these books half (of) those books

each either few a few many most neither none several some	of	the these those	NOUN – plural	each of the students either of those students few of the students a few of the students many of the students most of these students neither of the students none of those students several of these students some of the students

all both few a few many most no several some			NOUN – plural	all students both students few students a few students many students most students no students several students some students

a couple a lot lots plenty	of	the these those	NOUN – plural	a couple of the books a lot of these books lots of the books plenty of those books

all little a little much most	(of	the)	NOUN – noncount	all (of the) information little (of the) information a little (of the) information much (of the) information most (of the) information
no				no information
none	of	the		none of the information

Few/a few
1. Few people could pay the high price of the tickets.
   (Few = not many, emphasizing an insufficient number)
2. A few people attended the exhibit and bought paintings by the artist.
   (A few = a small number, but it does not imply an insufficient number)

Little/a little
1. There was little food left on the table after the reception.
   (little = not much, emphasizing an insufficient amount)
2. There was a little coffee left in the pot, so we drank it up.
   (A little = a small amount, but it does not imply an insufficient amount)

Lots of = informal English
1. The little kids were making lots of noise out in the yard.

Answer Key for Recognition Exercises

Exercise 1-2
1. feels 2. OK 3. know 4. need 5. OK 6. consists 7. has 8. OK 9. belong 10. OK

Exercise 1-5
2. F,?,?,T 3. ?,?

Exercise 1-9
1. T,?,? 2. F,T,? 3. F,F

Exercise 1-13
1. ?,T,F 2. ?,T,? 3. ?,T

Exercise 1-17
1. T,T,F 2. F,?,T 3. ?,T,F

Exercise 1-21
1. T,T,? 2. F,T,T

Exercise 1-24
1. C 2. A 3. C 4. A 5. C 6. B

Exercise 2-3
1. F,T 2. T,F 3. F,? 4. T,F

Exercise 2-7
1. ?,F,T 2. T,T 3. F,?

Exercise 2-13
1. ?,T 2. F,?,T 3. T,F

Exercise 2-21
1. c 2. b 3. a 4. b

Exercise 2-26
1. c 2. b 3. c 4. a

Exercise 2-29
1. C 2. C 3. N 4. N 5. C 6. C 7. N 8. C

Exercise 3-1
1. T 2. F 3. T 4. F 5. T 6. T

Exercise 3-9
1. a.F b.? c.T 2. a.T b.? 3 a.F b.T c.F

304 GAINING GROUND

Exercise 4-1
1. She works harder than most students.
2. correct
3. He spends more time in the library than his roommate.
4. That bike is better than mine because it is heavier.
5. correct
6. My sister eats more slowly than I do.

Exercise 4-4
1. That book is as expensive as this one.
2. He isn't as handsome as his brother.
3. Her lecture was as long as his lectures always are.
4. correct
5. She scored as well as I did on the exam.
6. He received the same score that he received last time.

Exercise 5-2
1. b 2. b 3. a 4. b 5. a 6. a

Exercise 6-6
1. S 2. D 3. S 4. S 5. D 6. D

Exercise 6-8
1. F 2. F 3. F 4. T 5. F 6. T

Exercise 6-9
1. T 2. F 3. F 4. T 5. T 6. F

Exercise 7-1
1. a 2. b 3. a 4. a 5. a 6. a

Exercise 7-5
1. a 2. b 3. b 4. a 5. b 6. b

Exercise 7-8
1. b 2. a 3. a 4. a 5. b 6. a

Exercise 7-14
1. unknown 2. unknown 3. the carpenter 4. unknown 5. the doctor 6. unknown

Exercise 8-2
1. *Boston* or *Washington*
2. *lying in the sun* and *walking along the shore*
3. *start exercising* or *stop eating so much*
4. *the plane which takes one hour* or *the bus which takes*
5. *during the day* and *at night*
6. *forgot to pack our umbrella* or *lost it in the airport*

Exercise 8-11
1. he could load it easily
2. the room would stay cool
3. he could finish reading them
4. she could see the weather forecast
5. the teachers could attend a conference
6. she could lose weight

Exercise 10-6
1. *lying on the floor*
2. *manufactured by Ford*
3. *written by Mark Twain*
4. *wearing the navy blue jacket*
5. *speaking in such a low voice*
6. *flying south for the winter*
7. *interested in keeping an oil reserve*
8. *launched on Friday*

Index

Ability
    negative 47
    past 47
    present 47
Absolute construction 290
Active sentence
    definition 168
Addition
    coordination 187
    correlative conjunction 189, 192
    preposition 221
    transition words 219
Adjective clause *see* Relative clause
Adjective complement
    infinitive phrase 97
    noun clause 242
Advice, advisability
    negative 38
    past 38
    present 38
    strong advice 48
after 11, 195
Agent *see by*-phrase
ago 7
already 14
Antecedent 134
Appositive
    gerund phrase 106
Articles
    a/an 298
    no article 299
    the 298
as 115
as . . . as 114

Bare infinitive *See* Infinitive without *to*
be going to 22
before 11, 195
best 118
by 30
by-phrase 171

can
    ability 47
    permission 32
    requests 35
Causative
    infinitive without *to* 93
    passive 180
Cause
    coordination 187
    preposition 201
    subordinating conjunction 198
Certainty *see* Possibility
Choice
    coordination 187
    correlative conjunction 189
Comma
    conditional clause 152
    coordinating conjunction 187, 228
    indirect speech 250
    infinitive phrase 102
    noun clause 229
    relative clause 127, 145
    subordinate conjunction 195, 228
    transition words 208, 228
Comparatives 110–112
compared to/with 112
Completed action 6

306 GAINING GROUND

Condition *see* State
Conditional clause *see If* clause
Continuous verb forms
    passive 176
    past 6
    present 1
    present perfect 17
Contrast
    coordinating conjunction 187
    preposition 205
    subordinating conjunction 202
    transition word 211
Coordinating conjunction 186
Correlative conjunction 189, 191
cost
    with infinitive phrase 99
could
    ability 47
    opportunity 47
    permission 32
    possibility 49
    request 35
Count noun
    comparative form 110
    equative form 114
    superlative form 118
    with *such* 120
    with *such a* 120, 124

Deduction
    negative 58
    past 58
    present 58
Demonstrative 300
Dependent clause
    subordinate conjunction 195–196
Determiner
    with *of* + relative pronoun 145
Direct object
    gerund 78–79
    infinitive phrase 84, 86, 88, 93
Doer *see* Subject
Duration of an action 7, 17

-ed participles 273
Effect
    coordinating conjunction 187
    transition word 209–210
either . . . or 188–189
Emotion verbs
    participle 273
    stative 3
Emphatic restatement 215

enough 97
Equative 114
-er . . . than 110–112
-est 118–119
ever 14
Exemplification
    adverbs 218
    transition words 216–217
Expectation
    negative 55
    past 69
    present 55

farthest 118
fewer . . . than 111
for 14
for + object 99
Formal English
    conditional clause 165–166
    coordinating conjunction 187
    noun clause 247
    participle 289, 291
    permission 33
    requests 35
Future
    passive 176
    perfect 30
    perfect continuous 30
    real conditional clause 147–148
    time 25, 32

Gerund
    appositive 106
    direct object 78–79, 90–91
    following preposition 76
    negative 73
    passive 184
    possessive subject with 73
    subject 72–73
    subject complement 81
get 180

Habit 1
had better 44
have
    causative 93
    passive causative 180–181
    present perfect 13–14
    present perfect continuous 17
have to
    lack of necessity 42–43
    necessity 38–39
    vs. *must* 38–39

Index **307**

if
in noun clauses   233, 236–237, 238–240, 259
If clause
mixed type   161–162
past unreal   157–158
present unreal   153–154
present/future real   147–148
question word order   165–166
unless   151
with *should*   164
with *would*   165
if . . . not   see unless
in   30
Incomplete action
participle   280
present perfect continuous   17
was/were going to   20
Indefinite time   14
Independent clause
coordinating conjunctions   186–187
subordinating conjunctions   195–196
transition words   207–208
Indirect object
for   174
passive subject   174
to   174
Indirect speech
changes in form   249, 253, 254
changes in verb tense   230, 249
command   264–265
main verbs   256, 260
passive   269
request   264–265
statement   249, 252
wh-question   261–262
word order   259, 262
yes/no question   259–260
Infinitive phrase
adjective complement   97
adjective phrase   95–96
adverbial   102
definition   93
direct object   84, 86, 88, 90–91, 93
indirect speech   264
negative   83
passive   184
perfect   106–107
subject   99, 100–101
subject complement   82–83
Infinitive without *to*   93
Inference   *see* Deduction

Informal English
coordinating conjunction   187
noun clause   247
permission   33
relative clauses   127, 131, 137, 138, 141, 146
request   35
subordinating conjunction   203
-ing participle   273
in order to   102
Intention   20
Intentional action   3
Interruption of an action   7
Inverted word order   *see* Question word order
it—substitute subject
infinitive   99–101
noun clause   239–240

just   14

least   118
less . . . than   110–111
let   93
like   115
Logical conclusion   *see* Deduction
Logical connectors   226–227
Logical sequence   207

make   93
many
in comparatives   112
in equatives   114
may
past possibility   49–50
permission   32–33
possibility   49–50
Measurement verb   3
Mental perception verb   3
might
past possibility   49–50
possibility   49–50
Modals
can   32–33, 35, 47
could   32–35, 47–50
had better   44–45
have to   37–39, 42–43
may   32–33, 48–50
might   48–50
must   37–39, 42–43, 58–59
ought to   37–39, 54–55, 69
should   37–39, 55, 69, 164–165, 247, 264
will   22, 34–35
would   34–35, 153–154, 157–158

308 GAINING GROUND

more . . . than 110–111
most 118–119
much
  in comparatives 112
  in equatives 114
must
  necessity 38
  present deduction 58–59
  prohibition 42–43

Necessity
  lack of 42–43
  past 38–39
  present 38–39
Negative
  gerund 73
  infinitive 83
  participial phrase 278
neither . . . nor 192
never 14
Non-count noun
  comparative form 111
  equative form 114
  superlative form 118
  with determiner 297–301
  with *such* 120
Non-restrictive
  clause 127, 131, 135, 138, 141, 146
  participial phrase 277
Noun clause
  adjective complement 242
  definition 230
  direct object 229–230
  if, wh-words 233
  object of preposition 243–244
  subject 238–240
  subject complement 236
  that-clause 229–230
  uninflected verb 246
  verb tenses 230
  word order 233
Noun complement
  noun clause 270

of with object + infinitive 100–101
on 30
Opinion verbs 3
Opportunity 47
ought to
  advice, advisability 37–39
  past expectation 69
  present expectation 55
  strong advice 44–45

Participial phrases
  contrast 283
  manner 286–287
  reason 283
  time 283
Participles
  absolute construction 290–291
  adjectives 272–273, 289–290
  adjective phrases 277–278
  adverbial phrases 283, 286–287
  passive meanings 273
  perfect 290
  verbal complements 280–281
  verbs of emotion 273
  verbs of sense perception 280
Passive
  causative 180–181
  continuous 176
  definition 171–173
  future 176
  gerunds 184
  indirect object as subject 174
  indirect speech 269
  infinitives 184
  modals 178–179
  perfect 176
  with *by*-phrase 171–172
  without *by*-phrase 167–168
Past 6–7, 10–11, 13–14
Past continuous 6–7
Past perfect 10–11
Past progressive *see* Past continuous
Perfect forms
  gerund 106
  infinitive 106–107
  passive 176
Permission 32–33
Planned action 20, 23, 25
Possibility
  negative 48–50
  past 48–50
  present 48–50
Prepositions with verbs, adjectives and nouns
    295–296
Present continuous
  indicating future time 24–25
Present perfect
  definition 13
  modals 69
Present perfect continuous 17
Probability 49
Progressive *see* Continuous
Prohibition 42–43

Promise 22
Purpose 198–199

Quantifiers 300–301
Question word order
    correlative conjunctions 192, 225
    if-clauses 165–166
Quotation marks 250

Reason 102
Recent action 14
Relationship verbs 4
Relative clauses
    definition 125
Relative pronoun
    in prepositional phrase 136–138
    no pronoun (ϕ) 131, 138
    object 130–131
    possessive 134–135
    subject 125–126
    that 127, 130–131, 138
    when 140–141
    where 140–141
    which 125, 130–131, 136–138, 145
    who 125
    whom 130–131, 136–138, 145–146
    whose 134–135
    why 140–141
Repeated action
    expressed by participle 280–281
Reported speech *see* Indirect speech
Requests
    indirect speech 264–265
    making, answering 34–35
Restrictive clauses 127, 131, 135, 138, 141, 146
Restrictive participial phrases 277
Result
    coordinating conjunction 187
    transition words 209–210

the same . . . as 114
say 256–257
Semi-colon 208
Sense perception verbs
    infinitives without *to* 93
    stative 3
Sequence of actions 10, 91
Sequence of tenses
    noun clauses 230
should
    advice, advisability 38–39
    indirect command 284
    noun clause 247
    past expectation 69

present expectation 55
    strong advice 44
    type I conditionals 164–165
Similarity 213–214
Simultaneous action 7
since 14
Skill *see* Ability
so . . . that 120
Specific time 7, 17
Spelling changes
    comparatives 111
    superlatives 118
State *see* Stative
Stative verbs
    as participles 277
    with simple verb forms 3–4
still 14
Subject
    gerunds 72–73
    noun clauses 238–240
    participles 283, 291
    passive 167–168, 174
    substitute subject *"it"* 99–101, 239–240
Subject complement
    infinitive 82–83
    noun clause 236–237
Subordinate conjunction
    cause 198–199
    contrast 202–203
    purpose 198–199
    time sequence 195–196
Substitute subject
    infinitive 82–83
    noun clause 236–237
such . . . that 120, 124
Superlatives 118

take
    with infinitive phrase 99
tell 256–257
that-clause *see* Noun clause
Time contrast
    past perfect 10–11
    perfect gerund 106
    perfect infinitive 106
Time expressions 7, 14, 30
Time sequence
    subordinate conjunctions 195–196
    transition words 207–208
too 97
Transition words
    addition 219–220
    cause/effect 209–210

contrast 211–212
emphatic restatement 215–216
exemplification 216–217
logical sequence 207–208
similarity 213–214
time sequence 207–208
Type I conditionals 147–148, 151–152
Type II conditionals 153–154
Type III conditionals 157–158

unless 151–152
until 10, 195–196

Volunteering 22

was/were going to 20
were
   in type II conditionals 154
wh-words 233, 238–240, 244, 262
wh-ever words 236–237, 238–240, 244

when
   relative pronoun 140–141
   subordinate conjunction 195–196
where 140–141
whether 233, 236–237, 238–240, 259
which 125, 130–131, 136–138, 145
while 7
who 125
whom 130–131, 136–138, 145–146
whose 134–135
why 140–141
will
   future 22
   requests 34–35
worst 118
would
   in type II conditionals 153–154
   in type III conditionals 157–158
   requests 34–35

yet 14